The Latino Male

D0760287

Luis José Avalos (right) and Ramón Avalos, the author's father and uncle, respectively, circa 1926. This photograph was taken shortly after the brothers arrived in the United States from Michoacán, Mexico.

The Latino Male

A Radical Redefinition

David T. Abalos

LYNNE
RIENNER
PUBLISHERS

BOULDER
LONDON

Published in the United States of America in 2002 by
Lynne Rienner Publishers, Inc.
1800 30th Street, Boulder, Colorado 80301
www.rienner.com

and in the United Kingdom by
Lynne Rienner Publishers, Inc.
3 Henrietta Street, Covent Garden, London WC2E 8LU

Library of Congress Cataloging-in-Publication Data
Abalos, David T.
   The Latino male : a radical redefinition / David T. Abalos.
   Includes bibliographical references and index.
   ISBN 1-55587-906-3 (alk. paper)—ISBN 1-55587-934-9 (pbk. : alk. paper)
   1. Hispanic American men—Social conditions. 2. Hispanic American
men—Psychology. 3. Sex role—United States. 4. Machismo—United States.
5. Social change—United States. 6. Hispanic American families. I. Title.
E184.S75 A625 2001
305.38'868073—dc21   2001019800

British Cataloguing in Publication Data
A Cataloguing in Publication record for this book
is available from the British Library.

Printed and bound in the United States of America

      The paper used in this publication meets the requirements
 ∞ of the American National Standard for Permanence of
      Paper for Printed Library Materials Z39.48-1984.

5 4 3 2 1

In loving memory of

Salvador J. Abalos
May 16, 1937, to April 4, 1992

and

Manfred Halpern
February 1, 1924, to January 14, 2001

Contents

~~~

Acknowledgments

—*mm*—

This book is dedicated to my brother Salvador J. Abalos, who died of AIDS in 1992. It was Sal, a gay Latino male, who above all taught me how to be a loving and nurturing man. My mother often referred to him as *El Salvador del Mundo,* the Savior of the World. She had given her son, my brother, one of the most important names used for Jesus in the Mexican tradition. At his birth she had an intuitive understanding as a mother that this son would be special, that he would be a deeply caring and sensitive man who would love and protect her and the members of the family, which he did until his untimely death. In his name I also want to dedicate this book to all of those Latino gay men who have been battered and wounded by our community and by the wider society. In our quest for masculinity many of us lost our way and saw manhood primarily as the justification to overpower and dominate. Maybe, just maybe, the gay men in our community hold the key to re-creating for the first time what it means to be a masculine, manly, macho Latino male in the service of transformation. *Querido hermano, Salvador, Chava, que descanses en paz.* Beloved brother, Salvador, Chava, may you rest in peace.

—*mm*—

The book is also dedicated to Manfred Halpern. Manfred and I saw our relationship transform from that of student-teacher to one of colleagues joined in friendship. He guided me into the world of underlying sacred sources wherein each of us can participate in making life more loving and just by giving concrete expression to the deepest source of transformation. He taught me how to participate in the process of theory building by leading me to my own experiences and to my own creative imagination. It was he who taught me that to be a Chicano and Latino man is to have the courage to live in fullness the personal, political, historical, and sacred faces of my being.

---*m*---

I would like to honor the women and men in my life who have helped me on my journey to becoming a man in the service of transformation. The men and women whom I name below have struggled to discover the relationship between the feminine and masculine aspects of their being in order to become whole human beings. Each of them has been for me a great source of inspiration and strength. They are men and women who are at every moment of their lives somewhere on the journey through the core drama of life as they pursue the fundamentally more loving and just stories. I have been blessed because I was able to draw from them the courage, the heart, to become the kind of man who knows he is vulnerable yet strong. They have assisted me in discovering new and better ways to be a man.

I owe so much of what it means to be a Chicano and Latino man to my wife, Celia, who struggled with me for many years and gave me the gift of refusing to accept my patriarchal ways. Together, we began fighting for a new and more loving marriage and family once we realized how destructive the story of patriarchy had been in our relationship and in the raising of our three children. David Jerome, Veronica, and Matthew suffered with me through the worst years of my being a patriarchal husband and father. At times they were confused and angry with me and deeply hurt, but they continued to love me and to trust in me until I was ready to become a new and better husband and father.

My surviving brother, Louie, and my brothers-in-law, Leroy, Jim, Bill, Louis, Chuck, Miguel, Tom, and Bud, whom I consider my brothers, have been a source of strength and affection. On many occasions my brother Louie fought for me and protected me with his own budding manhood. Leroy, my sister Vicki's husband, was always ready to help, and I especially remember one occasion when he got up out of a sickbed to attend to my needs; Jim, Angie's husband, was there when I needed a man to be my godfather for confirmation; Bill, Marge's husband, gave me my first watch, which I deeply treasured; Celia's brothers, Louie, Chuck, and Miguel (Chaparro), became my brothers as we grew up together; Tom and Bud, who married Celia's sisters, Sylvia and Dolores, were always there for me. I am deeply grateful for them all.

My colleagues Frank Morales and Dick Scaine respected me and loved me so much that I wanted to become what they inspired in me: a good and compassionate man. Over the years, I closely observed Frank Morales as he expressed his manhood by fighting for the Latino community and for those from all communities who needed him to assist them in their struggle for justice. Dick Scaine taught me about manhood in a simple yet wonderful manner. He taught me that to be a man is to be strong enough to be patient and gentle. Dick, through his love for animals and plants, guided me to help build a world where people know they are interconnected as a human community within an ecosystem that sees all life as sacred.

My colleagues at Seton Hall have inspired me to discover ever anew that to be a man is to serve others. Among those who have especially graced my life are Gisela Webb, Carlos Rodríguez Matos, Jack Ballweg, Chuck Carter, Janet Easterling, Kathy Rennie, Phil Kayal, Dick Adinaro, Joyce Strawser, Joe Palenski, Jerry Pire, George and Paula Tzannetakis, John Morley, Evelyn Plummer, Jeff Levy, Rosalie and Teresa Yannazzone, Patricia Kuchon, Amar Amar, John Mitchell, Athar Murtuza, Phyllis Russo, Cheryl Thompson, Larry Frizzel, Bob Wister, Harry Ashworth, Bill Sales, Richard Blake, Mary Williams, Virginia Servo, John Saccoman, Jane Zagorski, Barbara Brennan, Linda Hsu, George White, Kathy Keszkowski, Robin Cunningham, Walter DeBold, Johnny Rodríguez, Charles Yin, Larry Greene, Al Hakim, Ruth Hutchison, Linda Ulak, Gail Iglesias, Bernadette Wilkowski, Kusum Ketkar, Marty Kropp, Anthony Lee, Dick Liddy, Tony Malone, Dawn Williams, Bill McCartan, and Michael McMahon. I want especially to recognize Carol McMillan-Lonesome, the director, and Ingrid Hill, the assistant director, of Seton Hall's award-winning Equal Opportunity Program for their outstanding commitment on behalf of students. It has been a distinct honor for me to have been involved with this program.

My students continue to be a source of grace in my life. I am grateful for Rosaura Bello-Hoepelman, Kathy Rosado, Eugene Mulero, Kim Van de Walle, and Coryn Snyder. I am also thankful for Bill Rebhan, Jim Rebhan, and Patty Rebhan, a gift to me and to Seton Hall from their late mother, Ann Rebhan, our beloved university nurse for over twenty-five years; Zeneida Cruz and Arminda Moreno; three wonderful brothers who walked into my life, Carlos, Ignacio, and Juan Oliver Cruz; Joshua Curtis; Sara Lacagnino; Yesenia Cruz; Robin Cunningham;

Joseph Smolinski; Tracey Garripoli; Kelly Smith; Matthew Demian; Kimberly Kish; Kathy Rosado; and Joanna Tavarez.

I wish to recognize my colleagues, friends, and students at Princeton University: David Carrasco, an outstanding teacher and friend, as well as deeply caring faculty such as Jameson Doig, Nancy Bermeo, and the wonderful staff of the Politics office, Cheryl Oestreich, Linda Kativa, Kristen Wade, Karen Federico, Charlaine Claxton, Jane Hale, Monica Selinger, and especially Dorothy Dey, guide and friend to faculty and students for the past thirty years. My students in "Latina/Latino Politics in the United States" have, over the years, challenged me to be a better teacher as I applied theory to practice. I am in debt to Myrna Santiago, Luz Calvo, Suzanna Villalón, Jeff Avila, Ivette Santiago, Joel Barrera, César Gallegos, Juan Chavez, René Flores, Mike Montoya, Roberto Barragán, Michael López, Miriam López, Jacqueline Rodríguez, Anthony Marín, Michael Alemán, Ernesto Rivera, Elizabeth Cincotta, Jamie Bartholomew, Vicente Cabeza de Baca, Laurie Dean, Lori Mihalich, Michael Long, Justin Luciani, Adrián Rosales, Mónica Solorzano, Awilda Rodríguez, Lori Bennet, Jennifer MacAulay, Darren Joe, Charles Alden, Shani Moore, Nicole Quiñones, Adam Benz, Find Findsen, Jeremy Kogler, Anna María Nuñez, Parker Altman, Adeline Peff, Peter Turk, Hallie Welch, Emmanuelle Soichet, Tara Spencer, Nicole Stoik, Sarah Small, Sofia Almeda, James Coughlin, Dan Hafetz, Lisa Lazarus, Jane Liu, Danielle Nuñez, Erika de la Parra, Zaraelia de la Fuente, Gabrielle Ibañez-Vázquez, Ana Cristina Hey-Cólon, Karabeth Randolph, Kimberly Brown, and Erin Wade.

In my work with K–12 teachers, there is a man, Bruce Normandia, the superintendent of schools of Brick Township in New Jersey, who stands out. He had the courage to use the authority of his office and the strength of his manhood to protect children from the hurts of discrimination. And he moved aggressively to create a new and more loving alternative education: He stepped forward, together with his wonderful faculty and staff, to nurture and enhance the personal, political, historical, and sacred faces of students with a truly wonderful multicultural and gender-fair curriculum.

Throughout the country I have met outstanding and courageous people who daily risk themselves in the pursuit of a more loving and just society not only for *la comunidad Latina* but for all of us. Among these deeply caring people are Judith and Alex MacDonald, Kita Rodríguez, Joe Garrison, Sal and Denise Soto, Susan Casillas, José R. Rodríguez,

Wilt Walenga, Juanita Barbosa, Jim Brady, Darryl Hendricks, Becky Escribano, Dorothy Dey, Mindy Berman, Mary Kay Miller, Nilda García, Barbara Hogan, Zaida Padilla, Teresa Bender, Rebecca Hernández, Silvia Villa, Ric and Mimi Pérez, Ondina Jeffers, Elina Hernández, Casto Maldonado, Mirian Jiménez Maldonado, Angel and Blanca Millán, Félix and Margie López, and Javier Cervantes.

I have been blessed with a wonderful extended family here in New Jersey. When Celia and I first came to the Garden State, we knew almost no one and had no relatives here. But we soon rediscovered the meaning of family as people who care deeply about one another. We are not blood but perhaps something deeper; we relate to one another as persons who share a common soul, a spirit of concern and compassion for one another and for others that draws us together: Vivian and Frank Morales; Dick and Mary Scaine; Jim Palladino; Marge and Nick Martucci; Carol, Rick, and Maggie Biunno; Josephine and Joe Carpenter; Dick and Sandy Adinaro; and, here in our new home of East Windsor, Luz and George Horta, Juan Morales, Bettie Witherspoon, and Jim and Jane Brady.

Finally, I owe a great debt to my editor, Dan Eades, for the encouragement and cajoling that made this a better book than it otherwise might have been. Thank you for supporting my work over the years. A special thanks also to Leanne Anderson of Lynne Rienner Publishers for her help in bringing this book to fruition.

Introduction

~~~

Latino men need to break out, to open new doors and close some, to ask new questions and provide more loving and compassionate responses to the issues that surround them daily.

> We Gotta Get Out of This Place. . . . Getting out means crossing boundaries, breaking grounds, dismantling machismo, debunking taboos, coming out, coming to terms, finding a home away from home, building community and coalitions. In order to reach freedom—that is, social change—we must accept and understand each other for what we are, for our differences. Acceptance and tolerance also must take place in the heart of the family . . . with love, support, and care.[1]

For some time now I have been wanting to write a different kind of book on the Latino male. I want to ask new questions, provide a voice for Latino men, open new ways of seeing and doing, and explore different ways to plumb the depths of both the feminine and the masculine archetypes as they have been lived by Latino men. I have discovered and come to understand that the real goal of both Latina women and Latino men alike is to become full human beings. But in order to accomplish this, "we gotta get out of this place" in which we presently find ourselves.

What I discovered as I researched and wrote this book is that the sources I read could describe the stories I was living as a Latino man and critique them, but nobody told me how to free myself from destructive stories. Most important of all, not one author addressed the most critical point—the solutions to the issues facing Latino men, and

1

how they can create alternative stories that enable them to transform their lives.

This, I believe, is the heart of my work and the greatest contribution this book makes to the scholarship on Latino men: From the perspective of a theory of transformation I offer solutions to the plight of Latino men not only by exploring the stories, the relationships, and the ways of life that have undermined their capacity to be fully present as persons, but also by describing how to rid themselves of the stories that no longer work and to create more just and loving alternatives.

Who are these Latino men? They come from twenty-one different countries; most of them are mestizos, persons of mixed blood derived from Native American Indian, African, and European roots. The majority remain bilingual, speaking both Spanish and English. Some are dark in complexion and still others have a light skin color. They come in all sizes and shapes. They represent the full gamut of sexual identities. Many call themselves Latinos, others Chicanos, Boricua, Cubans, Dominicans, Ecuadoreans, or Hispanics. There are Latinos who trace their heritage in the United States to the first Spanish settlements, especially in New Mexico and Texas. Other Latino men are the descendants of Mexicans who chose to stay in the United States after the Mexican-American War (1846–1848). Many of them are first- and second-generation U.S. citizens due to economic or political upheavals in Latin America such as the Mexican Revolution, the Cuban Revolution, and the civil wars in Nicaragua, El Salvador, the Dominican Republic, and Guatemala.[2] Currently, *los recién llegados,* the most recent arrivals, are literally coming every day, with and without documentation, to look for a more decent life for themselves and their families. A good number of Latino men have achieved the American dream, but most have not. They represent all levels of the socioeconomic ladder, with the majority on the lower rungs.

All of these facts are helpful and important to know, but they do not tell us anything about what is going on in the deeper levels of the lives of Latino men. How then can we speak about such diverse men in a way so that we can come to understand the Latino male? In spite of all the apparent differences, there are stories and ways of life shared among Latino men. It will be one of the tasks of this book to demonstrate how they live archetypal stories in the service of different ways of life that determine the ultimate meaning and value of who they are as men.

Presently many Latino men live desperate lives. Too often they romanticize the past by re-creating the fantasy of male power that dominates their lives. They live the story of the disappointed male. They hang on to this fragment of life, a wounded masculinity, in order to have a sense of power and find ways to get even with a society that daily turns them into objects. The response to this dilemma has been the story of patriarchal machismo. Machismo is Latino men's inherited understanding of being in charge, of taking command, *un hombre muy macho.*

This means that Latino men see the answer to their dilemma through a cultural lens that cannot help them to confront fundamentally new kinds of problems. Often unable to overcome their sense of loss by asserting themselves, some Latino men fall into despair: "I am useless, I am nobody." The search for a remedy for this despair can lead to forms of self-wounding such as drugs. For many, no new insights can come because they are not fully present and have no idea who they are. Latino men need to discover what is crippling them, to go beyond symptoms to the underlying stories that continue to undermine their ability to struggle with problems in their own lives and in the community. Latino men have not dealt with the deeper causes of their sense of loss. They need to create a new and better alternative as deeply caring and loving men who see the sacredness in their own lives and those of others. Latino men have it within their capacity to go beyond the inherited traditional stories of patriarchy and uncritical loyalty that leave them partial selves. They need their own selfhood, the ground from which they can bring forth the fundamentally new and better. What allows Latino males to redefine themselves radically is that each of them has a *sacred face* rooted in the deepest sacred source of transformation.

Chapter 1 is dedicated to my search for manhood as a Chicano/ Latino male. As I relate my own journey and the stories of my life I am inviting the reader to look deeper into his or her own experiences by traveling with me through the core drama of our lives, the journey of transformation, a journey we are all called upon to fulfill.

In Chapter 2, now that the reader knows me and my journey to manhood, I look at my experiences through a lens that opens up my life and that of Latino men to a whole new perspective. I present a theory of transformation as the context within which people like you and me can name and critique the relationships, the ways of life, and the stories of the Latino tradition that for many have undermined masculinity and humanity. But analyzing and critiquing the past is not enough. Latino men need to go beyond criticizing themselves. What they can and need to do together is participate in the process of transformation, a process by which they can bring an end to those aspects of Latino culture that are destructive, a process that enables them to create fundamentally new and more loving stories to heal Latino manhood.[3]

From the perspective of the theory of transformation presented in Chapter 2, the Latino male at risk is the concern I address in Chapter 3. At this point, I ask new questions. What happened that brought about the wounding of the personal, political, historical, and sacred faces of the Latino male? Where did they get lost on their journey? Why have Latino men allowed themselves to continue to be badly wounded by practicing stories in the service of fragmented ways of life that have arrested them as partial selves on the journey of their lives? What aspects of Latino culture and the wider U.S. culture have been detrimental to our journeys? How in daily life do the archetypal stories of uncritical loyalty, romantic and possessive love, and the deadly spin-offs of patriarchy such as the disappointed male, machismo, and the *mujeriego,* the womanizer, which are inherited stories from *la cultura Latina,* devastate our relationships with Latina women? How do the stories of capitalism and tribalism that permeate American society collude with each other to block our journey as men and that of *la comunidad Latina?* Why do I call these stories archetypal? Why is it not enough to change only the concrete manifestations of these dramas and ways of life? Why must we go to the roots of the stories that lie in deeper, formative sacred sources? What are the four radically different choices available to Latino men? Why have Latino men lived their stories in truncated ways of life? What is the price they pay for not knowing these stories and ways of life? How can they fight back and refuse to participate in the replication of these stories? What do they need to know so they can empty their souls of these crippling stories and ways of life and create more loving and compassionate alternatives? Why is it that only in the service of transformation can Latino men critically and creatively participate with the fullness of the four faces of their being?

Perhaps the most creative contribution of this book is Chapter 4, in which I answer the questions that are raised in Chapters 2 and 3 by explaining the process by which Latino men empty themselves of the stories that block their journeys through the core drama of life, and then explore the stories that Latino men can create that would prepare them to become men in the service of transformation. Latino men need to identify actual stories that can be lived daily to deal with the issues they face. As alternatives to worn-out, broken stories, they can create fundamentally more loving and just stories in the service of transformation.

Chapter 5 examines how this new Latino male can help to transform the family. Having emptied themselves of destructive stories such as patriarchy and possessive love, Latino men are enabled to practice the personal, political, historical, and sacred faces of their being in order to achieve wholeness in all aspects of their lives. After telling the story of the family caught in the web of traditional relationships and stories, I move to address the issue of how, in daily practice, Latino men can help to transform the family.

Finally, Chapter 6 is dedicated to understanding men from all backgrounds who have been misled about what it means to be a man. We need again and again to ask the question, "In the service of what way of life am I living my manhood?" My brothers and colleagues will be not only men from my own ethnic and racial background but also men of all other heritages who care deeply about our humanity and who work to heal the personal, political, historical, and sacred faces of others' traditions in the service of transformation.

Throughout the book I have sought to apply theory to practice so that when the reader is done she or he will know not only about stories and ways of life and the sacred sources that inspire Latino men, but also how she or he can theorize, that is participate, in the process by choosing between destructive and creative stories of transformation.[4] As we redefine who we are, we are free to co-create with the deepest source of transformation again and again to bring about fundamentally more loving and compassionate alternatives in all aspects of our lives. This kind of radical participation, getting to the underlying sacred roots of things, is our true revolutionary heritage as human beings.

Notes

1. Alberto Sandoval-Sánchez, *José, Can You See? Latinos On and Off Broadway* (Madison: University of Wisconsin Press, 1999), pp. 146–148. I have learned a great deal from reading this book. It is a brilliant analysis of the politics of the theater and the politics of exclusion as it affects the Latino community in the United States. Sandoval-Sánchez goes beyond our current dilemma to reflect on a future open to the imaginative responses of the community as mirrored in the new kind of theater especially as the community responds to the AIDS crisis.

2. I am grateful to Juan González for *A History of Latinos in America: Harvest of Empire* (New York: Penguin Books, 2000), a very concise and insightful book providing us with an overview of Latinos in this country. He has also returned to a fruitful dialogue on the issue of the causes for increased Latin

American immigration. He places much of the blame on the economic and political policies of the United States together with our military involvement on the side of the elites in Latin America.

3. As I wrote the final pages for this book, my friend and colleague Manfred Halpern, who introduced me to the theory of transformation that I apply to the Latino male, died on January 14, 2001. He asked me to finish his book in progress, *Transforming Our Personal, Political, Historical, and Sacred Being in Contrast to Our Other Three Choices in Theory and Practice.*

4. Sheldon Wolin, in the pivotal article "Political Theory as a Vocation," *American Political Science Review* 63 (December 1969), made a great impact on me. He argued that we need to learn how to theorize, to participate in the creation of theory as our calling.

1

—*mn*—

My Journey to Manhood

I want to tell my own story as a Chicano/Latino male struggling for transformation. Let your own experiences serve as your guide as I re-vision, reinterpret, and re-create my own experience as a Chicano/Latino male in the United States. By proceeding in this personal way my hope is that it will help the reader to see not only my journey but also that of the Latino male as a member of *la comunidad Latina* struggling to re-create a more compassionate and just culture.

I would also like to revisit and re-vision terms and concepts that have profoundly affected our lives as Latino males, such as *patriarchy, matriarchy, macho, masculine,* and *feminine,* to consider how we as Latino males can achieve wholeness, that is, become human beings capable of participating in persistent creation. Many Latino males do not know what terms like *masculine* and *feminine* really mean. Even when they try to discuss the feminine or the masculine within each person, they are burdened with a specific masculine interpretation that permeates our language.

For a Latino male, to be a whole person is to be both masculine and feminine. By feminine or masculine I do not mean some human trait that can be arbitrarily designated as feminine or masculine. There has never been a single or monolithic way, nor even just a few ways, to express the masculine or the feminine. The terms represent two archetypal forces within each human being that have been radically deformed through the politics of gender roles, which attributes certain characteristics to women and others to men. The masculine and feminine make sense to us as a result of this distortion only as opposites, but they can remain in a potentially creative tension that may result in wholeness.

These two aspects of our individual being are both crippled when separated from each other. For this reason both Latino men and Latina women need to participate in the process of creating and growing new and different concrete manifestations of their femininity and masculinity.

Historically men have monopolized all connections to those masculine archetypal forces that are useful for their dominance and in the process have limited both feminine *and* masculine archetypes that are not conducive to male domination. As a result of the dominance of impoverished concrete manifestations of the masculine, not only were men and women cut off from other creative manifestations of the masculine, but all humans were deprived of the experience of the feminine ground of our being. Not to be both masculine and feminine, simultaneously, is to have one's personhood deeply wounded, fragmented, resulting in partial selves cut off from the complementary forces within each of us that create the tension necessary to be fully human—masculine and feminine:

> Transformation in our being cannot proceed without the full participation of both masculine and feminine archetypal forces in all human beings. . . . The liberation now being initiated above all by women to free the fullness of the masculine and feminine capacity of being thus inescapably challenges the legitimacy and power of all fragments that seek to arrest and contain people.[1]

It is a mistake for me as a Latino male and other Latino men to project onto Latina women the lack of our feminine self; similarly women must not seek their masculine self in men. In relationships based on mutuality, men and women awaken in one another the desire to be whole. Yet the wider society and our inherited Latino culture militate against this mutual fulfillment. Therefore, the choice of Latino males must be clear, not to reform the old but to create the fundamentally new and better by returning to the radical, to the underlying, formative roots of things, to the archetypal grounding of their concrete manifestations. To go home is to enter into our deepest source within and to find the means to redefine and re-create new concrete manifestations of the masculine and feminine reality within.

The Contributions of Chicana/Latina Feminists

Present-day Chicana/Latina feminists have performed a crucial service in contributing a voice that has long been excluded from the conversation.

In my effort to understand the story of patriarchy and the relationship between this kind of story and other dramas of domination, I have been deeply inspired by the scholarship of Chicana/Latina feminists. I want to specifically name some of the Chicanas and Latinas who provided me with not only the conceptual language but also encouragement and affirmation: Demetria Martínez, Maria Lugones, Gloria Anzaldúa, Cherríe Moraga, Teresa Córdova, Elizabeth Martínez, Alma Villanueva, Sandra Cisneros, Leslie Marmon Silko, Deena González, Pat Mora, Aída Hurtado, Tey Diana Rebolledo, Rosa Martha Villareal, Antonia Castañeda, and Ana Castillo. Their work and scholarship have demonstrated the need to see the intersection of race, class, and gender in order to better confront the interwoven forms of oppression. They have done this by using their bodies, their selves, their stories as they introduced with clarity and brilliance an autobiographical scholarship that fully revealed that the personal is political, historical, and sacred. They questioned in a fundamental way the Chicano/Latino culture that had silenced them. They opened up new stories and put to rest the taboo against declaring and celebrating one's sexuality, especially gay and lesbian sexual liberation. Once many Chicana/Latina feminists made this breakthrough, it liberated them to see and expose the other stories that had diminished their humanity.[2] Their work sensitized me to recognize how physical and sexual abuse give rise to an atmosphere of violence, fear, and intimidation. What has especially influenced me is what I call the creative anger I experience when I read their work. Their anger has helped to free me so I can drop my own fears and inhibitions and continue to write my own story. Many Latino men and Latina women have remained caught up in the language of the struggle between men and women so that they have lost sight of the deeper sources of the dramas arresting them. The present concrete reality being enacted in most Latino male–Latina female relationships have had devastating effects.

I would like to open doors leading to a new and better understanding of the Latino male and the transforming of the personal, political, historical, and sacred faces of our being by speaking of my own journey as a Mexican/Chicano/Latino male.[3] I want to begin by asking the question, "*¿Quien soy? ¿Quienes somos?* Who am I? Who are we?" My Latino colleagues and I are far richer in being than our current society allows us to understand, much less practice.

To tell my story is for me at once a personal, political, historical, and sacred task. The details of my life are necessary for me to reveal so that the reader can know me and the stories that shaped my life. As a child I was the recipient of a tradition that provided the structure of life for my culture and my parents. By the time I was eight and nine I began to make choices. I intuitively understood that my life was in danger. And now I want to know how and why Latino men and the Latino community have been badly wounded by the archetypal stories of patriarchy and machismo. And because the lives of Latino males have become arrested in these fragments of life, we cannot know who we are, since we remain partial and wounded men. Both our Latino heritage and our adopted culture in this country continue to socialize us into stories that prevent our personal wholeness as males, cripple our political capacity to shape a more just and compassionate society, deny us the right to create a new and more compassionate history, and cut us off from the sacredness rooted in the deepest source of transformation, the source of the fundamentally new and better. Now I want to go beyond understanding to see how in actual practice Latino men can transform their lives so that the wholeness of the four faces of our being becomes a reality in all aspects of our lives.

The struggle of the Latino male with his heritage of domination inherent to the story of patriarchy, I know only too well from my own experience. I was raised as a male in the Chicano/Mexican tradition that gave me permission to dominate women as an all-knowing lord. In addition, my Catholic training reinforced patriarchy and male domination by teaching me to transcend the body and to use willpower and prayer to control my own desires by resisting the temptations of the world, sexuality, and women. As a youth I was caught between the two competing worlds, both of which were hostile to women. My culture raised me to enjoy sexuality as pleasure *from* women not *with* women. Women were a sexual challenge, a mystery that could be solved if men could lay them low, that is, sexually conquer them. We were taught to move from one woman to the next. But in the midst of this drama there was a dichotomy. Catholicism taught me that sisters and wives were like mothers, saints who deserved to be put on a pedestal. But when a Latino man marries his "mother," he cannot be fully sexual with her. Marriage is necessary for continuing and maintaining the carefully crafted facade of the traditional family. The saintly/motherly wife stays home to nurture children. But because she is now a mother to the husband too, she often ceases to be a lover. Because women are sexual conquests or because they are put on a pedestal, Latino men often stop relating to their wives with sexual passion. So they turn to other women for their sexual needs. When their lives go sour, many men take revenge on their wives and children. It is the only realm where they believe themselves to be in control.

In the other world of the Catholic Church I was taught to resist the body and to save my soul. I was deeply attracted to the Church because of my desire to be accepted into American society. In addition, as a youth I had seen so much conflict between Latino men and Latina women that I came to identify sexuality with violence. I did not want to grow up to be an abuser, but I did not know how to remain a Latino male and create an alternative. The racism directed against me as a Mexican led me to believe the lies and the stereotypes that said only Latino men were guilty of female domination.

The Church presented the priest as hero. The world of the priest, in turn, led to the repression of sexuality and of women. I was only too glad to accept the world of the Church, since it relieved me of the dilemma of not knowing how to deal with sex and women and placed me in the world of the powerful. This repression of my own sexuality and of women as threats meant that I denied the feminine within me. But it led to the disabling of the masculine as well. I was so polarized living in the masculine patriarchal drama that I had no awareness that the goal of transformation was to heal the wound between the feminine and the masculine. I fought to survive in a very dangerous world filled with racism in the wider society and violence against women in my own culture. I ran from the confusion permeating my Mexican heritage. I believed that I could get away from the past by repressing my sexuality, since I identified sexuality itself with the dominance of the Latino male.

My personal face was repressed, since my ideas and needs were not important when compared to the demands of authority figures wrapped in a mysterious shroud; my political being was dominated by a desire to be totally, even blindly loyal, so that I had no right to question and thus initiate change; historically, I was dominated by the inherited past that I had no right to challenge, so I could not be the agent of new stories or turning points but only the recipient of a dead past, and my sacred face was filled with the blush of sin, shame, and guilt whenever my anger caused me to momentarily break through the repression in which I was held and in which I held myself.

My inability to confront the feminine in myself stemmed in large part from my culture's inability to deal with homosexuality. To be feminine was debased into being effeminate, a very derogatory term that meant that a man had no sexual prowess. To be a man was to sexually conquer women; if you did not have the ability to penetrate a woman, you could not prove your masculinity. This cultural world was a breeding ground for homophobia that manifested itself in the ridicule and bashing of gay men. Because of the stories in which I was raised, especially a negative machismo and the story of patriarchy, which I experienced daily, I suffered a deep hurt within my own body and psyche. I did not know how to confront my sexuality. I believed that it was necessary to obliterate the dangerous aspect of my masculinity, which for me meant sexuality. I experienced the Mexican men in my community with profound ambivalence. I saw them bloodied after a fight, drinking and singing with the most incredible sadness and longing for their *patria,* their fatherland. I wanted to be protected by them. But on the whole they disappointed me. I was searching for a protector and father, since my own father had died when I was two years old. I witnessed their rage against women, the mothers of our community, including my own mother, with a sense of despair. I felt that my anchor was giving way. How could I possibly identify with such men or become such a man? I knew nothing of the conflict raging within me between two worlds, one the European, Spanish victimizer and the other, the world of the Indian as victim. In this country I experienced racism as I felt shame and anger against those who called me a "dirty Mexican." Thus my conflicted Mexican past became a stigma in this country. My response was to romanticize women and demonize men. I wounded myself by choking my sexuality, refusing to be a penetrating, dominant male, and choosing instead to live a life of discipline that would make me acceptable to the powerful around me, especially the magical priests of my home parish.

This denial and repression only led to more hurt and confusion. I was not redeeming anything, only alienating myself. I was afraid of sex. There were times when I managed to break out of this trap. I loved being affectionate with young women. On the whole I treated them with respect and they liked me. But as I got closer to a decision to go to the seminary, the carefree affection that I had enjoyed became increasingly somber and eventually absent from my life. Even without intimacy with women, however, I became what I thought was a sensitive and caring male, especially dedicated to protecting the honor of women as I avoided physical contact with them.

There was much self-righteousness in all of this. I actually thought of myself as being superior to those young men who needed sex. I would shake my head in disappointment and wonderment at their pursuit of sex. It was all a fake. I had no clue how to face the passion that threatened me except to deny, deny, and deny some more what I was feeling. I felt anger because, in spite of all of my attempts to be what I called a good man, I still had these ever-present desires to be like the other young men in my group from whom I had separated myself. Rather than face the terror I went further into the "good" masculine-patriarchal world of the Catholic priesthood. Why was this the answer? Because it was a world without the pain I identified with passion, sex, the body, temptation, and the domination of others, especially women.

How did I prove myself in this new arena? By becoming more patriarchal than they, my fathers, through dedicating myself to long hours studying and learning so that I could compete with the white, European American boys. Once I had decided to become a priest, I transferred to an all-boys Catholic prep school. In order to survive there and to prove myself, I studied at least three hours every evening after working for at least four hours. On weekends I studied a minimum of five hours. I had never been so studious in my life. But once I had focused on my goal of the priesthood, I was determined to make it. This academic show of force allowed me to prove my worth to them, the others, the better, the best.

When I entered my first year in the seminary, I heard some were saying that I would not be able to make it academically. That was all I needed to hear. Once again the Mexican boy in me rebelled against the stereotype; I fiercely competed with the white boys to show them that I had the right stuff. I became one of the "best" as I studied and worked for most of the day. Another irony was that I thought that patriarchy was only a story that belonged to my Mexican past and not to European American white males. In this way the war between my Spanish and Indian/Chicano roots and the ideal of manhood in American society raged in the midst of a white, patriarchal, Anglo-Saxon world without my knowing it.

But there was something else; priests were attractive to me not only because they were potential fathers but also because they were pure, that is, they didn't have sex. They were transcendent beings above the fray, the muck of things. They were heroic figures in a world filled with sexual demons. They appealed to my sense of adventure and challenge, and I sought to join them as an escape from the suffocation of my own matriarchal mother. I replaced the story of matriarchy with the story of patriarchy with my adopted fathers. I had not really experienced change for the better. I, however, believed I had put myself in a situation where I could silence the issues of my identity and sexuality by entering into relationships whereby I became a mere extension of mysterious others who justified my escape from sexuality and thereby gave me an identity, their identity. There was something else going on. I was rebelling against my Mexican heritage and Mexican men. This attempt to replace one world for another resulted in my ending up where I had begun: living in a dying world of uncritical loyalty in which I sought to find and hold on to the truth. Why is this significant? As I tried to give up my identity as a Mexican youth who saw himself as an extension of a powerful mother and community, I sought a new identity as an extension of priests representing my father, both symbolically and literally. This was the search for the father I never knew accompanied by the desire to serve these fathers as my own father would have wanted, with loyalty and dedication. In this way I sought to replace a web of life that was breaking with a more secure one. I had no idea that I had gone from one container to another just as moribund.

But I was also living in a new world of power and competition. I was caught in a new way, in a relationship to another way of life. To study for the priesthood, coming from a life of poverty as I did, was to place myself in a powerful position in the wider society. In this way I joined the world of privileged white males and sought to assimilate myself into their world. To study and get good grades allowed me to compete and to surpass my fellow seminarians, especially the Irish Americans. This was my way of becoming accepted, becoming negotiable, becoming powerful. My form of capital was my intelligence: I disciplined myself and then sold myself as a highly competent and skilled teacher. In this way the story of capitalism invaded the holy walls of the seminary. The drive to achieve more power through academic performance, coupled with my flight from my Mexican past, intensified the repression of my sexuality.

The Archetypal Drama of Uncritical Loyalty

The story of uncritical loyalty disarmed me and incapacitated me from fighting back. Since I had become disillusioned with my Mexican heritage, I transferred my absolute loyalty to the Catholic Church, hoping this community could give me the kind of all-embracing identity in which I longed to lose myself. I wanted to be accepted and to give myself totally to whomever or whatever had provided me with an overarching sense of being safe and that freed me from my sexual confusion. I could not bring myself to criticize the Catholic Church and I idealized the members of the community, especially the clergy, whom I hoped to join. But I wanted them to be real; I needed them to be real. Because if they proved to be untrustworthy, I would have no place to go.

I was depressed because I had no sense of self; I was in full flight from myself. I was looking for perfection in myself and others, and when I failed to find it I would become more depressed. It would be years before I would come to see myself as another face of the deepest sacred. Until then I dealt with the crumbling of my identity by doing everything that I could to breathe new life into the false image of myself constructed by others.

As I lived the story of uncritical loyalty I came to recognize its characteristics:

- I believed that the truth had been given to us once and for all; therefore, there can be no dissent.
- I always gave deference to authority, because without structural assurance I feared chaos.
- I was apologetic on behalf of the institutional Church whenever I or others saw a problem.
- Experimentation was on the verge of sin, since it threatened to take me out of the realm of the good.
- Dogma was my answer to life's problems.
- Nothing could change because it would undermine divine immutability.
- My view of the good was oriented toward an ideal past.
- I feared change and wanted to maintain the status quo.
- My personal interpretation was not important.
- My creative imagination lay fallow and was indeed aborted in favor of the Catholic Church as an organization and institution, but especially as an all-embracing mother.

Living this story as I did demonstrates how badly I wanted the world of the Church to work for me and others. I felt abandoned by the death of my father, by a mother who was not present for me, and by a Mexican heritage undermined by the society in which I lived.

Fortunately, because of the inherent inability of closed institutions to respond to new kinds of problems, my attempt to repress and suppress myself failed. I recall praying to "God" to please save the Catholic Church from harm and to deliver me from sexual desire so that I could do "His will." This is an excellent example of a prayer to the masculine lord of patriarchy. This experiment in self-alienation failed; it collapsed as I found myself against my will feeling angry because I continued to experience sexual desires. I was flirting with danger—my

Chicano identity and sexual passion were bursting to express themselves. I was painfully split at the root of my person. Self-wounding had been an attempt to maintain my loyalty to an institution that consumed my life. But I experienced more doubts that led to an awakening. No matter how much I prayed and fasted, the sexual desires did not go away. As my belief system crumbled and the power that I sought failed to eliminate my desires, I used more violence against myself in order to maintain self-control. And this is precisely why patriarchy and uncritical loyalty cannot respond to fundamentally new kinds of problems. I could not maintain the stories of patriarchy, uncritical loyalty, and capitalism, which continued to deny my needs as a person. Because these stories became unbearable and unfruitful for me, I could no longer hang on to them without doing violence to myself. But this is exactly what I did—hurt myself by denying and diminishing my own humanity. My attempts at rebellion did not lead to my emptying myself of the stories of patriarchy, uncritical loyalty, and capitalism but rather to wounding myself. I punished myself with guilt, humiliating myself with confessors whenever I looked at a nude picture. I studied longer and sought to hide myself in academic honors. I thought I was weak because I could not control, that is repress, myself, even more effectively.

I finally realized that I could not maintain this collusion between stories that threatened to make my life fundamentally worse. My personal face went from denying and hiding my sexual needs to trying to erase my passion; the politics of unquestioning loyalty and the pursuit of power were now replaced by a politics of revenge, anger, and hostility against my own sexuality; my Mexican past, which prompted me to repeat stories of uncritical loyalty and patriarchy, now led to a story of self-wounding, of deformed sexuality, and loyalty. With regards to my sacred self, I could not hear from the deepest realm of transformation since false lords blocked the deepest sacred from my life with feelings of shame and sin and the thirst for power.

When I left the seminary I told a friend that I felt free from all of the inhibitions that had inflicted me from my Latino past and from the study for the priesthood. I further said that I was ready to let loose for a year or two and then settle down after belatedly sowing my wild oats. Nothing of the kind happened. I failed to face myself again. I was not ready to be free just because I had declared my liberation. I was too deeply caught in the stories of my life. I could not fight them because I was unconscious of them.

The Politics of Intimacy

In no way do I wish by taking this autobiographical route to substitute emotion for political analysis, but rather to demonstrate the political implications of the sexual and emotional lives of Latino males. What I seek to explore is how my personal struggle with the sacred and with sexuality as described above made it impossible for me to connect as a whole person to the deepest source of my being so that I could participate in creating a new politics that would bring about a new and more loving and just history for myself and others. Each person has his or her own story to tell. And even though many Latino males have not experienced the specific details of my story, I believe the issues I raise are archetypal. That is, the fundamental grounding of the experiences of Latino males are the same no matter how different the individual men may seem. I know from my reading and conversations with Latino men that all of us have felt in our bones the need to dominate and the need to love and be loved; we have all felt the split between the love for our mothers and the desire to be loved by a woman or lover for ourselves as an equal; we have felt deep disappointment when our wives became our mothers, such that we no longer considered them as sexually desirable women; we have felt the need to conquer women and then go running home where it is safe; some of us as gay, transsexual, and bisexual men have experienced the frightening cost of being outcasts in our own community, forced to go underground; we have all felt the rage that comes with being unhappy and angry with our lives and not knowing what to do; most of us, if not all of us, have experienced self-doubts when competing with white males allegedly superior to us; many of us have felt the guilt that leads us to deny our conflict and to give up the struggle as we drown ourselves by compensating, paying ourselves for our sadness with drugs, booze, gambling, endlessly watching, but often not participating in, sports, all down payments on the way to becoming self-castrated males.

The fragments of the dying stories that sanction male privilege and that inspire men to relate to women in terms of power cannot help us to heal these injuries. All the power in the world cannot command us to love or be loved by another. In order to trust and to grow, to find myself, I need love. But because of the contradictions I experienced while practicing stories and relationships that left me only a partial person, I had no idea who I was or how to relate to others who said they loved me.

I am convinced that I and Latino men, and men in general, find it difficult to be intimate. *Intimacy* is a word that derives from the Latin word *intimus,* which is the superlative of *intus,* meaning "within"; another derived meaning is "most private or personal." Combining these two interpretations, intimacy refers to the highest degree of *withinness,* closeness to one's innermost person. Intrinsic to the stories of patriarchy, machismo, possessive love, capitalism, and other forms of exploitation based on male power is the inability to be close to one's own self. Of its very nature, domination veils a deep fear, a profound insecurity about one's own self, one's own personhood. Many Latino men are not fully present because they are literally possessed by stories that prevent them from reaching their inner selves. Afraid to let go of these stories, they have no idea what lies on the other side except the terror of facing emptiness. At the heart of this inability to experience intimacy is a deadening solitude and fear that power, rage, violence, drugs, and alcohol cannot overcome.

I spent years being afraid of intimacy. I avoided myself; I failed to be present to myself and others because I was insecure as a man. If I am afraid to be present to myself, to love myself, because of a story that possesses me, then I cannot be fully present to or love people who need *me,* not a caricature of myself. I was taught a silent agenda with which to protect myself from women by both my Mexican culture and the culture of Western society. Whenever I became insecure or threatened by a woman, it was acceptable for me and for men in general to ridicule them or to look for flaws. Ever since I can remember I looked for the ideal woman, which is another way of saying that I never looked for an actual woman, to love and to love me. When I found myself attracted to a woman I looked for something in her I did not like. Seeing a flaw in her ended the threat of being sexually overwhelmed, swallowed up. Part of my fear was based on the relationship I had with my mother. I wanted to free myself of my mother's demands. She often ignored my needs, and at the same time of course, I wanted her to love me.

As a high school student I had some affectionate and caring relationships with young women. But whenever I thought that a young woman was getting too close or needy for me, I would feel a sense of desperation. I would even resort to being rude and mean in order to end the relationship. I needed to be physically loved but saw such love as dangerous. I would go to confession and admit to the most natural and innocent physical response that occurred with sexual arousal. I was especially close to one young woman throughout my high school years. The reason I felt safe with her was that I expected her to collude with me in my repression. Whenever I became too attracted to her I would find a reason to be turned off. I looked for small things to disappoint me, the way she wore her hair or how she was dressed.

Just as I wanted to get away from my mother, I also wanted to escape the entanglements of sex so that I could live the life of the hero who transcends such "mundane" concerns. I was after big game: My destiny as a warrior lay in the army of the Church. I had no idea my dreams for myself were moving me more deeply into the story of patriarchy I thought I had left behind in my Mexican community.

At our yearly retreats in high school the priests admonished my peers and me to stay away from the sins of the flesh. "If you want sex, get married," was their advice to us, as if marriage was the answer to all of our problems. Years later, after leaving the seminary and getting married, I thought that I had succeeded in ridding myself of the fear of women and of sexuality intrinsic to the stories of patriarchy, capitalism, and the negative machismo in the wider society as well as in my Latino culture. I had rejected the tradition of my father as the dominating male and the example of my brother, who belonged to a gang. In that tradition, one learned to be a man by not needing women. A man's indifference is what allowed him to use women and walk away from them, a free agent. But I woke up one day and realized that I was just like them. I had become an intellectual revolutionary who knew the right words, but I was still ensnared by the story of patriarchy. My awareness made me increasingly angry with my life.

Disappointed, I withdrew from my wife. I was angry and unhappy but did not know why. My wife did everything to keep me from being disappointed, attempting to please me however she could. I was aloof, cold, and detached. I could not believe I was so unhappy. I now recognized I was a Latino male with all of the traits I had rejected. I realized I had rebelled against particular men in my background, but I had not emptied myself on the deeper level of the cultural stories that held me in their grip. My wife was also lost because she was caught in the same stories that were afflicting me. She responded to me the way that she used to relate to her own father, with love yet resentment and fear that her life would again be controlled. She believed when we got married she would be able to leave behind the compromises she had seen modeled by Latina women all of her life.

The Story of the Disappointed Male

One of the most dangerous spin-offs of the archetypal story of patriarchy in the Latino community is the story, also archetypal, of the disappointed male. I have encountered this story myself and have observed it in many of the men in my community as well as in the society around me. What makes this story so deadly is that it is a form of neopatriarchy, that is, an attempt to restore the lost glory and power of the male. As this story is everywhere disintegrating, however, men find it more difficult to legitimize their power over women. After all, what is bringing about the death of this cultural story is that people are no longer willing to deny their own experiences. All over the world women and children are asking, "What about me, what about my needs as a person?" Their questions signal the end of repression wherein women agreed, although usually not consciously, to participate in their own domination.

As this world of repression dies, a new culture based on self-interest and power inherent in the story of capitalism continues to substitute for the old traditions, whether in Mexico, Peru, Puerto Rico, Colombia, or the barrios of the cities and towns in the United States. In this new world of money and power, the majority of Latino men are not succeeding. Many Latino men feel powerless, both in the countries of their heritage and in U.S. communities. As a consequence some Latinos turn to movements that promise them an identity and allege a restoration of their power. But these fundamentalist movements promise only a return to a world that is gone forever. Because they still believe in the return of a cyclical past, many men feel justified to use violence to bring back the lost heritage of male privilege. In their attempt to repair the torn web of tradition through violence, they fail and make everyone's life worse.

Looking Inside the Story of the Disappointed Male

The disappointed male holds the following characteristics:

- He is angry and wounded.
- His ego is threatened by the collapse of male privilege inherent in the story of patriarchy.
- He tries to restore the past and is tempted to turn to violence against himself and others.
- He does not know how to transform his life.

- At best he compromises by reforming existing relationships.
- He mellows out and loosens up, using bargaining and limited forms of autonomy in order to maintain his power.
- He also uses fragments of the dying tradition, sin, shame, and guilt, to maintain the status quo to prevent radical change.
- To him, reformation means changes *within* the existing relationship, whereas transformation demands a change *of* relationships and stories.
- To him, there is no conversion, only behavior modification.
- He is a master of manipulation, not transformation.

For example, Latino men who move to this country from small towns throughout Latin America often live the story of the disappointed male. They start off looking for a better life. Many Latinas are also coming. But when these Latinas and Latinos marry or live together, all of the frustrations of being caught between two ways of life are brought into the open. In the politics of the family this contest between competing cultures and traditions is acted out. The disappointed male feels the loss and abandonment of his own culture and the assault of U.S. culture. The stories of his new country, especially capitalism, treat him as a commodity, as an abstraction. He no longer has worth, only what he can produce and purchase. He often cannot speak the language and has little formal education. His lack of skills means menial jobs and poor living conditions with no health benefits. His wife or lover may find it easier to get a job. He feels useless. He often finds himself at home, perhaps with small children for whom he is expected to provide care. As the children go to school they begin to master the language and the culture. The man of the house is further alienated. When he does find work, he takes orders from the white males who are usually his bosses. In this context, caught between two worlds, neither of which work for him, the disappointed male often resorts to violence to deny the disintegration of his very being.

To assuage the ego of the disappointed Latino male, the Latina woman is forced to become an expert in covert manipulation. She has to know when to speak, when to be quiet, how to use food and sex as a bargaining tool, how to live a private life on the side, how she should never question a male in public or in front of the children, how to read a man's moods, dress for him, pinch, tuck, and fast her body so that she remains attractive to her man. This has profound consequences for a Latina woman. She represses her own personal desires and needs. With her political face, she practices a politics of uncritical loyalty to her man, which ensures that the next generation of Latina women will repeat the same historical stories that she is living as her inheritance from her own foremothers. Her sacred face continues to be obscured by a husband who believes he owns her.

Latino men, in spite of the attempts of Latina women to buffer them from their pain, become increasingly angry with their lives. They do not know who they are: The culture that gave them their identities as machos is breaking apart and they often do not have the skills to succeed in U.S. society. The turn to violence comes as an attempt to prove they are still in charge, worthy of respect and obedience.

Latina women who refuse to repress their own personal faces in deference to a husband or father or lover, who refuse to practice a politics of uncritical loyalty to men, who refuse to blindly obey the stories of an inherited history, who refuse to deny their own sacredness, and who reject the ultimate authority of men to dominate them become the subjects of male violence. Rather than letting go of the old, inadequate stories and creating fundamentally new, transformative stories, men make their lives worse as they turn to physical abuse.[4] The use of violence is a rearguard action played out by men who sense, but who are afraid to admit, that their hegemony has ended.

This kind of marital politics practiced within a family dominated by a disappointed male carries over into the wider society. Women and children living in such an environment are learning a politics of sexism that is ever more violent. The children are being prepared to accept and repeat the same domination and victimization, depending on their gender, not only at home but also in the society at large. And the community is impoverished.

For generations Latina women were discouraged by men from becoming fully involved in the politics of their communities. Prior to the 1960s, Chicanos in the Southwest and California were politically active. Mexican and Latino veterans returning home after World War II took the lead to establish unions.[5] In Texas, the GI Forum was founded in 1948 to guarantee that Chicano veterans would receive their full GI Bill benefits. Once they had organized around this issue, the veterans turned to other concerns facing the Chicano community, especially voting rights.[6] Chicana/Latina women, meanwhile, were very much involved in the Puerto Rican and Chicano movements, especially the United Farm Workers and civil rights movements sweeping the country in the 1960s. But most of the leadership was male, as was true in other communities of color. One of the costs of racism is that men of color too often practice a harsher form of patriarchy and machismo to compensate for the lack of power outside the home. Latina women continue to be taught that to be involved in the public realm is to neglect their children and to place their husband in a potentially embarrassing situation.[7] Moreover, women's historical and cultural heritage had conditioned them to take their cues from men. They were trained to believe they had nothing to offer in the public realm.

The politics of the family and of male-female relationships is symptomatic of the issues being faced in the Latino community. Latinos cannot go back to an idealized past, a past that never really existed. Moreover, *la comunidad Latina* needs to resist assimilating into the story of capitalism. The story of capitalism allows us to join the powerful, but it is a drama that condemns many people to perpetual poverty. Even those who make it will remain a sad fragment of who they could have been. The story of capitalism is enacted at the expense of many. Those of us who are successful, who climb into the middle class, often turn ourselves into people who cannot afford to be generous. The answer for Latinas and Latinos is not to turn to revenge against European American whites. Revenge is always destructive. Nor is the answer for Latina women to become powerful in the wider society in order to become independent of Latino men, so that they may in the end dominate them. And certainly the answer is not to resort to underground capitalism by becoming involved in the drug trade, which destroys our own youth and devastates our communities.

Historical Roots of Male Domination in the Latino Community

Antonia I. Castañeda introduces historical evidence that aids the quest to understand how and why the Latino male became so prone to violence against women. She describes the politics of sexual violence during the Conquest and argues that this legacy of domination and oppression developed historically as a backdrop to contemporary society. The Spanish invasion of California began in 1769. With the founding of missions and presidios throughout California, both the military authorities and the clergy found it difficult to control the sexual exploitation of American Indian women by soldiers. Under the threat of military punishment and excommunication, which could mean eternal damnation, the soldiers continued to assault the women. Why? Castañeda believes rape, in this case, was not about personal pleasure. Rape is about power. Rape during wartime is a violent political act of aggression against women designed to undermine a whole community, a constant reminder of the alleged racial superiority of the Spaniards over the Indians, a means to keep the Indian family and community in chaos, and a reminder of the Conquest.[8] The Indian male was humiliated and psychologically castrated by the Spanish soldiers. He could do nothing to assist his wife, sister, or mother. The systematic rape of women, and the subsequent loss of honor, undermined the family and the community. The men avoided the women. When the men became angry, they expressed their rage against the women who had cost them their "honor."

There is historical precedence for the use of rape as an aspect of the Conquista of Latin America in Spanish history. During the long reconquest of Spain by the Christians, which took 700 hundred years, Muslim women were raped when a town was recaptured from the Moriscos as a sign of Christian dominance and superiority.[9] In the New World, *mestizas* and *mestizos*, persons of mixed blood and heritage, are the result of the intermarriage between the indigenous population and the Spaniards. To this day, throughout Latin America, there is an ongoing conflict between those who try to maintain their pure Spanish blood and those who work to keep their Indian blood from being mixed with the Spanish. For this reason the *mestizos*, who make up the majority, are at times held in contempt by the two racial extremes. In countries such as Bolivia and Mexico, which are still deeply connected to their indigenous past, calling an Indian who is trying to fit into the larger society or a *mestizo* who is succeeding economically *un Indio*, is considered an insult. On the other hand, if an Indian asks a *mestizo* or an Indian if he or she is a Spaniard, it is a question filled with hostility.

What does this historical background have to do with Latino males living in the United States now? Latino males, the majority of whom are *mestizos*, carry within them simultaneously the arrogance and feelings of superiority of the Spanish soldier who raped women out of a sense of superiority and the blood of the Indian victims who experienced the helplessness and rage of such humiliation.

I remember my own anger when I was with a group of students visiting the winter headquarters of Hernán Cortés, the conqueror of Mexico, in Cuernavaca. In the main passageway hangs a large painting portraying Cortés in the nude, with his white skin, blonde hair, and blue eyes, embracing a naked, dark-skinned Indian woman, la Malinche, the concubine of Cortés, who allegedly betrayed her people to the Spanish. This painting represents the sexist, patriarchal, and racist norms that dominated the relationships between Spanish men and indigenous women.

Since the Conquest indigenous men have used Malintzín as a scapegoat, as a buffer for their own anger at their inability to defeat the Spaniards. Chicana and Latina women still suffer from the results of this historical trauma because too many men find justification in this story for their rage against women. To this day in Mexico, the popular term *Malinchista* refers to a coward who betrays others.[10] And the term continues to be an attack on women. With all of these cultural and historical antecedents swirling around me when I saw the painting, I thought of the white men who were attracted to Latina women. I even thought of my wife as the potential target of a white male. And yet I felt an opposite anger as well. I also saw my mother, who had very light skin, and the darker males who pursued her. Because of the racism that I had experienced as a young man growing up in Detroit, I preferred to go out with light-skinned young women, to prove my worth and acceptance.

Skin color, race, heritage, mixed blood, history, and personal experiences all became knotted together. I couldn't separate my feelings. What I do know is that many Latino men share a similar confusion. On the one hand they embody the Spanish soldier in their sexual exploitation of women and in their desire to stand alone to prove their worth in battle just as the bullfighter proves his manhood as he faces the bull alone.[11] But they are also the Indian male as they see themselves as victims of white, blonde, blue-eyed males in the United States who symbolize the Spaniards raping Indian women. Anger, violence, and guilt are intertwined. Because many cannot resolve the tension they turn to drink, drugs, womanizing, and other forms of escape. As a result they do not find alternatives. They either romanticize a golden past that never existed or try to assimilate. Or they join a gang in an attempt to restore pride through power games. Or they carry out their own counterrevolution in the family, a choice that leads to violence. Very few choose to be honest by admitting that they have lost their way and need to give up the stories and the partial ways of life that have failed them.

Archetypal Models of Manhood

When I and other Latino men and men of color, indeed all men, look for an archetype of masculinity, of maleness, of being a male interested in transforming his life for the better, to whom shall we turn? There are four men who come immediately to mind: César Chávez, Gandhi, Malcolm X, and Martin Luther King Jr. And yet, for all of their brilliance and courage in facing some of the most fundamental problems of our time, none of these men was good at relating to women. Martin Luther King Jr. was dominated by his own patriarchal father well into his adulthood.[12] He was in love with a white woman while attending Crozer Seminary in Philadelphia. They wanted to marry but knew that his father would never approve and so they mutually agreed to end their relationship.[13] Until the very end King had a series of affairs with white women. He knew he was endangering the movement, and his guilt about his imprudent behavior may have been part of the reason he sought to risk his life even more.[14] African American women risked their lives in the civil rights movement by going into the streets to confront racism. But it is also clear that, notwithstanding their contributions, they usually were not involved in the decisionmaking. There is no question about the contributions that were made by women like Rosa Parks and Coretta Scott King, but in the Southern Christian Leadership Conference, which Martin Luther King Jr. helped to found, women still made the coffee and did the secretarial work.[15]

It is impossible to say how the history of this country would have been different if outstanding men like King had resolved their relationships with women. I believe that King practiced transformation in his life in regards to the story of racism from which he did much to free this nation. But transformation is a continuous process that is never complete. I have faith that if King had lived he would have come to see sexism as another form of oppression as serious as racism, just as he came to realize the connection between the war in Vietnam and the struggle of the poor in the United States.

César Chávez, a Chicano/Mexican man of impeccable personal courage and integrity, led the struggle for human rights for the most exploited workers in the country, farm workers, especially migrant farm workers.[16] Chávez followed the philosophy of nonviolence and helped to bring the plight of farm workers to the attention of the nation. He was deeply religious and used fasting, as Gandhi did, not as a weapon against others but as a tool to awaken his own inner strength and to inspire his union members. For thirty years he carried on an extraordinary and courageous struggle for the civil rights of farm workers and workers in general until his death in 1993. Once again, though, we encounter ambivalence and hesitation when it comes to Chicana/Latina/Asian women. The United Farm Workers, the union founded in 1965 to organize farm workers, was dominated by Latino and Filipino men, despite the protests of high-ranking women who complained of the way decisions were made.[17]

Malcolm X, following the teachings of the Honorable Elijah Mu-
hammad, accepted the role of women as handmaids to men in the Nation of Islam.[18] He was from all accounts a dedicated and loving father
and husband within the intrinsic limits of the story of patriarchy. There
is no evidence in his famous autobiography, however, that he saw
women as equals; he saw them as people who had been exploited by the
white man and therefore as persons deserving protection by strong
black men. He did speak with love and admiration for his older sister,
but she was the exception. As in the case of King, I have faith that if
Malcolm had lived, he would have turned his great gifts to the liberation
of black men, hopefully of all men, in their relationships to women, just
as he freed himself of both white and black racism.

In his experiments with truth, Gandhi gave to us all the message of
nonviolence based on *satyagraha,* the soul force, the power of the soul
to discover the truth.[19] He wanted no man or woman to be lesser than
any other. He took on the whole of the British Empire with its arrogance, military might, and glaring imperialism based on racism. In his
struggle to bring about the transformation of a passive and obedient
people to a militantly nonviolent people, he went so far as to disarm his
own masculinity. He knew that masculine power was another form of
domination. He was suspicious of phallic desire because he saw it as a
weapon that threatened his evolving philosophy of nonviolence.[20] Yet,
in his own relationships with women, Gandhi leaves me deeply trou-
bled. In the face of his own teachings of nonviolence he *unilaterally* declared and therefore violently imposed on his wife a demand that she
open her house to strangers and that she cheerfully share the tasks usually done by Untouchables. When she objected to emptying the cham-
ber pot of a guest who was not only an Untouchable but who was also
a Christian, she showed her displeasure by making a face. Gandhi then
proceeded to command her to do it cheerfully and, when she resisted,
Gandhi showed her the door.[21] On another occasion he ordered that the
hair of two young women be cut lest it become a temptation to young
men.[22] This is an example of Gandhi imposing on others his own fear of
sexual passion. As a young husband he had demanded constant sex from
his wife and blamed this obsession on his father. Gandhi believed that
he had been cursed by his father, whom he considered to be oversexed,
because Gandhi's mother was his father's fourth wife and was consid-
erably younger than his father.[23] As he neared the end of his life,
Gandhi was often depressed due to the civil war that had broken out between Muslims and Hindus. His wife now dead, Gandhi sought warmth

and comfort by sleeping between two young women. This was scandalous behavior in the view of many of his admirers at the time. Gandhi insisted that his sleeping arrangements were not sexual but merely the need of a depressed man to be nurtured and protected, the behavior of a man who was still testing his resolve not to give in to sexual desire. Until the end Gandhi continued to struggle to transcend his sexual needs for the sake of fulfilling his destiny to free India from the British and prepare his people for home rule, rule of the self as well as of the nation. But at no time did Gandhi see the possibility of sexuality as joyful intimacy.[24]

To this list of men who demonstrated extraordinary courage and achievement can be added many others. But the point here is that there are few, if any, men to provide us with guidance when it comes to the question of how to create the new man. Men have traditionally defined and proved their manhood and masculinity by being a provider, protector, and impregnator. These three roles legitimized men to become warrior heroes, skilled and fearless hunters, and sexual predators who came to see it as their right and duty to protect women, to dominate them, to batter them, or to manipulate them with the right words or gifts.

Participating in the Creation of a New Latino Male in the Service of Transformation

If the doors of perception were cleansed
everything would appear to man as it is, infinite—
For man has closed himself up, till he sees
all things thro' narrow chinks of his cavern.[25]
—*The Marriage of Heaven and Hell,* William Blake

I want to continue in an autobiographical vein in order to show how I have attempted to free myself of the worst aspects of the Latino culture so that I could participate in creating a new and more just and loving alternative. Like Blake, I want to free myself of the old perceptions and see masculinity and femininity with new eyes. As a youth I was taught to fear the body and to save my soul. It was the devil who sought to capture me and to send me to hell; I lived in fear of this possibility. In a similar manner I had split off the feminine from the masculine and saw the feminine and women as owing men love and nurturing as mother and sister but as temptation in regards to other women because of the entanglement in sexuality. I had no way of knowing that this was all a historical and political construction of the powerful in both Church and culture to keep men in a narrow cavern. I have learned much from William Blake, who taught me the words and the images to express the reality that was always in me, what he refers to as the poetic genius. I can participate in creative imagination by opening my own doors of perception. For me in this context it means letting go the conceptions that have held me arrested for so long. In *The Marriage of Heaven and Hell,* Blake writes in the persona of the Devil: "All bibles or sacred codes, have been the causes of the following Errors. 1. That man has two real existing principles Viz: a Body & a Soul." Blake then gives another perspective:

> But the following Contraries to these are True. 1.
> Man has no body distinct from his Soul
> for that called a Body is a portion of Soul discernd
> by the five Senses, the chief inlets of soul in this age.[26]

If I accept this understanding of my soulful body, then I can see my way to reexperiencing and redefining my feminine masculinity and by so doing assist others like me who are looking for good language to express what we intuit.

What Is to Be Done?

It is time to conquer the Conquest.[27] Latina women and Latino men have it within their capacity to end the victimization. Yes, it is important for us to acknowledge the traumas and problems of the past that have hurt us as members of *la comunidad Latina.* We faced the destruction of our indigenous culture and the racism of the Spaniards; we faced the injuries from being poor and from being members of an allegedly backward culture in a class- and color-conscious society both in Latin America and in the United States. We continue to suffer because of who we are. But we cannot afford to spend time lamenting and becoming more angry over what society or whites or our own Latino people do to us; we are more than victims.

I agree with Rosa Martha Villareal, who writes about how Latino men have to redeem their past by taking the best from their Spanish and indigenous heritages.[28] As Sandra Cisneros maintains, the time of the *llorona* and the *llorón,* those who endlessly complain and lament their loss, is over.[29] Latinos need to become a community who shout a new

Grito de Lares, a new *Grito de Dolores,* and a new *Grito de Yara,* yells of protest and resistance that signaled the beginning of the Puerto Rican, Mexican, and Cuban uprisings against the Spanish Empire. Just as Ramón, one of the main protagonists in *The Plumed Serpent* (Quetzalcóatl, the god of culture and transformation in Mesoamerica), took the images that represented the old tired gods of the people out to the middle of the river to a small island and then burned them, in the same way Latino men can end the tyranny of the old sacred sources that cripple their ability to see and enact visions of the fundamentally new and better.[30] In the process of creating more loving and compassionate relationships and stories, they can transform the four faces of their being: The personal face now emerges into wholeness as they accept and celebrate who they are while loving and respecting the personal face of others. Now that they are connected to their deepest selves, they are able to practice the politics of compassion by asking what it is that humans need to do together to bring about a more just society. The historical face of Latino men is freed from the tyranny of the past so that they can create new and more compassionate turning points that shape a new history. Finally, their sacred face is now connected to the deepest creative source of transformation, who asks us to participate in finishing the task of creation.

In a conference in Miami, Florida, dedicated to the Health of the Latino Male and sponsored by Aspira, a Puerto Rican national civil rights organization, I gave a presentation, "Latino Men in the Struggle for Transformation."[31] During that address I stated that

> No new insights can come because we are still hanging onto the patriarchal drama that European Americans reinforce. The answer to the health needs of Latino males is not only to provide more clinics, more access to counseling services, more employment, better drug treatment and so forth; all of this will help but above all what must change and what is crippling the Latino male is his belief that his honor and well being depend upon his ability to dominate and to provide security for women. Latino men need to reject patriarchy in favor of seeing the sacredness within their own lives and that of others. Such sacredness and its corresponding creativity can only emerge if my self is free to reject inherited dramas that cripple us and choose the archetypal story of mutuality, of transforming love which means that nobody is an extension, or owes their life to another; each of us is a face of the deepest sacred; what radically grounds each of us as women and men in our own autonomy is that each of us has his or her own holy spirit, each has their own creative imagination waiting to come forth. The strength has to come from within the deepest self of the Latino male.

In this task of bringing about the fundamentally new and more loving, Latino men need guides who have experienced transformation in at least one aspect of their lives. This can be someone in the barrio, the neighborhood, or the guide could be a wife or lover. To begin the process of transformation it is crucial for small groups of Latino males to meet regularly to share their lives so they can assist each other in resisting the destructive stories that still hold great power. In the tasks of daily life they need to be honest. This happens only with discussion, by dialogue about how they feel and how the battle is going.

For example, I recently spoke like a patriarchal male to both my wife and my mother-in-law. The presence of my wife together with my mother-in-law brought out feelings of a need to assert my authority that surprised me. At that moment I represented, and actually became, another concrete manifestation, a living example of the patriarchal male who was continuing the story of masculine domination that reaches back generations. All of this was triggered by a seemingly insignificant issue, those kinds of details that in fact make up the sinews of the daily interactions between Latina women and Latino men. I complained that my suggestions for eating dinner with a large number of invited guests had not been accepted. My mother-in-law later told me that I spoke to her in the same domineering manner in which her husband and father had spoken to her. I immediately felt bad, but I resisted the guilt and self-bashing that merely push us deeper into despair and instead decided to speak about it so that together we could expose the story that was still very much alive. We also did something very important: We talked about it with humor so that we could disarm the bitterness of this heritage. I also readily admitted to the truth that my mother-in-law had expressed. Many times after similar outbursts of patriarchy on my part I would apologize to my wife. Her response was: "You are always sorry." What she meant was that apologizing for the same behavior is no longer acceptable; what she was asking for was change. In this fight to rid ourselves of the stories of oppression, there is no other way other than to be utterly honest with ourselves and with each other.

Initiating behavior that fulfills the contours of a new and better story is another dimension of this strategy. My spouse and I can practice together what it means to be equal by sharing the task of nurturing children. Every evening we need to take time to speak to each other about how we are, about our job, our feelings, our relationship. This demands intimacy to one's self and to the other. It would be dishonest to hide our feelings for fear of hurting the other when in fact we do not want to face our own fears and the problems in the connections between us. But we need to be critical. A Latino man can wash clothes, mop, and do dishes and still be patriarchal. Again and again we have to ask ourselves, "Why am I doing what I am doing?" This kind of question and analysis assists us to resist merely reforming the old stories. We need to do more than rearrange the furniture; we need to transform ourselves by actually ridding ourselves of the stories that no longer work.

Another urgent issue in our community that most of us as Latino men have not addressed is the traditional rejection and bashing of homosexual, transsexual, bisexual, and transvestite Latino men, men who continue to experience great suffering in the Latino community because of their sexual preference. They are frequently rejected by their fathers, if not the whole family, and by the men in the community. And they are condemned by the Catholic Church and other churches as well.

But it is primarily Latino gay men, who have suffered because of the violence of a negative machismo, who can help heterosexual men to overcome their homophobia and to redefine what it means to be a man in the Latino community. What Latino men need now is to open a dialogue with their gay brothers so that together they can redefine their masculinity. This conversation can be very fruitful because it will take them away from the usual sterile and tired definitions of manhood.[32] Men have much to learn about their own capacity to practice and understand the deeper meaning of love as caring for self, others, the community, and the planet on which we live. The issue of sexual preference for Latino males will be further developed in Chapter 4.

Re-visioning and Transforming Machismo

I have written about the necessity of Latino men transforming culture by taking those stories that are destructive and putting them out of our lives in order to create new and better alternatives. I believe that it is possible to subvert aspects of *la cultura Latina* so that we turn it around from below. This means that we can take the archetypal story of the macho and remove it from the service of domination and redefine and rediscover it in the politics of transformation.[33] Let me share what has led me to this approach. Gandhi saw the penis as the problem because he saw it as the phallic weapon, as the inevitable tool of male domination. But this view leads to another kind of violence just as deforming: the emasculation of the male, both literally and symbolically. It seems as if Gandhi saw no possibility for mutuality in which the male organ could become the means not only for procreation but also for a joyful and pleasurable connection between men and women. The problem is not men; nor is it the male anatomy or the masculine or even machismo. The problem originates in the *distortion* of the masculine, the macho, and man.

What I am getting at here is that there is a strong possibility that by condemning the sins of men we might end by destroying machismo, which has its roots in masculine energy. Latino men can vigorously condemn and end the misuse of machismo as a force to maintain the dying story of patriarchy, refuse to use machismo as domination in the quest for power, and empty themselves as individuals and as a community of any use of the power of the macho to abuse women and children and one another.

At the Conference on Rescuing the Latino Male, I addressed an audience on "What It Takes to Make a Man from the Perspective of Transformation":

- Go back and reconnect to *las venas abiertas,* the open wounds, of our heritage in order to heal ourselves and reach out to others.
- Become a feminist male, that is, a whole person.
- Rediscover the sacredness of the self.
- Create relationships of mutuality with women.
- Reject the sickness that there is nothing that we can do to change our lives.
- Go home to our own deepest sources within our own self.
- Turn our anger into the necessary courage to bring about a better life.
- Reject the pornography of the male organ as a weapon and substitute for it intimacy; let go of the masturbatory sex of the patriarchal world in exchange for a sensuous, erotic love of giving and receiving in wholeness.
- Rediscover the body, nature, emotions, feelings, the feminine, and fiesta as a search for community.
- De-educate ourselves, throw out the lies regarding our culture by re-educating ourselves to celebrate our emotional and affectionate nature.[34]

Now I will reopen the discussion on machismo not as the use of our strength to dominate women nor to free them but as the energy of a Latino man who *together* with Latina women steps forward to protect and defend our humanity in the setting up a co-op, establishing a scholarship fund, tutoring, spending time with the sick and senior citizens, and nurturing children.

More recently I spoke about machismo in the service of transformation in a presentation given to the National Council of La Raza. I told the story of Mexican GIs who were stunned when returning to their hometowns in the Southwest after World War II to see the same old racist signs in the windows of many businesses: "No Mexicans Allowed." These veterans had fought and bled for their country. However, they did not take their anger, their male pride, their machismo and use it to attack European Americans on a personal basis. They were much more radical than that; they organized the people and were the heart of the union movement that ended more than fifty years of systemic exploitation based on race and class. They used their anger and macho energy to challenge, if not yet to end, the stories of racism in collusion with capitalism.[35]

I do not want Latino men to become pacifists but to become militantly nonviolent in the struggle for political and historical justice. Pacifism is the same as fatalism with a new name. One cannot be calm and peaceful and apolitical in the face of a tribalism that renders us invisible, inferior, and worthy of exile and extermination if we do not assimilate. We need Latino machos everywhere in our communities who are prepared, together with women working as their equals, to step forward to protect our communities from violence, crime, drugs, racism, poor housing, and other forms of deformation.

Let us look at the task facing this new kind of Latino macho. Within Latino communities the disappointed Latino males continue to abuse. This leads Latina women and the young to ask, "Why?" and "What about my life?" In the wider society the powerful feel the threat and fear of genuine competition as our communities ask to be included. This crumbling of the foundations in both the Latino past and the refusal of the powerful to recognize our humanity tempts the traditional Latino male and the powerful in our society toward increased violence. This threatens to make life fundamentally worse. The poor and excluded in *la comunidad Latina* are already facing the reality of deformation both at home in the barrios and in the outside world. In the United States, the Latino jobless rate is 12 percent, double that of non-Latino whites; only 50 percent of Latinos have a high school education in comparison to 84 percent of the non-Latino white population; 10 percent of Latinas and Latinos hold a bachelor's degree while non-Latino whites are at

24 percent. The median income of Latino families is about $24,000 as opposed to $40,500 for non-Latino whites; about 28 percent of all Latinas and Latinos were living in poverty as of 1990. Latina young women are especially at risk to be caught in a cycle of poverty since they represent fully 25 percent of high school dropouts nationwide. This high dropout rate is related to another concern: 24 percent of all Latino families are headed by women, and 53 percent of all single-parent Latino households headed by women live at or near the poverty level. Of all Latino men and Latina women, 30.1% have no health care at all, which means that close to seven million lack access to health care. Twenty percent of women reported to have AIDS/HIV are Latinas, and in the Puerto Rican community the disease is an epidemic, with the rate of AIDS seven times higher than among the non-Latino population.[36] These statistics are alarming because *la comunidad Latina* in the U.S. is already the largest ethnic group in the nation. The future well-being of the country is inextricably tied to the growth and development of the Latino community. And yet the numbers of teenage addicts, children born with AIDS, school dropouts, unemployed, and people living in poverty continue to grow.

The structures and attitudes of U.S. society, especially institutionalized racism, cause serious violence to the Latino community. Much of the destructive behavior is a suicidal rebellion against the violence of racism being practiced by the wider society: Latinos are excluded from proper housing, education, employment, and access to health care. It is very difficult to measure to what extent the community is wounding itself from within due to a refusal to let harmful aspects of the culture die, and to what extent the harm is being done by the violence of the external society. What is clear is that it is due both to the internal wounding and to the external assault. As a community Latinas and Latinos are facing the breaking of their inherited culture as they try to live as human beings in a society permeated by discrimination and racism, creating an environment in which Latinos and Latinas and others are turned into faceless persons who often respond to violence with violence.

But Latino men, allied together with Latina women, can respond to this challenge. Masculine energy belongs to women at the very core of their humanity. Thus Latina women also need to express their masculine strength as *marimachas,* as the Chicanos call Chicana women active in the fight for civil rights in the service of transformation. Just as Dorothy on her journey in *The Wizard of Oz* discovered that her companions, the Lion, the Tin Man, and the Scarecrow, were dimensions of her own undeveloped masculine self, so in like manner Latina women and Latino men can find their feminine and masculine wholeness through action in the community.[37]

Growing Our Own Masculinity in the Service of Transformation

Latino males must not give up their masculinity without creating a more loving and just alternative to transform their lives. To do so would be to replace the sadism of male power with an equally destructive masochism. Nothing will have changed for the better. Some Latina women have also given up. Believing it is impossible for men to change, they become bitter and cynical. They even mock the Latino male for his uselessness. I have listened to Latina women students speak about how their mothers were abused by men and how they plan to never repeat the experience of their mothers: They will not allow a man to get too close to them.[38] One young Latina woman told me recently that she used to be angry with her father for the harm to the family caused by his patriarchal rule. Then she said she realized her mother had to share the blame because she had colluded in his behavior. Her mother taught her how to cope with men based on the following strategy: Do not trust men, assume they are ignorant, see them as useless, and recognize they always think with their penises. As a result she always goes into a relationship with her guard up and never lets it down, minimizing the possibility of getting hurt.

Young Latina women raised with these attitudes toward men will find it very hard to risk faith in a relationship in which both can love and care for each other. Latina women have every right to be angry and to be cautious, but they have no right to seek revenge, to hurt men, to ridicule them, to prove how strong they have become by living without men. This course of action is really a form of rebellion in which men continue to dominate the consciousness of women. Latina women who seek revenge by inflicting pain and control over men cannot be intimate and find out who they are without shaping fundamentally new and more loving relationships with men. For Latinas who are lesbian there is still the challenge of rediscovering the masculine in their own persons and of relating to men as friends and colleagues. The gender of the sexual partner may have changed, but the issues of one's wholeness remain. The community needs Latina women who are strong within themselves and, because they know who they are, are willing to struggle with their fathers, husbands, sons, lovers, brothers, uncles, and male colleagues. To daily choose to challenge a Latino male who you care about is to love him in such a way that you demand that he be a different and better kind of man.

Marx had no blueprint for the future society. However, he saw two clear indications of a new and better society: (1) people can fulfill their inner need to create; (2) more significant from our perspective, sex must no longer be a commodity. Rather, sexual relations are the means by which men and women discover that they need the other in order to be fully human. For Marx, men and women involved in the most intimate moment of sexual love become human (Mensch) as social and cooperative beings:

> The relationship of men and women is the most natural relation of human being to human being. . . . In this relationship is also apparent the extent to which man's need has become human, thus the extent to which the other human being, as human being has become a need for him, the extent to which in his most individual existence he is at the same time a social being.[39]

In the movie *Lucía,* a Cuban revolutionary film by Humberto Solas, the protagonist, Lucía, fights with her husband and refuses to let him regress to the same old story of patriarchy: "I am going to stay with you and you are going to let me love you." But Lucía will no longer accept the domination of the relationship. As Tomás pushes her away, she warns: "Not like that; no more of that or else I am going to stop loving you."[40] I am not looking for Latina women to save Latino men or to make them their project but rather to struggle with those of us who are trying to re-create ourselves as Latino males by practicing a politics of transformation. Whether they want it or not, Latinos and Latinas are irrevocably linked to each other. They can try to regress to the same old stories, compete with each other, and hurt each other, or they can choose to build new and better relationships. Women and men owe that to each other. After all, for generations Latinas colluded in the story of patriarchy by raising young boys, giving them privileges not given to girls and young women, to take the place of their husbands and fathers as the next generation of patriarchs. To discontinue this aspect of their heritage, Latina women and Latino men need to take co-responsibility for creating a new kind of family. Most people know by now that there is no such thing as an ideal family, an ideal marriage, or an ideal male-female relationship. Women and men can and need to grow their own sexual identities and sexual relationships. And we need families grounded in love, mutuality, and passion for each other, not power and domination.[41]

Redeeming Our Fathers

Latino men's attitudes toward their fathers is also in need of redemption. For most of my life I have had only clouded images and vague feelings about my father, since he died when I was too young to really know him. I listened to accounts by members of my family: Although he was a loving and hardworking man, he was patriarchal and domineering. My mother found it very painful to tell me he had controlled her life. But in my attempt to be the opposite of my father, I was still possessed by the same story of patriarchy, since I had not created a new and better alternative. Lately I have been re-visioning my father. He came to this country and took a risk for all of us and attempted to make it in a new society permeated by the stories of capitalism and racism. My father was shot in Chicago, defending himself against a policeman who tried to take his money. He was assaulted because he was a Mexican man, a man of color, an immigrant, a poor man, a man without education, a man without power and connections who was considered invisible, inferior, unworthy of assimilation: someone to be exiled and marginalized to the point of death.

As I write these words I mourn for my father and for myself and for all others who continue to undergo the same kind of deformation in this country. The only way for me and other Latino males to redeem our fathers is for us to become our own father and the father of all those who are turned into orphans by impersonal systems and bureaucracies. What I am getting at is that my father and all Latino fathers need me and all Latino sons to finish the journey that they began. For the most part our fathers got lost living between the old world of uncritical loyalty and the present world of power and self-interest that often diminished their humanity; they did their best, but most of them did not know how to create a new and better family and community. It is the task of Latino men to complete their journey so that we find our fulfillment in transformation. As Latino men carry their fathers within them into a new age, they need to be prepared to protect the community from the blows their fathers experienced. Men do this by becoming their own fathers, originators of a new people. Latino men will then be fully present because they have freed themselves from the dead hand of the past and of the stories and relationships that wounded their fathers and mothers. They need to give themselves permission to be the fathers and mothers of the future. The new kind of fatherhood and manhood as Latino males is centered in *la comunidad Latina;* but from that center we can now go beyond our own blood family and our own racial and ethnic family to include as our children all who are in need of nurturing and care. In this way, we as Latino men redeem the personal, political, historical, and sacred faces of our being and those of our fathers by bringing about a new creation: males who are both masculine and feminine, both fathers and mothers. As whole human beings we will find fulfillment by bringing together in a fundamentally new and more loving way our feminine and masculine capacity, our ability to nurture and care deeply about others.

Sexual Love, Eros, and the Capacity to Play

One of the most important strategies in creating a new kind of Latino male who is capable of intimacy and caring is to engage in sexual love and passion as play. Play is a way to undermine patriarchy. When we are intent on mutual sexual relationships, giving and receiving pleasure, we do not lose ourselves; but rather we rediscover ourselves as persons who can choose to be vulnerable with and for one another. To find themselves, Latino men need to give up control, the heart of patriarchal domination. To be spontaneous, to engage in long, sexual foreplay is to honor the lover's and one's own ability to play, to be open to the moment, to be open to change. I continue to be deeply moved by a novel I read as a student, *Siddhartha,* in which a beautiful courtesan, Kamala, tells Siddhartha that he knows how to make love but he does not know how to love. But neither did Kamala. For both Kamala and Siddhartha love had become a game of power and techniques.[42] As their relationship grew, Siddhartha realized how closely passion was related to death.[43] In death and passion, as in play, we need to give up domination, to release our fear of the next moment and to allow ourselves to experience a dying of our old sense of self. We need to experience rebirth through a sexual passion that is intimate, in which we let go our roles and risk faith by sharing ourselves. Men need to learn how to risk saying yes to life, to become pregnant with new feelings and ideas as well as with more fulfilling connections to women. Such mutually fulfilling love is impossible given the inherent restraints of the stories of patriarchy, homophobia, possessive love, capitalism, and other stories of exploitation. Living in these stories, we are not fully present: Intimacy is impossible.

Only when we become vulnerable are we as Latino males present, ready to enact new and better relationships.

Latino men can be fully passionate in a way that includes but goes beyond, without in any way disparaging, sexual intercourse. They can practice the story of erotic love, a story that finds its fulfillment in an infinite number of different connections. When they experience a bi-unity, a knowledge and experience of being at one with another person, with the deepest sacred, with nature, with music, with words that end emotionally charged as poetry, with color and form that express the deepest emotions and thoughts in a painting, all of these are experiences of erotic connection. Each of us has by our very nature as humans a creative imagination. Within each of us there is a continuous flow of inchoate ideas, intuitions, feelings, emotions, and passions that seek to become more fully human as they take their shape by being shared with others. When we find the right words, sounds, forms, and colors to express our deepest insights, we are making creative connections, that is, we are being erotic. To be erotic is to discover the joy that comes when one understands something for the first time and finds the right words and format to tell and share that knowledge no longer only in one's bones but in a new way. Eroticism is the pleasure that comes with connecting the previously unknown to the knower, who in that creative, erotic moment loses control and plays with risk and openness, becomes vulnerable. An erotic male cannot rest until he brings to fruition what he feels in the depths of his being. In this way the erotic male activates the creative imagination as he responds to inspiration, literally the breathing of the sacred within him. In this way men become intimate with themselves, with others, with nature, and with the deepest source of their being. The erotic Latino male is always open to new ideas, new feelings, new strategies. He is ready to risk his personal and political being so that he can bring about a new turning point in the history of his family, community, and nation. In such a context each person can concretely experience the eroticism of the creative imagination in his and her own life.

I shall return to the task of creating more loving and compassionate stories for the Latino male in Chapter 4.

Conclusion

In Spanish there is a very beautiful word, *amanecer,* which can be translated as "the dawn," the coming of the new day, "sunrise." There is a greeting that is spoken throughout the Latino world based on the word *amanecer*—*"¿Como amanecíste?"*—for which the usual translations are: "How did you sleep?" "How do you feel this morning after your evening rest?" But I prefer the literal translations: "How did you dawn?" "How did you rise up?" These literal translations better capture the reality of the indigenous heritage of *la comunidad Latina*. Like many other ancient peoples, the indigenous people of our past believed the sun went down every day and during the night had to fight to be reborn against the forces of eternal death. As the sun came up, they performed ceremonies to celebrate once again the victory of life over death. Some groups, such as the Aztecs, deformed this transformation by sacrificing human captives and virgins to the gods to ensure the return of the sun.[44]

I would like to return to this symbol and heritage. We know the indigenous people throughout Latin America worshiped the sun and the moon as coequal principles of life and death. The moon and silver symbolized the tears of the feminine moon goddess, and the sun and gold the sweat of the masculine sun god. Latinos and Latinas are the daughters and sons of this culture. They have inherited as well the ancient art of alchemy, the process by which base metals are purified into gold and silver, a purification that symbolizes the transformation of the shattered personality into the pearl of great price, the child in each of us waiting to be born, the self.[45] We can once again share the fears and tears of the feminine as the sun descends toward possible eternal death. But the feminine does not watch passively; she stands guard and provides her light. These two cosmic forces, the feminine and the masculine, celebrate the new dawn. The golden victory of the masculine principle and the silver victory of the feminine principle allow Latina women and Latino men to have *esperanza,* hope, from daily resurrection. Only through the daily commingling of our sweat and tears, our gold and silver, our sun and moon, our masculine and feminine selves will Latinas and Latinos be able to reveal the sacred as we transform male-female relationships. Unlike our indigenous forebears, we need not be inspired by a false lord to believe the new sun will only rise if we use human sacrifice. On the contrary, the enemies that seek to obstruct the new dawning within each of us and within the community as a whole are the destructive stories, patriarchy, capitalism, and racism. Inspired by the sacred source of transformation, we Latinas and Latinos can choose to let die daily the stories and relationships that cripple us. We rise daily: *amanecer.* And we experience a new dawning of more loving and just relationships between Latino men and Latina women, relationships that are the key to a new and more loving family as well as a more loving society.

Notes

1. Manfred Halpern, "Why Are Most of Us Partial Selves? Why Do Partial Selves Enter the Road to Deformation?" paper delivered at a panel on "Concepts of Self: Transformation and Politics" at the annual meeting of the American Political Science Association (Washington, D.C., August 29, 1991), p. 12.

2. The best readers in which one can find the writings of the Chicana/ Latina feminists mentioned are: *Living Chicana Theory,* edited by Carla Trujillo (Berkeley: Third Woman Press, 1998); *Chicana Feminist Thought: The Basic Writings,* edited by Alma M. García and Mario T. García (New York: Routledge, 1997); *Chicana Critical Issues,* edited by Norma Alarcón, et. al. (Berkeley: Third Woman Press, 1993); *Making Face, Making Soul, Haciendo Caras: Creative and Critical Perspectives by Women of Color,* edited by Gloria Anzaldúa (San Francisco: Aunt Lute Books, 1990); *Between Borders: Essays on Mexicana/Chicana History,* edited by Adelaida del Castillo (Encino, CA: Floricanto Press, 1990); Teresa Córdova et al., eds., *Chicana Voices: The Intersections of Class, Race and Gender* (Austin: University of Texas Press, 1990); *Building with Our Hands: New Directions in Chicana Studies,* edited by Adela De la Torre and Beatríz Pesquera (Berkeley: University of California Press, 1993); *This Bridge Called My Back: Writings by Radical Women of Color,* edited by Gloria Anzaldúa and Cherríe Moraga (Watertown, MA: Persephone Press, 1981); *The Latino/Latina Condition: A Critical Reader,* edited by Richard Delgado and Jean Stefancic (New York: New York University Press, 1998). See Bibliography for additional books and periodicals on this topic. For a more general feminist perspective that does an excellent job of relating race, class, and gender, see *Racism and Sexism: An Integrated Study,* edited by Paula Rothenberg (New York: St. Martin's Press, 1988).

3. See chapters 1, 4, and 5 in David T. Abalos, *La Comunidad Latina in the United States: Personal and Political Strategies for Transforming Culture* (Westport, CT: Praeger Press, 1998).

4. See chapter 4 in David T. Abalos, *The Latino Family and the Politics of Transformation* (Westport, CT: Praeger Press, 1993).

5. See in regards to the politics of resistance before the civil rights movement, Mario García, *Mexican Americans* (New Haven, CT: Yale University Press, 1991); Juan Gómez-Quiñones, *Chicano Politics: Reality and Promise, 1940–1990* (Albuquerque: University of New Mexico Press, 1991) and *The Roots of Chicano Politics, 1600–1940* (Albuquerque: University of New Mexico Press, 1994); and the excellent film *Los Mineros,* directed by Hector Galán, telescript by Hector Galán and Paul Espinosa, narrated by Luís Valdéz, and introduced by David McCullough for the American Experience Series, PBS (1990), which tells the stories of the returning Chicano GIs and their subsequent fight for unions and civil rights.

6. In this regard see Henry A.J. Ramos, *The American GI Forum: In Pursuit of the Dream, 1948–1983* (Houston: Arte Público Press, 1998). In the fall of 1985 I was asked by the Chicano Cultural Center at Yale University to give a series of four public lectures in honor of Dr. Hector P. García, the founder of the American GI Forum. I agreed to do this, but since I had never met Dr. García I traveled to Corpus Christi, Texas, in the summer of 1986 to meet and discuss with him what had led him to become involved in the founding of the American GI Forum. I had heard about Dr. García and of how some considered him to be somewhat conservative. But in our discussions I learned a great deal about his involvement in Chicano political activity in the 1940s and 1950s. He spoke of how he and some of his colleagues had set out after the war not only to make sure that returning Chicanos were receiving their GI Bill benefits but also to register Chicanas and Chicanos to vote. In one of our talks he recalled that "rednecks" would show up and not say anything or do anything as he went with his colleagues from house to house to encourage people to register to vote. These Anglos, who often showed up in small pickup trucks, did not say a word but conspicuously carried shotguns. Until his mid-seventies Dr. García continued to make house calls as he had all of his professional life as a doctor. I traveled around Corpus Christi with him on two separate visits and saw him in action both in the community and in his clinic. He often charged nothing for his services and until the end of his active life as a doctor drove an old car in which the air conditioning was not adequate to cool one in the legendary heat of a Corpus Christi summer. For all of his concern for veterans and duty to this country, he cared deeply about the issues of *la Causa*, from unemployment to bilingual education. He never failed to support a rally in which issues of justice were involved for *nuestra gente*. I came away from my encounters with Dr. García with feelings of respect, affection, and gratitude for what he had done in the struggle to achieve justice for *la comunidad*.

7. The crucial participation of Chicana women in the fight to establish a union for mine workers is the subject of the film *The Salt of the Earth,* directed by Herbert Biberman and produced by Independent Productions Corporation and the International Union of Mine, Mill, and Smelter Workers (1953), San Marcos (Zinc Town), New Mexico. For further historical documentation into the key part played by Latinas/Chicanas, see the article and bibliography provided by William V. Flores, "Mujeres en Huelga: Cultural Citizenship and Gender Empowerment in a Cannery Strike," pp. 210–254 in *Latino Cultural Citizenship: Claiming Identity, Space, and Rights,* edited by William V. Flores and Rina Benmayor (Boston: Beacon Press, 1997).

8. Antonia I. Castañeda, "Sexual Violence in the Politics of Violence," in *Building with Our Hands: New Directions in Chicana Studies,* edited by Adela de la Torre and Beatríz Pesquera (Berkeley: University of California Press, 1993), pp. 15–33.

9. Health Dillard, *Daughters of the Reconquest: Women in Castilian Town Society, 1100–1300* (Cambridge: Cambridge University Press, 1984).

10. See Norma Alarcón, "Chicana's Feminist Literature: A Re-Vision Through Malintzin, or Malintzin: Putting Flesh Back on the Object," in *This Bridge Called My Back: Writings by Radical Women of Color,* edited by Cherríe

Moraga and Gloria Anzaldúa (Watertown, MA: Persephone Press, 1981); and Sandra Messinger Cypess, *La Malinche in Mexican Literature: From History to Myth* (Austin: University of Texas Press, 1991).

11. Américo Castro, *The Spaniards,* translated by Willard King and Selma Magarettem (Berkeley: University of California Press, 1971), pp. 588–600.

12. Howell Raines, *My Soul Is Rested: The Story of the Civil Rights Movement in the Deep South* (New York: Bantam Books, 1978), p. 57.

13. Taylor Branch, *Parting the Waters: America in the King Years, 1954–63* (New York: Simon and Schuster, 1988), pp. 88–90.

14. Ibid., p. 860; see also Taylor Branch, *Pillar of Fire: America in the King Years, 1963–65* (New York: Simon and Schuster, 1998), pp. 530, 533, 545, 557.

15. Raines, *My Soul Is Rested,* pp. 432–434.

16. Peter Matthiessen, *Sal Si Puedes: César Chávez and the New American Revolution* (New York: Random House, 1972).

17. Based on personal interviews with a former colleague who worked as a volunteer for the United Farm Workers (UFW) and a Chicana who worked for twenty years with the UFW.

18. Malcolm X, *The Autobiography of Malcolm X* (New York: Grove Press, 1966).

19. Erik Erikson, *Ghandi's Truth: On the Origins of Militant Non-Violence* (New York: W. W. Norton, 1969), pp. 410–418.

20. Ibid., p. 194.

21. Ibid., pp. 237, 403.

22. Ibid., pp. 237–242.

23. Ibid., pp. 127–128.

24. Ibid., pp. 121–122, 403–406.

25. Plate 14, *The Marriage of Heaven and Hell,* from *William Blake,* vol. 3, *The Early Illuminated Books,* edited with an introduction and notes by Morris Eaves, Robert N. Essick, and Joseph Viscomi (Princeton, NJ: Princeton University Press, 1993), p. 166.

26. Ibid., Plate 4, p. 146.

27. Rosa Martha Villareal, *Doctor Magdalena* (Berkeley: TQS Publications, 1995), pp. 72–74.

28. Ibid., pp. 71–72.

29. Sandra Cisneros, *Woman Hollering Creek and Other Stories* (New York: Random House, 1991), pp. 43–56.

30. D. H. Lawrence, *The Plumed Serpent* (New York: Vintage Books, 1954), pp. 313–315.

31. Aspira annual conference, Miami, Florida, February 27, 1991.

32. There are many other Latino and non-Latino men who have helped me to understand manhood and masculinity in the Latino community. In this regard see especially Alfredo Mirandé, *Hombres y Machos: Masculinity and Latino Culture* (Boulder, CO: Westview Press, 1997); Rafael Ramírez, *What It Means to Be a Man: Reflections on Puerto Rican Masculinity,* translated by Rosa E. Casper (New Brunswick, NJ: Rutgers University Press, 1999); Rick Najera, *The Pain of the Macho and Other Plays* (Houston: Arte Público Press, 1997);

Ray González, ed., *Muy Macho: Latino Men Confront Their Manhood* (New York: Doubleday, 1996); Joseph Carrier, *De Los Otros: Intimacy and Homosexuality Among Mexican Men* (New York: Columbia University Press, 1995); Matthew C. Gutmann, *The Meanings of Macho: Being a Man in Mexico City* (Los Angeles: University of California Press, 1996); Stephen O. Murray, *Latin American Homosexuality* (Albuquerque: University of New Mexico Press, 1995); J. G. Peristiany, ed., *Honor and Shame: The Values of Mediterranean Society* (Chicago: University of Chicago Press, 1966); chapter 5 in David T. Abalos, *Strategies of Transformation Toward a Multicultural Society: Fulfilling the Story of Democracy* (Westport, CT: Praeger Press, 1996); and chapter 2 in Abalos, *La Comunidad Latina*. In regards to Latino men and homosexuality, bisexuality, and transvestism, see the authors cited in note 22 of Chapter 4.

33. Chapter 5 in Abalos, *La Comunidad Latina*. For other works on understanding machismo, see works cited in note 32 above, especially Mirandé, *Hombres y Machos;* González, *Muy Macho;* Ramírez, *What It Means to Be a Man;* and Gutmann, *The Meanings of Macho.*

34. David T. Abalos, "What It Takes to Make a Man from the Perspective of Transformation," paper presented at the Conference on Rescuing the Latino Male (Atlantic City, NJ, December 9, 1991).

35. National Council of La Raza, annual meeting (Chicago, July 12, 1997).

36. This statistical profile outlining some of the dangers facing *la comunidad Latina* was largely drawn from two papers: Curt Idrogo, "Hispanic Americans," in *A Guide to Multicultural Resources, 1997–1998,* edited by Alex Boyd (Fort Atkinson, WI: High Smith Publications, 1997); and Rev. Ferdinand Fuentes, "An Overview of the Hispanic Context in the United States," a United Church of Christ Latina and Latino Leadership Summit working paper (Cleveland, 1994).

37. Ann Belford Ulanov, *The Feminine in Jungian Psychology and in Christian Theology* (Evanston, IL: Northwestern University Press, 1971), pp. 277–285.

38. Chapter 4 in Abalos, *La Comunidad Latina*. For a fine insight as to the issues facing Latina and Latino students, from male-female relationships to concerns with education, identity, and how to survive in an Anglo world, see Félix M. Padilla, *The Struggle of Latina/Latino University Students: In Search of a Liberating Education* (New York: Routledge, 1997).

39. Shlomo Avineri, "Marx's Vision of Future Society," *Dissent* 20 (summer 1973): 330.

40. *Lucía,* a Cuban film directed by Humberto Solas (1968).

41. Chapter 5 in Abalos, *The Latino Family.*

42. Hermann Hesse, *Siddhartha* (New York: Bantam Books, 1971), p. 73.

43. Ibid., p. 81.

44. Octavio Paz, *The Other Mexico: Critique of the Pyramid,* translated by Lysander Kemp (New York: Grove Press, 1972), pp. 71–112.

45. Titus Burckhardt, *Alchemy* (Baltimore: Penguin Books, 1971), pp. 11–22.

2

~~~

Setting the Context:
A Theory of Transformation

Now that the reader knows me and my journey to manhood as a Latino man, I want to retell and re-vision my story and that of Latino men in general from the perspective of a theory of transformation. Latino men come in all colors and sizes. Although most have been raised Catholic, they are religiously diverse. Some are gay and bisexual. They speak a variety of languages, not only Spanish. They come from twenty-one different nations. Some are Indian, others are closer to European roots. The majority are *mestizos,* that is, men with a rich and colorful heritage from mixed racial and ethnic backgrounds. Those who have Spanish blood have always been multicultural, with a heritage that is Jewish, Christian, and Muslim, joined in the New World with Native American and later African blood. When Columbus arrived in the New World there were 500 indigenous cultures in what is now called Latin America. Many Latino men from Argentina, Paraguay, Uruguay, and Chile have Italian, German, and East European blood in their veins. Latino men from Peru could easily have Japanese ancestors as well as Incan and Spanish ancestors. To this day there are Latino men who speak no Spanish and who continue to communicate in ancient tongues such as Nahuatl, Quechua, or Quiche Maya as a result of the struggle of their ancestors to resist Spanish domination. Latino men are truly *de colores,* men of many colors.

But the facts about Latino men, their socioeconomic status, their levels of employment, their income, their level of participation in the workforce, how many years they went to school, tell us little about such complex individuals. We know almost nothing about them. We need to know on a deeper level what is happening in the lives of Latino men.

47

Latino men and the people who live and work with them can only know what their lives are like if they ask new questions: What are the stories that the Latino male is now practicing? Where are Latinos in the core drama of life? What do the four faces of their being, the personal, political, historical, and sacred, look like as they struggle for wholeness? And the most important question: In the service of what way of life are they enacting the stories and relationships of their daily living? In the midst of the changes swirling around us, Latino men have much in common. All of them share many of the same underlying archetypal stories and relationships, even though those stories and relationships may be practiced in the service of radically different ways of life. I want to tell this deeper story. I want to reveal the struggle to be a man, a person, a self, what we share as Latino men by looking at our lives through a new lens, a theory of transformation.

A Theory of Transformation as Our Guide

Modern social science has reduced its pursuit of the understanding of the Latino male to statistics, variables, and the use of questionnaires. Many social scientists want to quantify the facts about Latino men in an attempt to create a mathematical certainty they hope will capture the meaning of Latino culture and people. None of their methodologies or instruments have proven capable of revealing what is really happening on the deeper levels in the lives of Latino men. Many sociologists and political scientists study the institutionalized power of male privilege without knowing about the realm of the archetypal, the underlying sacred, formative sources. Nor do they understand the difference among these sacred sources. As a result they can only describe the outward manifestations of the lives of Latino men and the stories that they enact by counting, looking for variables, and interviewing. But they cannot help Latino men to free themselves from powerful stories such as patriarchal machismo that are a manifestation of a deeper force. Nor can they tell Latino men how they can participate in the process of transformation that enables them to know and reject the stories of domination so they can create fundamentally more loving and just alternatives for relationships between men and women.

Because scholars continue to rely on traditional social science, we know very little about who Latino men are, why their lives are breaking, and where they are going. In fact, postmodernists, or poststructuralists, have left all men completely bereft. Practitioners of these theories are opposed to the theory I use here because it points to living, underlying, patterning forces, or archetypes. Poststructuralists consider this kind of theory essentialist, universal, and structured, which discounts individual freedom. But the theory of transformation being used here has no intention of upholding any kind of established order, the order that benefits those in power; nor does it seek to replace the old theories with a new power theory. Moreover, this is not an attempt to set up a new dogma as theory. Yes, it was necessary, as many feminists and others have argued, to demolish the structures and functions of the dominant theory that upheld the power of the old guard in the academy and in policymaking. But once this was accomplished, we were left with no theory by which to reconstruct our lives and world. Any theory that seeks to make sense of our lives on a deeper level, illuminating a structure to our lives, is quickly dismissed. So what I ask is that readers remain skeptical and yet open as they are invited to personally participate by testing this theory with their own experiences, evaluating whether or not this theory in fact allows us to see, understand, and participate in creating alternatives that are new and more just. Do I ask that readers make a leap of faith? No, not if this means blind acceptance as belief. But yes, I do, if faith means taking a risk by opening ourselves to a new experience.

Although this theory is indebted to Jung and his understanding of archetypes, it fundamentally disagrees with his work. Jung had almost nothing to say about the process of transformation. He was silent on the political and historical faces of our being and wrote nothing at all about archetypal ways of life in which we enact the relationships and stories of our lives and from which we draw the deeper meaning and value of what we enact.[1]

This theory is not an abstraction. It is an invitation to understand and participate in a sacred story at the heart of human existence. My exploration with readers of how we can rediscover the deeper reality of the Latino male is based on the discovery that there is a fundamental structure to life that is given to us by the core drama of life, a drama with three acts. Many Latino men either arrest themselves in a fragment of this journey, the partial ways of life of emanation, incoherence, and deformation, or they move toward its fulfillment by journeying through all three acts of the drama until they reach transformation.[2]

The Core Drama of Life and the
Origin of the Four Ways of Life

The source of transformation, the deepest source of our being, has created the most important story: the core drama of life. Only this story fulfills the need for persistent transformation. The core drama of life is a three-act drama that must be enacted again and again. Why? Because the deepest source is still creating the universe. From the beginning, creation was intended to bring forth the fundamentally new and better. The core drama of life, as fulfilled by the story of transformation, requires participation in all of its three acts between the deepest source and human beings. Our deepest source is what I call the first source. It is not perfect or finished; it continues to create. We and the deepest source need to continually choose to respond to new problems by journeying through the core drama of life. We, together with the deepest sacred source of transformation, are the only creatures able to persist in transformation because we can choose new and better answers to new problems as we journey through the core drama of life. Only humans can, drawing upon the sacred source of transformation, participate in transformation without a preprogrammed outcome.

But there are three other sacred sources: the lords of emanation, incoherence, and deformation. Unfortunately, they have the power to arrest us in fragments of the core drama of life and thus to frustrate the work of transformation. Why are lesser sacred forces or lords able to arrest our lives in different acts and scenes of our journey and thereby frustrate the story of transformation created by our deepest source? This is not a puppet play. The story of transformation has to offer us, and the lords of emanation, incoherence, and deformation, the capacity and freedom to say no and yes to this story that constitutes the heart of creation. The partial lords of emanation, incoherence, and deformation try to prevent us from hearing the voice of the deepest source, who reaches out to us in order to further transformation.[3] To reach the goal of the core drama of life, the third act involves the practice of transformation, the practice of continually saying no to the archetypal lords who enchant us and hold us in fragments of the core drama of life. We need to free ourselves from these lesser sacred sources and the ways of life they inspire in order to be filled anew by the deepest source of transformation. To choose to make life fundamentally more loving and compassionate is to participate with each other and the source of transformation, the deepest ground of our being.[4]

So let me continue to tell the story of the journey through the three acts of the core drama of life, to explain the four fundamentally different ways of life, and to provide examples of the stories and relationships available to us by which we shape the personal, political, historical, and sacred faces of our being in our daily lives. On this journey through the three acts of the core drama of life I invite readers to test this theory with their own experiences in order to determine if it is in fact a path that leads to the fundamentally new and better.

The Three Acts of the Core Drama of Life

Telling the story of this drama tells us something we are rarely told: How in actual practice can we transform ourselves? How can we actually find a fundamentally better way and test it by translating it into practice together with our neighbors?[5]

The core drama of life is a journey with three acts (see Figure 2.1). There are no deeper acts of life than the three acts of this drama. When Latino males arrest life, and therefore their masculinity, in one of these acts before reaching the third act, they stunt their manhood in a fragment of the core drama. And because it is only a fragment, it leaves Latino men as partial selves: fragile, wounded, and angry no matter how much power they may accumulate within it. Each time someone enacts this drama in its fullness as the archetypal journey of transformation, he or she together with the deepest sacred source are mutual participants in the process of continuous creation.

The core drama of life requires a mutual participation in its three acts between the ground of our being and the individual. In this drama all human beings, but specifically Latino males, can by the very nature of their humanity consciously, critically, creatively, and caringly participate in fulfilling the core drama of life. But this co-creation can only take place if Latino men realize their own story by overcoming arrested and fragmented aspects of their maleness and embarking on the journey of transformation.[6]

Arresting Life in Act I, Scene 1: The Way of Life of Emanation

We always begin in emanation in Act I, Scene 1, at the very least in the relationship of emanation. Emanation is a relationship in which we are held as extensions of powerful others such as our mother or father, who provide us with security, love, and nurturance. We need emanation as a relationship to survive. But what should be a temporary and loving initiation into the journey of life is too often frozen and dogmatized into a

Figure 2.1   The Core Drama of Life Symbolized

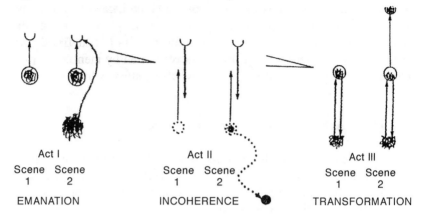

permanent relationship and the end of one's journey. For most of recorded history, emanation as a relationship became not a step forward in a quest but was arrested as a whole way of life. Because the lord of emanation is the sacred source that legitimizes the established order, human lives were arrested in the first scene of Act I. They were caught in the overwhelming embrace of mysterious others like their mothers and fathers. They were raised to be uncritically loyal to an established lord that legitimized the power of their mothers and fathers and the stories of patriarchy, uncritical loyalty, and machismo. Because they were told to believe that the final truth had been given to us, their lives were arrested here, and Act I, Scene 1, was a finished drama, an entire way of life in the service of emanation. Those who remain in this overarching way of life are forbidden to ask new questions about masculinity or femininity because these ideas and what they represent in the real world have been determined as true for all time. To doubt their eternal truth is to be threatened with sin, shame, and guilt. In this way the stories of patriarchy and masculine power were and continue to be legitimized by the lord of emanation. Under the influence of this lord, men dominated women and denied their own femininity as the will of this lord. This smaller, petty lord, split off from the deepest sacred source of transformation, is worshiped as a masculine lord in the three world religions of Christianity, Judaism, and Islam. He inspires (literally, breathes within) followers to repress any idea that would go against masculine hegemony. This lord, the lord of emanation, is the sacred origin of the archetypal domination of the masculine over the feminine. One of the most important stories enacted in the service of emanation in the Latino community that maintains the supremacy of men is the story of patriarchy.

Looking inside the archetypal drama of patriarchy. Simply defined, patriarchy means the systematic domination of women by men. It is important for us to know the characteristics of this story, which has devastated the Latino community for generations:

- Women are seen primarily as producers of children.
- Women carry the honor of the family in their sexuality.
- Women's main task in life is to be housewives.
- Women are expected to be sensitive, emotional, soft, and gentle.
- Women are never allowed to be economically autonomous.
- Women are subjected to a double moral standard.
- Women are forced to become manipulative in order to survive.
- For the lifelong repression women have endured they gain their part of the bargain by driving their men to provide for them.
- This story is always in the service of emanation, incoherence, or deformation, destructive and partial ways of life that arrest the lives of women and men in the core drama.
- The four faces of both women and men are undermined by repression.
- This story wounds the next generation.
- The sacred source of emanation blesses this story as the fate of women.
- This story cripples both men and women because neither can become full persons.

Many Latinas and Latinos continue to practice the inherited story of patriarchy that determines male-female relationships as final and ultimate because they are the revelation of a mysterious lord. This is how the status quo comes to be final: Latinas and Latinos are forbidden by the stories they live to create conflict or change; their sense of justice is perverted to become the enforcement of revealed dogma. The cost they pay is the repression of the personal, political, historical, and sacred faces of their being. Because they do not question this tradition, their entire lives are arrested here. Life begins and ends with emanation in Act I, Scene 1.

Since many Latino men are radically wounded, cut off from their deepest source, arrested in the possessive embrace of the lord of emanation, they cannot develop a new consciousness. Their creativity is denied. They are forbidden new relationships to others outside their family and community, and they cannot pursue shared goals with others. They diminish their own humanity and that of others in order to protect and maintain an alleged male superiority.

Act I, Scene 2

But Latino men can hear the deepest source even in the midst of their repression. However powerful, the emanation that threatens to arrest us in Act I, Scene 1, is fragile precisely because we have an inner need to experience the fundamentally new and more loving again and again in order to turn the fundamentally new toward the fundamentally better. For this reason there are two scenes in Act I. In Scene 2, we are filled with new ideas and intuitions that have their origin beyond the official voice of conscience formed by our culture and society. This inner voice, rooted in underlying sacred sources, undermines our repression. But we cannot assume that these new voices are to the good. We need to test them to discern whether or not they are fundamentally new and better or if they are destructive. We can choose to risk faith that the new inspiration comes from the deepest source of transformation. If we respond to these new feelings and give up trying to repress them, we leave Act I, Scene 1. We rebel and break with significant others who have held us in the embrace of emanation.

The way of life of emanation is everywhere dying. Many people are no longer willing to deny their fundamentally new experiences, ideas, and hopes. When Latina women begin to move toward rebellion by acting out their own desires, too often Latino men respond by attempting to restore their inherited privilege. Many resort to violence when women and children dare to raise questions. Many Latino men cannot accept the challenge, because the story of patriarchy and machismo together with the story of uncritical loyalty makes it very difficult for them to see any other possibilities.

Arresting Life in Act II, Scene 1:
The Way of Life of Incoherence

When individuals do take Act I, Scene 2, that is, new doubts and intuitions, seriously, they enter into Act II, Scene 1, wherein they break with parents and other authority figures and embark upon a path of open rebellion. But the first scene of Act II also threatens to arrest the journey and institutionalize rebellion. As a community, Latino men and Latina women are currently facing perhaps their greatest challenge: how to create a new and more compassionate culture as they find themselves living in the midst of the story of capitalism. Because they live in a hostile world, rather than continuing their journeys many create fortresses to escape a world they do not understand.

Another sacred force is present: the lord of incoherence, the lord of power, who attracts us and inspires us in the first scene of Act II. This lord replaces the lord of emanation. But like the lord of emanation, the lord of incoherence is a partial and lesser lord who hinders Latino men's ability to reach the deepest sacred. Latino men pay a heavy price for assimilating into the story of capitalism. The lord of incoherence inspires them to practice their masculinity in the pursuit of power and self-interest. This way of life takes them over and their relationship to this overarching drama is one they cannot understand. They get trapped in stories that turn them against each other in a perpetual competition that sours relationships into contests of mutual suspicion and fear. Assimilation is deadly for *la comunidad Latina*. When its members join the powerful they too become possessed by the story of capitalism. In addition they are filled with the self-hatred that comes from believing they are inferior until they become manly, as defined by white, European-American men. If Latino men fail to compete, to achieve power (and the structures of racism make their failure likely), too often they compensate by turning to domination in the home, the last resort of their wounded masculine pride.[7]

Looking inside the archetypal drama of capitalism. Let us consider what practicing the story of capitalism does to the humanity of Latino males and the price they pay for assimilating into this story. The following are the characteristics that they actually live and practice:[8]

- In order to survive, Latino men are all tempted to become immoral and insincere.
- Nobody can afford to be intimate.
- We are always looking over our shoulders lest we be overtaken.
- We wear masks.
- All of our relationships are in danger of being corrupted by the competition for power.
- We belong to impersonal systems that turn us into fragments.
- Nobody knows the individual in his or her wholeness.
- The bureaucracy of the system is based on anonymity.
- This story is always in the service of incoherence or deformation.
- We cannot practice the four faces of our being in their fullness.

This is the official story of U.S. society, which arrests our lives in Act II, Scene 1.⁹ This way of life is often in collusion with deformation. In order to practice the story of capitalism we have to be prepared to hurt those who threaten us. When European Americans become annoyed that I do not want members of *la comunidad Latina* to assimilate, I explain that I do not want them to accept and practice the story of capitalism. I explain the deeper meaning of this story, how it wounds our humanity. Capitalism is not the United States at its best: U.S. society fulfills its promise when its members practice the story of participatory democracy.

In the story of capitalism, we agree on procedures that keep us from physically assaulting or killing each other as we struggle with one another in the name of self-interest. To overcome our vulnerability, we seek power, which, of course, increases our anxiety. There is no security. We turn this attempt to organize insecurity, without being able to name it, into a whole way of life, a way of life I call incoherence. Everyone is had by this story. The powerful, the less powerful, and the powerless are all wounded but still collude with each other to believe this is the only way to live.

Latino men wake up day after day knowing what this way of life is doing to them and to their community. They get angry and sit with one another and talk about how the Anglos are using them. Again and again they rebel against them in their conversations and, at times, through actions. But since they are only breaking with actual antagonists in Act II, Scene 1, they remain caught by the lord of incoherence, by the archetypal story of capitalism. By merely rebelling against Anglo power and bosses, they seek to replace Anglo male domination with Latino male domination. But nothing has really changed. The color of the people seeking power has changed, but, on the deeper level, people are still being held and exploited by the same story of capitalism. Since these individuals are arrested in the first scene of Act II, they cannot in fact know themselves, nor can they know their own best self-interest. Many Latino males know themselves only as fragments, unable to realize their deeper manhood.

It is not enough to break with European American male domination; Latino men need to experience a deeper breaking. They need to empty their souls of the archetypal story of capitalism in the service of incoherence that inspired and gave mysterious power to their white or brown bosses. They need to focus their anger by becoming radical, that is, going to the roots of the problem. Otherwise they will become just like the bosses. They are not the enemy; they are also victims of a story that destroys their humanity when people become obsessed with greed and power. The real enemy is the story of capitalism and a way of life inspired by the lord of incoherence. Because Latino men do not understand the power of these sacred stories that are concrete manifestations of underlying sacred forces and the necessity of emptying themselves of them, they repeat history, that is, live the same stories in the service of ways of life that constitute mere fragments of the core drama of life. Even though most Latino men remain unaware of the world of archetypal, sacred forces that possess them, they wake up one day to realize that only the outer appearances have changed. The story remains as powerful as before.

Moving Into Destructive Death at the Exit from the Core Drama in Act II, Scene 2: The Way of Life of Deformation

Deformation is the exit from the core drama; deformation diminishes our humanity and places us in the service of destructive death. At the second scene of Act II, Latino men have a choice: Either they empty themselves of the stories and partial ways of life that have possessed them or they turn to violence in order to hang on to the old stories, thereby hurting themselves and others. In this scene men move from being the victims to become the victimizers. In the modern age, deformation is becoming increasingly more prevalent. Because of the inherent fragility of emanation and of incoherence as ways of life, people whose security is threatened often turn toward violence to preserve their way of life, thus exiting the core drama of life in the service of deformation. Violence, of course, always fails to make things better and even fails to return them to the way they were. Because many Latino males are excluded from the realms of power, they feel increasingly powerless. At home fragments of the way of life of emanation continue to break. What deformation promises is not just power, but absolute power. If Latino males join a gang, deal drugs, or give in to fantasies of restoring male privilege, they feel they have the power of life and death over others. Power now becomes total power. What people who seek power are really after is security, even as the ground shifts and opens beneath their feet.

A Latino male who is not making it in the power game in society often seeks to assert his power by restoring the stories of possessive love, uncritical loyalty, and patriarchy in male-female relationships and thereby seeks to return women to the dying way of a life of emanation. But emanation as a way of life is losing its meaning for many Latina women; they are no longer willing to submit to the traditional culture. As a consequence, they and their children are often physically or psychologically abused. What began as a return to the past and the way of life of emanation is really a pseudo-emanation, a false world that ends in deformation. Latino men are caught between two crumbling ways of life: In the life of emanation they are trying to uphold the legitimation of masculine power, and in the other world of capitalism they are failing to succeed. Thus many Latino men are driven to violence against themselves and others at home and in the wider society. What began as an attempt to restore the story of patriarchy in the service of emanation in order to compensate for powerlessness in the Anglo world now becomes patriarchy in the service of deformation, destructive death at the exit from the core drama of life. This explanation exposes the lie that "family values" and the restoration of the old respect are ideals worthy of honorable men. Many Latino males are angry with their lives because they are losing contact with their own Latino roots, and, even though they are trying to assimilate, they are not getting ahead. Too many of them vent their rage on the women whom they want to keep below them in the hierarchy of power.

But violence was always a part of the strategy to preserve the way of life of emanation. Deformation has always been available as an ally to men who tried to maintain the container of emanation. Many wives were abused as a matter of right by Latino men. It was not necessary for a woman to be in open rebellion to be assaulted. The greatest and ever-growing danger in these circumstances is that the hidden resentment of the husband will erupt at any time without warning in an irrational manner in the form of violence. The Latino culture has given men permission to abuse their wives both psychologically and physically, just to let them know who is boss. It was the Latina woman's duty to accept this violence. Both Latino men and Latina women in the Latino community have colluded in practicing the relationship of deformation as victim and victimizer for generations. But practicing deformation as a way of life differs from deformation as a relationship. In deformation as a whole way of life, violence becomes systematic and threatens to destroy families both physically and psychically. Latina mothers and wives have been raised to believe that they must have done something to cause such an eruption of anger, so they are always prepared to blame themselves and forgive the male abusers. Latina women entered into a conspiracy with men that guaranteed that violence would go on in a morbid sadistic-masochistic drama in the service of deformation.

The male ego is badly bruised by its inability to make it in U.S. society. The Latino man's self-image is distorted by the exalted role that *la cultura Latina* gives him. Too often Latino men are unhappy but do not know what to do except to try to compensate for their sense of powerlessness by exercising total power over children and wives. When they fail to intimidate Latina women who have the courage to resist them or leave them, they escalate the violence or see themselves as failures and turn to violence against themselves. Latino men live on the edge of the abyss. Why is this so? Latino men dedicated to this arrested way of living cannot allow any new feelings within themselves or in those around them. They continue to repress, deny, and destroy new ideas, feelings, intuitions, and stories that question their privilege. They are prepared to hurt themselves and others in order to keep their families and worlds intact. The inability to acknowledge crucial aspects of their lives is what constitutes the danger of being a partial self. In order to preserve a stunted identity in a truncated world, the road to violence opens up again and again.

The present expressions of the archetype of masculinity in the Latino community are but a few of the possibilities Latino men might create. Men's current models and expressions of maleness are profoundly flawed because men have historically practiced maleness as a way of being superior to women. This view was affirmed by the most recent statement of the Southern Baptist Convention, which declared that it is God's will that women should submit, albeit graciously, to their husbands.[10] The Catholic Church and other Christian denominations encourage the same submission of women to men. In this atmosphere the essence of femininity becomes the negation of the feminine self for the sake of enhancing the masculine. To ask women to efface themselves for the sake of men who have no idea who they are is to move more deeply into ignorance. As Tina Rosenberg points out:

> Machismo still reigns. Sexual and physical abuse is common among all social classes in Latin America. It is less and less acceptable to say so publicly, but many people, including many women, still view a woman as a man's property. Moreover, they see sexual violence as besmirching the honor of a woman and, if she is married, the honor of the husband to whom she belongs. This view is still found in the law. In at least ten countries, a rapist can escape punishment by marrying his victim. Her family often pressures her into agreeing, to restore her honor and assure a husband for a woman considered tainted.[11]

Killing a woman to recover one's honor is still practiced in some Muslim countries. This practice is justified on the premise that a woman's body is not her own but the property of the men in the family. Sexual relations outside of marriage are totally unacceptable. The honor of a man is physically located in the vagina of the woman. Any alleged unclean act dishonors and humiliates the men in her family.[12]

Looking inside the story of the wounded self. Many of us were hurt as children by disappointed men and sometimes disappointed women who, because they could not cope with their lives, lashed out in violence against themselves and us. I have discovered by asking my students to write about the politics of their own family that the vast majority of them have suffered from one or several of the following traumas: sexual abuse, physical or psychological abuse, alcohol abuse, drug abuse, and desertion. I have found this to be true of children from all backgrounds.

What this means is that many of us walk around hemorrhaging from within. And because we live the story of capitalism we dare not admit our pain, our hurt. To admit vulnerability is dangerous in the midst of a contest for power. Many people try to compensate for the deformation they have experienced by filling the void with that very power. But all the power in the world cannot heal the story of the wounded self. Neither should individuals return to the stories of patriarchy and uncritical loyalty to heal their broken lives. We need to do something with the hurt and the corresponding anger before we can go on with our lives.

I, for example, was abused as a child. For years I did not see this experience as the basis for my anger. Because I wanted to be acceptable to others, I repressed this part of my life. But it did not go away. I finally entered therapy and told the story of my abuse and began the process of emptying myself, in Act II, Scene 2, of the story of the wounded self and the way of life of deformation. Because I had not faced this story I was in danger of repeating it with my own children as I lived my own version of the disappointed male.

The Latino community needs to recognize the stories and ways of life that strangle its members and void itself of the archetypal dramas of patriarchy, uncritical loyalty, machismo, the disappointed male, homophobia, capitalism, and the wounded self. It is these underlying ways of life and stories that are the enemy. Latino men have a right to be angry because of what was done to them. But there can be no revenge in the story of transformation. These men need only the courage released by their anger to first engage their oppressors. Then they need to go beyond those who oppress because they are also victims. It is the deeper causes, the stories and the partial ways of life, that are wounding the lives of Latino men. Once they have emptied themselves of these destructive stories lived in the service of emanation, incoherence, and deformation (Act II, Scene 2), Latino men can send the stories, not themselves or others, into the abyss at the exit from the core drama. Now freed, they can begin Act III, Scene 1, to hear anew from the deepest source of their being. Subsequently, the second scene of Act III offers the chance to practice with our neighbors this new vision.

Moving On in the Core Drama of Life in Act III, Scenes 1 and 2: The Way of Life of Transformation

The fundamentally new and better cannot come from current cultural stories or religious institutions. They inspire Latino men only to a life of fragments in which they fantasize about an ultimate truth or about power to control others or absolute power over the life and death of those others, the outsiders. Latino men need to turn to the deepest sacred source in order to shape a more compassionate and inclusive world. The participation of all sons and daughters of the deepest sacred is necessary to transform the personal, political, historical, and sacred faces of life.

To journey through the story of transformation as the core drama of life is the vocation to which all humans are called. A decisive breakthrough has been accomplished when Latino males realize that their greatest freedoms are to (1) become conscious of the archetypal ways of life, stories, and relationships they are living, (2) prepare themselves to choose some and reject others, and (3) participate in creating more loving and just archetypal stories and relationships in the service of transformation. In Act III, Scenes 1 and 2, the final act of the core drama of life, Latino men can now cooperate with their deepest sacred source in order to share in the continuous work of creation.

The story of transformation is radically different; this sacred story needs the conscious and creative participation of all who endeavor to live it. They need to rebel against their actual antagonists, the men and women in their lives from whom they learned how to dominate women. This allows men to break from the underlying stories and partial ways of life in which they and the men and women of their lives were caught.

The way of life of transformation provides the only context within which Latino males can express the wholeness of the personal, political, historical, and sacred faces of our being. But the deepest source is free to continuously re-create the world only when people are prepared to personally decide to be political in order to create a new and more open and just history. The sacred face of our being incarnates the sacred source of transformation that inspires us. Participation in persistent transformation belongs to each of us by the very nature of our humanity.

What I am coming to understand is that the emerging stories of the Latino male as a political innovator, faithful partner, guide, and nurturing parent, which I will describe fully later in Chapters 4 and 5, are grounded in transformation. People like you and me give a new expression to what it means to be human by coming to know ourselves and by emptying ourselves of destructive stories and ways of life, and by creating new and more compassionate stories in the service of transformation. Latinos and Latinas, people of color, women, men, and individuals from all backgrounds are manifesting the four faces of our being by making a personal decision to create new and more compassionate stories, thus rejecting the stories that previously diminished our humanity. Through our political faces we can give shape to an environment in which we are free to enact what is necessary to bring about justice. Together we can create a new turning point for our nation, a new history, a new story of democracy, a multicultural diversity that affirms that each of us has a sacred face. Most Latinos and Latinas were never told that each of them has a personal, a political, a historical, and a sacred face by which to shape daily life. Furthermore we were not taught to question our culture so that by critique and dialogue they could constantly renew and transform their heritage through conscious participation. Latino males too often became a part of the culture and lost their ability to empty themselves of the destructive stories and partial ways of life by allowing themselves to be made into uncritical participants who carried out pre-programmed behavior. In this way our *cultura Latina* took on a life of its own, and we as its members became the mere recipients of the past, rather than the persistent creators of an evolving culture.

Now let us go on to see how in the context of daily life Latino men connect themselves to Latina women and to the world around them and how these relationships often fail to allow Latino men to respond to new kinds of problems.

Nine Archetypal Relationships Enacted Within the Four Different Archetypal Ways of Life

What constitutes our first worldwide revolution is the breaking of the concrete, inherited manifestations of archetypal relationships as well as the dying of the way of life of emanation. Everywhere in the world societies and cultures founded on a final truth are being undermined and subverted. This collapse of meaning and purpose gives rise to a profound anxiety that opens up both horrible and creative possibilities.

In all encounters between self and other in recorded history and in all societies, there are according to the theory of transformation being developed here only nine forms of relationship that give people the capacity to deal simultaneously with continuity and change, collaboration and conflict, and the achieving of justice. These nine archetypal relationships apply to all intrapersonal, interpersonal, and intergroup relations. These nine relationships apply to all groups, from families, or affinity groups, to political parties, nations, and the human species. Individuals also connect themselves to those forces that have been called the sacred, the unconscious, or god. We can know how others in our past have related to one another because there are only nine relationships in recorded history and in human society. You and I can test the claim that this hypothesis applies to all human experience by examining our own experiences.

What are the archetypal patterns of relationship that connect the lives of Latino men? From one moment to the next, the theory of transformation sensitizes us to the realization that our task is to deal with constant change. Our lives are always in the process of creation, nourishment, enforced preservation, death, and re-creation. This perpetual process of change is given shape by nine specific archetypal relationships, and they in turn are given their deeper meaning by the four archetypal ways of life in whose service men and women enact relationships. Practiced in the service of a particular way of life, each of the nine archetypal relationships has its own capacity to relate ourselves to the self, to the other members of our society, to problems, and to the sacred.

Let us now proceed to an explanation of the nine forms of encounter enacted in the service of the four radically different ways of life: emanation, incoherence, deformation, and transformation. Identifying which relationships are allowed by a particular society tells us what any person or group is free to express and what they are forced to repress. Presently there are very few persons in the world who are free to create all nine relationships. With the exception of deformation, no current society encourages or even allows the free use of the other eight relationships in the service of transformation. Currently all human societies discourage full human capacity.

Figure 2.2 provides a symbolic representation of the nine archetypal relationships by which we can shape daily life. Emanation, subjection, isolation, buffering, direct bargaining, autonomy, incoherence, deformation, and transformation: These are the patterns by which we shape daily life and act out the stories of our lives. We encounter problems in

Figure 2.2 The Nine Archetypal Relationships Symbolized

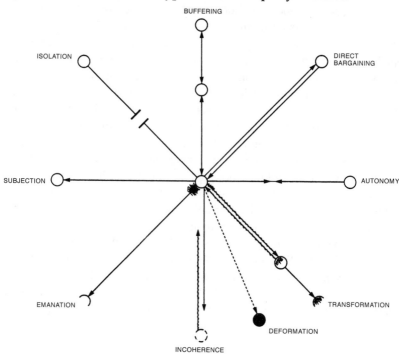

our lives when the concrete, inherited forms of these underlying patterns no longer give us the ability to deal with the five issues of daily, human performance: continuity and change, collaboration and conflict, and justice. Each individual has five aspects of capacity, and each relationship differs in its ability to connect the individual to them: new consciousness, creativity, linkages to others, the experience of shared justice with others, and the ability to reach the deepest source of our being. Each concrete form of an archetypal relationship gives us a different ability to cope with the five issues of performance and the five aspects of capacity.

These relationships will be fully explained with examples in this chapter and throughout the book. My goal is to demonstrate how to take the concrete, inherited manifestations of these nine archetypal patterns into our own hands so that as patterns break we can create new concrete combinations of these archetypal patterns in order to restore for ourselves the capacity to change. We can identify those patterns that have to be struggled against by naming them clearly as patterns that, in their present concrete form, undermine our human capacity to reexperience self, other, and our creative sources.

Emanation

In the relationship of emanation one treats another person, such as a son or wife, as an extension of oneself. If a wife accepts the denial of her own separate identity because of the mysterious and overwhelming power of the source of this emanation, the husband has a mysterious power over her. If a wife dutifully obeys her husband in the relationship of emanation, she is rewarded with security. All humans began life as children vulnerable to the powerful others in their homes. We had no choice but to yield our identity to the mysterious and overwhelming power of our mothers until we felt strong enough to risk our security by freeing ourselves. However, some of our fathers or mothers want to keep us in the container of emanation, seeing their children as carbon copies of themselves, that is, as emanations of themselves. In the Latino culture when a woman marries, she often transfers this emanational relationship with her father to her husband. It could be said that she never left home. Others treat their property or their employees in this way. Many individuals remain eager to surrender themselves as loyal extensions of a political movement, a dogma, or a lover.[13]

The relationship of emanation is the most prevalent and, perhaps, the most powerful relationship in the Latino community to this day. It points out an unexamined, unconscious, uncritical relationship to a mysterious and overwhelming source that contains Latino men and Latina women, and within which they live inherited stories. Indeed most are not even conscious of archetypal stories; they practice unconsciously the relationship of emanation. Moreover, many Latino men see themselves as the expression of their father's personality. Most Latino men and Latina women were raised under inherited stories, especially patriarchy, and were trained to believe that the limits of their lives are determined by their fathers or matriarchal mothers. What was good enough for their mothers and fathers is good enough for them. With this perspective, change cannot possibly arise.

Many Latinos agree to repress conflict. Both parties agree to achieve continuity by rejecting change, taking their cues from fathers, mothers, or other authority figures. In this way they grant mysterious and overwhelming power to them in exchange for security. Emanation keeps individuals firmly embedded in Act I, Scene 1, of the core drama of life. No other relationship among the other eight offers a Latina woman as much security as emanation. Many Latinas are tempted to remain in its embrace in order to avoid participating freely in conflict and change. Thus they submerge their own lives and live as an extension or shadow of a mysteriously overwhelming male figure, father, uncle, husband, or brother. But the relationship of emanation is not in itself destructive. The relationship of emanation can be enacted in profoundly different ways that are determined by which of the four different ways of life it serves. For example, in the service of transformation, emanation can be used temporarily to nurture the young; in this way the flow of emanation can be redirected to allow for emergence rather than containment. This is why it is necessary for us always to ask the question: "In the service of what way of life am I practicing the stories, four faces of my being, and relationships of my life?"

Subjection

In the relationship of subjection both the Latino male and his partner are fully present, but in reality both are denied a full presence and an identity of their own. The relationship is still unequal; it still rests upon the experience of overwhelming power. But this power, which was mysterious in emanation, becomes naked in subjection—the man can clearly see that he blocks his wife's freedom, and she also recognizes this fact. She sees how the denial of access to money controls her, and he identifies his efforts to keep her under control. We see subjection enacted when Latino men—husbands, fathers, and sons—command women as their birthright. It is a father or husband controlling the spending of the family's finances. In subjection, conflict is no longer unconsciously repressed but consciously suppressed. In the wider society Latino men are in turn subjected by the powerful. They often cannot be themselves by speaking their mother tongue and telling the stories of their heritage. Rules defined by the dominant culture tell them how to behave. The powerful everywhere often combine emanation and subjection when relating to the less powerful. Newly arrived Latinos are prepared to show authority figures in this country their traditional respect for those in command, and they retain their fear of being hurt by the powerful. The dominant group controls the society by determining continuity and change in accordance with what is necessary to preserve its power. Latino men are aware of having lost their right to step forward and initiate change. Their ability to get along in the society at large is based on the rules of the game defined solely by the powerful. Justice in the relationship of subjection consists of a harsh message: To this day in order to survive the majority of Latina women accept what they believe to be the supremacy of male power. But Latino men in the wider society also continue to survive by bowing to the power of the white male. This lack of power in the wider society is what often leads to a more desperate use of the relationship of subjection at home on the part of Latino men who are compensating for their humiliation at the hands of other, more powerful males.

Buffering

This is a relationship in which conflict and change are managed by intermediaries. Buffering is carried out by a mediator, a broker, or a concept.[14] Buffering is very important in *la comunidad Latina. Comadres,* or godmothers, and *padrinos,* godfathers, are very important mediators for Latino young men as they seek to break away from the control of their parents. As in all patriarchal societies, Latinos and Latinas use buffering to create conflict and change in a socially acceptable manner by having others, who are seen as the peers of their parents, intervene on their behalf. In this way they avoid directly questioning or contradicting their parents. To do so is considered a sin. Justice in the use of the relationship of buffering allows young women and men to obtain a better situation through the intervention of an aunt or grandmother. Thus, godparents, teachers, or clergy are able to win considerable exceptions from the strict rules of the family. When Latino men marry, they become the source of emanational authority with whom buffers intervene on behalf of wives and children. In this way the next generation is lamed by the relationship of buffering in the service of emanation, a relationship that is intended to perpetuate the power of authority, especially male authority. For generations the freedom of Latina women relied on the ability and skill of the mediator. Buffering became a central relationship to maintain male dominance. As a result men and women were deprived of the ability to confront problems face to face.

Isolation

Isolation is a relationship that Latina women who live in emanational relationships to Latino men cannot bear to endure. In this relationship, two people or groups agree to leave each other alone. Both sides agree to avoid any conflict that would lead to change between them. In this case justice means a degree of freedom, the right to be left alone. But both parties agree not to bring about any change in the other. Isolation cannot be achieved alone. The other must agree to cooperate. If a Latina woman attempts to isolate herself so that she can be left alone without an agreement with her male guardians, then she is not practicing the relationship of isolation. Instead of isolation, there is a consciousness of broken connections.[15] As patriarchal males possess their wives in the relationship of emanation, they assume that their spouses will always want to be near them, since they are the source of mystery who give women their reason for living. They need to control women's every move and refuse to allow them physical isolation. Latina women can and do practice emotional isolation, a kind of detachment by which they are allowed to withdraw into themselves as a substitute for not being able to physically withdraw. Latino males have always reserved the right to go out alone and to travel alone, a right that was never conceded to their wives. It is another example of the double standard applied to men and women.

Direct Bargaining

In this relationship, a Latino male and his lover agree to allow conflict in order to bring about change with each other directly. Justice consists in the better bargain that one side or the other may achieve, but both agree with the result of the bargain. This relationship allows a Latino male in relationship to his father, or a Latina woman resisting her husband or father, the right to advance his or her self-determination by struggling with another to gain a more advantageous bargain and thereby change the balance of power between that person and themselves.

By means of gifts or favors, the less powerful spouse looks to gain bargaining leverage by creating a sense of indebtedness between herself and her lover or husband. In fact the one who provides the favor is implying that: "You owe me something in exchange for my gifts or good behavior." Throughout history, Latina women have known that the way to get a better deal from men was through the leverage of sex and food. In exchange for these services, their husbands often relented and allowed them favors. But the use of direct bargaining in the service of emanation is one of the most effective ways to head off real transformation. When Latino men sense that their wives are becoming dangerously close to rebellion, they offer their wives a better deal within the story of patriarchy. They give them some valuable gift to make their wives feel indebted and guilty for questioning their love. Too often men attempt to return women to "normal," that is, to the relationship of emanation enacted in the story of patriarchy in the service of emanation that kept them arrested in Act I, Scene 1, of the core drama of life. In this way Latino men reformed the story of male dominance, that is, they made the story easier but by no means did they let the story of patriarchy die. Time and again they manipulated the anger of Latina women and reduced their rage to catharsis, emotional outbreaks that ended by sending them back to their enchained container. In this way they avoided real change and remained in command.

Autonomy

Autonomy is a relationship in which both a Latina woman and a Latino man are entitled to claim certain boundaries within which each of them exercises power based on education or competence. Both of them agree that justice in the relationship of autonomy is the right of each to sustain or enlarge their areas of power and autonomy. The key word here is *autonomy*. This relationship profoundly threatens male domination because it questions the relationships of dependency. A young Latina woman can now go to university and become a doctor or lawyer so she can achieve economic autonomy. Latino men want this relationship for themselves and for their wives, when two breadwinners are needed to support the family. But in domestic relations Latino men have often tried to deny autonomy to Latina women. In addition, to keep women dependent, when they work outside the home, Latina women are required to hand over their checks.

In the wider U.S. society the relationship of autonomy, together with direct bargaining, is the most powerful pattern. Both patterns are necessary to survive in this country. Autonomy and direct bargaining justify the attainment of power. But this relationship can be subverted and used in the service of transformation. A competent Latina doctor can choose to use her skills and the autonomy granted to her as a physician to protect the rights of her patients rather than to enhance her own personal power. The relationship of autonomy in the service of transformation is the relationship enacted when Latino men and Latina women assert their right to organize and participate in the building of a union, a union that truly represents the rights of working women and men.

Incoherence

Incoherence is a relationship in which a Latina woman and a Latino man face each other in the same place and at the same time but are unable to agree on how to relate. Incoherence is the painful recognition that the relationships that had previously connected them, emanation, subjection, buffering, and direct bargaining, are now broken. It is the experience of discontinuity rather than continuity; of change that is unintended and uncontrolled; it is conflict because they cannot agree on any form of cooperation, leading to injustice for both self and others. Recently a Latina woman told me that she was so angry with her husband when she discovered that he had had an affair that she rebelled against him. All of the inherited relationships by which she and her husband connected to each other were shattered: She refused to continue to relate to him as if he was the source of her mystery in emanation; she refused to obey him as he commanded her in subjection to stop her rebellion; she defiantly rejected his use of the relationship of buffering that allowed him to rationalize that "All Latino men are like me" as he attempted to disarm her anger; she would not bargain with him by allowing him to give her gifts or to make promises of a better life; and she also refused to consider his betrayal as the basis for getting concessions because of any guilt that he might feel. Both stood in the presence of each other and could not agree on how to relate, hence the relationship of incoherence.

What exacerbated the incoherence was that he was angry and threatened by an act of freedom: She had gone back to school and secured a part-time job without his consent. He eventually accepted the fact that she could use the relationship of autonomy in the wider society but when it came to their home life he was against her sharing the decisionmaking. Thus wife and husband stood in the presence of each other unable to agree on which relationship to use. This Latino man refused to listen to his wife, who now listened to her own inner voice in Act I, Scene 2. As she entered into rebellion in Act II, Scene 1, he was afraid she was breaking away from his control. She is now moving toward transformation. She intends to free herself not only from this marriage but from the underlying story of patriarchy and the way of life of emanation that gave her husband permission to be unfaithful. Her husband and her family are deeply opposed to what she is doing because they remain caught in the core drama in Act I. They want her to return to her husband in order to remain in the service of emanation, practicing the story of patriarchy as a mere extension of her patriarchal husband's life. They want her to continue to repress her own personal face by denying her own aspirations; she was required to enact her political face by practicing a politics of uncritical loyalty; her historical face was expected to repeat the stories of the past so that she would continue to be incapable of changing the stories that froze her life into a historical object; finally, she was not allowed to recognize her own sacred face—only the life of her husband was sacred.

When she asked her husband to leave, it was truly an act of incoherence; it was a sin from the perspective of the way of life of emanation. All of the psychic artillery of sin, shame, and guilt was used by her husband and family to attempt to restore her to her senses. Her mother argued, "If you love him, swallow your pride and let him come back; go back to normal." The woman missed her husband and loved him, but she would no longer accept him at the expense of her own life.

The result is that the man and wife are no longer able to relate because they are now living different ways of life and mean something fundamentally different in their use of the word *love*. The relationships of dependence that he wanted to continue are broken. His wife dared to practice the forbidden relationships that he refused to accept. She has moved from rebellion against him (Act II, Scene 1) to a deeper breaking. She moved into Act II, Scene 2, wherein she emptied herself of the story of patriarchy and the way of life of emanation. In Act III, Scene 1, she succeeded in creating the story of the transforming self. And she now looks to become a guide to her son in Act III, Scene 2, as she assists him through the acts and scenes of the core drama of life.

This woman has dramatically changed the four faces of her being. Her personal face has emerged whole. She has experienced herself for the first time as a person who can live without being dependent and helpless; her political face practices a politics of compassion, inclusion, and justice as she works to help young women and men experience the fullness of their lives; she has created a new and open history by putting in place a new and better story; with her sacred face she has become a co-creator with the sacred source of transformation to bring about the more loving and just.

Deformation

Deformation is a relationship in which a Latino male makes the decision to use violence to restore his power. Traditional society legitimized the story of patriarchy and gave men permission to use violence in order to restore order. The officially sanctioned use of violence by a whole culture is intended to preserve the status quo. Threatened males see their life and everything they stand for disintegrating; they want not only to punish women but also to cripple them. They are unable to respond to new demands on the part of their daughters, lovers, or wives. Pulled in two fundamentally opposed directions, they can either choose to create a truly open relationship or try to crush the women who challenge their privileged status. The latter choice brings men to use the relationship of deformation. Latino men resort to violence because they do not know what to do in a world where their authority is questioned. What they refuse to see is the dismantling of that world. But from the very moment they turn to violence, the relationship of deformation becomes an entire way of life of deformation. Emanation as a way of life colludes with deformation as a way of life through its readiness to turn to violence whenever anybody questions its ultimate truth. Because deformation attempts to restore the past, it is often confused with emanation. Emanation carries an overwhelming and mysterious power, but deformation is pseudo-emanational, a fake emanation that can possess individuals. The relationship of deformation connects Latino men to a demonic sacred source and means they are on the road to destructive death in key aspects of life. This relationship is often used when the relationships of emanation, subjection, buffering, and direct bargaining no longer work to keep a woman or child in her or his place. It is used as an attempt to force people back to the old relationships.

Fortunately, Latino males can be inspired to break with archetypal relationships and empty themselves of destructive archetypal stories and the partial ways of life of emanation, incoherence, and deformation. But that requires connecting to a more powerful sacred source, the deepest source of transformation. Only this sacred source is powerful enough to help men to empty themselves of both the concrete and the archetypal bonds that enchain them.

Transformation

The relationship of transformation connects us to the drama of transformation and to our deepest source. We no longer need external sources of emanation like our father or other father figures used. In transformation, we are conscious of those sources in the depths that constitute the archetypal ways of life and the stories of our lives. To enact this relationship is to participate in creating fundamentally new and better dramas and relationships. We can create, nourish, and end relationships that no longer help us to achieve justice; we can re-create new forms of relationships to deal with new problems; we can even woo new combinations into being. In Act III, Scene 1, Latino men, connected to their deepest source, are inspired by a new vision of how to shape life by enacting the story of the transforming self. In the second scene of Act III, such men reach out to assist others as guides. And this newfound wholeness enables them to enact not only all eight relationships (excluding the ninth relationship of deformation, which cannot be enacted in the service of transformation) but also an infinite number of concrete manifestations of each relationship. Time and again, they create, nourish, and destroy in order to create and transform.

Archetypal Relationships in the Service of Four Ways of Life

As I have said earlier, the nine archetypal relationships do not stand alone. Each of the nine archetypal relationships in its concrete manifestation derives its deeper meaning from a wider context, a whole way of life of emanation, incoherence, deformation, or transformation (see Figure 2.3). The four ways of life determine the quality of our stories and relationships; consequently, excepting deformation, the archetypal relationships are neither negative nor creative in themselves. But the relationship of transformation can never be used in the service of emanation, incoherence, or deformation; it is always to the good. And deformation can never be enacted in the service of transformation; it is always destructive. The quality, the ultimate meaning, of the relationships is given to them by the way of life in which we choose to enact them. Again, Latino men need to ask the question: "In the service of what way of life am I practicing the relationships and stories of my life?" For example, it is usually assumed that the relationship of subjection is negative. But subjection in the service of transformation is necessary. When we forbid a child to light matches when he or she is alone, we are protecting their life and the lives of others. Subjection in the service of emanation is the use of the relationship of subjection to keep somebody as an extension of oneself. In the service of incoherence, subjection is used to dominate others as a means to one's own end. Subjection in the service of deformation is enacted to hurt a person, even kill them, because the subjector sees the other as a threat to power. In the chapters that follow I give many examples of the use of the nine archetypal relationships and how they are enacted in the service of different ways of life. Emanation, incoherence, deformation, and transformation as archetypal relationships differ from emanation, incoherence, deformation, and transformation as whole ways of life. I will always specify which I mean, the relationship or the entire way of life.

Figure 2.3 Four Archetypal Ways of Life Symbolized

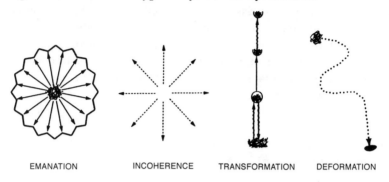

EMANATION   INCOHERENCE   TRANSFORMATION   DEFORMATION

Notes: Emanation represents the closed container of final truth in which the individual is secure but trapped. *Incoherence* represents a world of broken connections in which individuals pursue their own self-interests and power. The ascending-descending arrows (at base) represent the mutual relationship between the individual and the deepest source of *transformation*, co-creating together; the ascending arrows represent the self now whole who reaches out to others as a guide. *Deformation* represents the exit from the core drama of life into the abyss of destructive death.

The Personal, Political, Historical, and Sacred Faces of Being in the Service of Transformation

Each Latino man and Latina woman has a personal, a political, a historical, and a sacred face. But only in the service of transformation can they fully experience and express the four faces of their being. The process of transformation takes place first of all in the individual's depths, in her or his personal face. The archetypal sources that wounded the individual and used her or his ego as their incarnation are consciously recognized and rejected in Act II, Scene 2, so that the individual is prepared to be renewed by the deepest source of transformation. When Latino males reject a particular father or lover or ruler, there is a political dimension. Their personal and political faces were shaped by families and the larger society with stories, relationships, and archetypal ways of life. Therefore when Latino men say no, they are not only responding to particular persons such as fathers and mothers who represent family and society, but also, on a deeper level, they are breaking with the official politics, lords, and stories of these institutions. Only a person can choose to be political; the Latino man's personal face is necessary to choose a new turning point in the creation of a new history; the deepest source of being knows him as a unique and individual person. The four faces of being are always present, and if the Latino man ignores any one of them, he does so at his peril. Latino men need to reach beyond their personal lives to the political and historical networks that severely limit their personal capacity.

To resist the racism in one's personal life requires a struggle against structural deformation in the society that continues to cripple others. Latino men need to be political, that is, to ask always what they can and need to do together with their neighbors in order to liberate themselves from the dramas practiced by the wider society, both in their concrete manifestations and in the underlying sacred source of the stories. To cast out demons in their personal lives and society, means that Latino men must free their sacred faces from the lesser lords of emanation, incoherence, and deformation and connect them instead to the deepest sacred source of transformation. Latino men make history by enacting the historical face of their being and create a new turning point by struggling with the concrete tyranny as well as its underlying formative source.

Doing Archetypal Analysis

The description of the theory of transformation provided above gives us the tools to participate in archetypal analysis. At every moment of our lives we are somewhere in the core drama of life, in one of its acts and scenes, in one of the stories, in one of the nine relationships, in one of the four ways of life, practicing the four faces of our being. When we do archetypal analysis we realize that the concrete stories and relationships and the four faces of our being are manifestations of deeper, underlying formative sacred sources we call archetypes. We know only the surface, the concreteness of life, when we describe the external reality of our daily life. To get to the deeper, underlying meaning we ask the question: "In the service of what way of life am I practicing the stories and relationships and the four faces of my being?" The answer tells us where we are in the core drama of life. We learn what stories and relationships we are practicing and whether we are enacting stories, relationships, and the four faces of our being in their fullness or arresting our lives in fragments.

The task of Latino men is to know through archetypal analysis how to actually live and practice life by knowing and choosing to live the stories, relationships, and the four faces of their being as more loving and just manifestations of the deepest source. They need to relate theory to practice by learning how to enact ways of living that they never practiced before. Participation in the life and death of the stories that possess them and the resurrection of fundamentally more loving and just stories constitute the meaning of justice relevant for contemporary times. The old stories and ways of life needed men's involvement to remain alive and active. By withdrawing from them, they deny them life. By personally and politically allying themselves to the deepest source of transformation they can participate in making transformation concretely alive and present in all aspects of their lives. This is the newly won freedom of Latino men in Act III, Scenes 1 and 2, not only to choose among existing archetypal dramas but also to create new ones that do justice to themselves, to others, and to the deepest source. For example, by creating neighborhood centers that serve the young, the sick, the unemployed, and the elderly and by changing the parameters of what Latino men can and need to do together, they shape a new historical path. Breaking inherited patterns that condemned people to docility and silence and replacing them with new and better ways of relating to each other enables the community to participate in the decisions that affect their lives:

> Only in the service of transformation is our capacity—our unconscious, consciousness, creativity, linking with others, and our use of just means kept in lively tension with the changing realities of life, for in the way of life of transformation, the concrete realization of transformation is never experienced as a final solution. To enter into the relationship of transformation becomes the final moment of a particular turn in the process of transformation. Nourishing this new experience of transformation will inevitably reveal new suffering and threats and new joys and opportunities. To live in the service of transformation is therefore persistently to experience an archetypal process of breaking relationships, moving into incoherence, and entering into the relationship of transformation.[16]

I will now apply theory to practice as I respond to the questions posed earlier: Where did the Latino male get caught? How and why did he lose his way? What are the strategies that will be necessary for him so that he can rediscover and uncover the deeper capacity of his life as a Latino male to change his life for the better? The theory of transformation can help Latino men understand how the four faces of their being, the relationships and stories they are living as Latino men, are being used creatively and/or destructively. The theory enables Latinos to see that they fail to achieve the meaning of their lives by remaining arrested in Act I of the core drama of life, wherein they have unconsciously lived the stories of the Latino tradition. In Act II, Scene 1, they become caught in rebellion in the story of capitalism as the pursuit of self-interest. The journey through Act II, Scene 2, at the exit from the core drama, leads to deformation and violence that result in personal, political, historical, and sacred destruction. The only viable alternative is transformation in Act III, wherein Latino men can bring about a way of life committed to the persistent creation of fundamentally new and more loving sacred stories.

Notes

1. In this regard see C. G. Jung, *Man and His Symbols* (New York: Dell, 1970) and *The Collected Works of C. G. Jung,* especially vol. 9, *The Archetypes and the Collective Unconscious,* edited by Michael Fordham, translated by R. F. Hull (Princeton, NJ: Princeton University Press, 1980).

2. Manfred Halpern first taught me the theory of transformation, which he had rediscovered when I was a graduate student of his at Princeton University. This chapter owes much to his book, *Transforming Our Personal, Political, Historical, and Sacred Being in Contrast to Our Other Three Choices in Theory and Practice,* which I had the honor of helping to prepare after his death on January 14, 2001. For earlier versions and applications of the theory of transformation, see David T. Abalos, *La Comunidad Latina in the United States: Personal and Political Strategies for Transforming Culture* (Westport, CT: Praeger Press, 1998); *Strategies of Transformation Toward a Multicultural Society: Fulfilling the Story of Democracy* (Westport, CT: Praeger Press, 1996); *The Latino Family and the Politics of Transformation* (Westport, CT: Praeger Press, 1993); and *Latinos in the United States: The Sacred and the Political* (Notre Dame, IN: University of Notre Dame Press, 1986).

3. Manfred Halpern, "Why Are Most of Us Partial Selves? Why Do Partial Selves Enter the Road to Deformation?" paper delivered at a panel on "Concepts of Self: Transformation and Politics" at the annual meeting of the American Political Science Association (Washington, D.C., August 29, 1991).

4. Ibid.

5. Manfred Halpern, "Beyond Present Theory and Practice: Transformation and the Nation State," in Edwin Schwerin, Christa Daryl Slaton, and Stephen Woolpert, eds., *Transformational Politics: Theory, Study, and Practice* (Albany, NY: SUNY Press, 1998).

6. Halpern, "Why Are Most of Us Partial Selves?"

7. Abalos, *The Latino Family,* chapter 4.

8. Marshall Berman, *The Politics of Authenticity: Radical Individualism and the Rise of Modern Society* (New York: Atheneum Press, 1972), pp. 113–144.

9. Manfred Halpern, "The Archetype of Capitalism: A Critical Analysis in the Light of a Theory of Transformation," paper presented at the annual meeting of the American Political Science Association (San Francisco, 1996), pp.

18–19. This is the best analysis of capitalism that I have seen. It is an original and brilliant piece of scholarship that shows the devastating cost of this drama in the service of the partial and wounded ways of life that threaten to move humanity into the service of deformation as workers are turned into objects and exploited by the powerful.

10. The Baptists in Salt Lake City declared that women were to honor the commandment that they were to be the handmaidens of men, as found in the Report of the Baptist Faith and Message Study Committee to the Southern Baptist Convention, adapted June 14, 2000, on the website for the Southern Baptist Convention, http://www.sbc.net.

11. Tina Rosenberg, "Machismo Gives Good New Laws a Black Eye," *New York Times,* June 20, 1998.

12. Douglas Jehl, "Arab Honor's Price: A Woman's Blood," *New York Times,* Sunday, June 30, 1999, pp. 1, 8.

13. Much of the the section on emanation, including quotations from Halpern's theory, are taken from *Transforming,* chapter 7, "Archetypal Relationships" (forthcoming). I have also called on L. Carl Brown and Norman Itzkowitz, eds., "Four Contrasting Repertories of Human Relations in Islam: Two Pre-Modern and Two Modern Ways of Dealing with Continuity and Change, Collaboration and Conflict and Achieving Justice," in *Psychological Dimensions of Near Eastern Studies* (Princeton, NJ: Darwin Press, 1977), p. 62.

14. Abalos, *Strategies of Transformation,* p. 25.

15. Ibid., p. 39.

16. Halpern, *Transforming,* chapter 7.

3

~~~

The Latino Male at Risk

Why is it that so many of us get caught in living the stories of others and not our own? Why do we get so caught up in violence both at home and in the community? Why are we so angry? Why are we as Latino men hesitant to vote, organize, protest, and practice the politics of transformation? Because too many of us believe the inherent racism of the big lie—that Ecuadoreans, Puerto Ricans, Chicanos, Salvadorans, Guatemalans, Bolivians, Cubans, and other Latino groups are not as competent as European Americans. Too many of us have internalized the oppression by accepting the lies and then practicing the behavior that is expected of us according to the projections of the powerful. At times many of us have serious doubts about our own manhood. Why? For many of us our understanding of manhood was based on control, domination, and power over others, especially the female members of the community. Now that this power is crumbling, many of us feel insecure, lost.

Candil de la Calle, Oscuridad de la Casa

Since I was a child I heard this complaint from my mother about men and about me: "*Candil de la calle, oscuridad de la casa*, You are the light of the world but the darkness of your own home." She meant that men took their love, creativity, and the best of themselves elsewhere. In spite of praise from outsiders, many Latino men inspire disillusionment among family members. Many Latino men show their anger at home and take out their frustration on those closest to them. Increasingly, the men are simply missing. What has happened, what is happening to

Latino men? Why are they in danger? Perhaps they are not truly at home in the society or within themselves. Perhaps they do not know who they are.

We know that U.S. society is partially at fault for the pain and loss of the Latino male. The wounds of racism and capitalism deny many of the necessities of life. The corresponding anger that follows brings self-hatred and self-wounding, which end in crimes against family and community. The grim statistics regarding dropout rates, the number of young Latinos in jail, underemployment among Latinos, the use of drugs, the abandonment of families, the increase in AIDS: All of these cold facts together pound out the story of despair that Latino males daily encounter.[1]

Archetypal Analysis: Never Stereotypes

I want to stress that whatever I say about the Latino male is not peculiar to him; except for concrete cultural specifics, the stories and ways of life discussed in relationship to Latino men apply to all men from all other ethnic and racial backgrounds. Each culture has particular concrete differences as to how stories are actually enacted, but the underlying, deeper roots of the stories remain the same for all cultures. All human beings struggle with the same archetypal dramas. Patriarchy is patriarchy whether we find it in Mexico, Hong Kong, England, Saudi Arabia, France, Spain, Peru, Nigeria, or in the Latino barrios of the United States. Wherever patriarchy is found men systematically dominate women.

A stereotype freezes a person and violates them by depriving them of their personal worth grounded in the sacredness of their life. Stereotypes are essentially projections. But even false stories have a kind of power. If we can categorize people, pigeonhole them, "type" them, we can marginalize them. I do not wish to participate in the kind of stereotyping that wounded me as a Chicano youth growing up in the wider community of Detroit, Michigan. To do archetypal analysis, in contrast, is to see stories, ways of life, and relationships, to experience a person in motion. We as family members and friends can see where a person is caught and possessed by stories and ways of life. At the same time it is important to remember that their difficulties do not deprive them of their intrinsic capacity to change their lives for the better. When doing archetypal analysis we must never lose sight of the person. We ask:

Where are they in the core drama, in what act and scene are they arrested, what story has caught them, and in the service of what way of life are they practicing their stories? What do these stories and ways of life do to the four faces of their being? Are they in the process of leaving the story? What resources do they have to assist them? Are they receiving guidance from others? We need to ask these questions about each person, each situation, here and now.

Much contemporary social science comes close to stereotyping because the kind of knowledge produced by statistical analysis, interviews, and questionnaires can only take a snapshot of the reality of a person's life, leaving hidden the person's ongoing struggle to be a self. Often social science reveals nothing of the deeper meaning of a person's life, that is, where he or she is in the core drama of life, in what way of life he or she lives stories and relationships, and the four faces of his or her being. The kind of empirical data collected turns our lives into abstractions, fragments to be collected and studied and put on graphs for publication. Numerical correlations cannot, nor do they intend to, provide any strategies for change. Social scientists protest that recommending alternatives constitutes another realm of knowledge, perhaps ethics or religion but not science, which can only report on what it observes. Much of our current social science reveals only fragments of reality, never a look at the wholeness of the individuals being studied. These kinds of studies leave us totally bereft since they point out, for example, the number of abuse cases between husband and wife together with their ages and socioeconomic background or whether being unemployed heightens the possibility of domestic abuse. But this data can never indicate what to do in order to void oneself of destructive stories and partial ways of life, nor can it say how to transform people's lives for the better.

Archetypal analysis not only analyzes what is, but also points out choices available for creating new and better alternatives in place of those dramas that diminish our humanity. What is needed is a theoretical perspective that allows for the empirical work, that is, the collection of facts as well as a movement beyond facts toward the normative task of asking the question, "In the service of what way of life are these stories and relationships being practiced?" Which means, as discussed in Chapter 2, that we see and practice concrete stories, relationships, and the four faces of being never for their own sake but in the service of deeper underlying ways of life that give them their ultimate meaning and purpose. To do radical analysis, that is, to get to the underlying roots of the stories of the lives of Latino men, is to see which way of life has taken over. Finally, Latino men need to discover how they can free themselves from false ways of life so that they can go beyond mere reporting of what is wrong to the more important task of changing their lives for the better.

False Interventions

Conferences are held throughout the country to address the serious situations in which many Latino men find themselves. The workshops focus on problems such as unemployment, education, health, housing, psychological concerns, the family, and male-female relationships. These meetings are well intended. However, from the perspective of the politics of transformation, we need to look deeper to see what is affecting the Latino male. To look deeper is to critique both Latino and U.S. cultures. As I have discussed, the Latino male was raised with stories, especially patriarchy and uncritical loyalty, that allowed him to believe that he was superior to women and that he was to be respected as a source of emanational mystery. But even in Latin America the container of emanation has begun to disintegrate. People have for some time been questioning what used to be considered final truths. In this changing world, the Latino male has begun to lose his sense of direction. He knows that he is no longer a source of mystery; he knows he is not making it in the marketplace; he often feels confused, betrayed, angry. In the United States, Latino men, both immigrants and those whose families have been here for generations, face ever more destructive stories in their daily lives.

How the Stories of Tribalism and Racism, Capitalism, and the Wounded Self Reinforce Each Other

The Story of Tribalism and Racism

Like African American women, Latina women often overindulge men in order to compensate for the tribulations that men face in the wider society. It is heartbreaking for family members to see, day after day, their husbands, brothers, and fathers come home hurt by the story of tribalism. Tribalism is an archetypal drama, a sacred story in which a group takes a fragment of life, such as skin color, ethnicity, gender, religion, race, or age, and turns it into a fantasy that dominates the whole of life. Those who hold to this fragment consider themselves superior and privileged. There are only five ways by which the powerful relate themselves to the less powerful, or the outsiders: Because they are not Anglo or white the outsiders are (1) invisible, (2) inferior, (3) worth something only if they assimilate, (4) dismissed if seen as disloyal to the powerful, and (5) in danger of extermination because their safety, education, health, and human rights are considered not as important as those of others. Tribalism is always in the service of deformation because it diminishes the humanity of both the victim and the perpetrator.

The Story of Capitalism

Latino men, even those who begin to "make it" socioeconomically, are faced daily with the story of capitalism. In this story, the official story of U.S. society, participants are tempted to become immoral and insincere in order to survive; no one can afford to be intimate lest he or she be betrayed; personal energy is used to acquire more and more; relationships are corrupted by competition; no one knows each other in their wholeness; each person becomes a fragment who performs a function on an assembly line hour after hour. We are forced to wear masks to hide our pain; we look over our shoulders constantly as a matter of self-defense; and we are caught in an impersonal web wherein nobody accepts responsibility.[2] Our lives are arrested in the pursuit of self-interest and power.

The Story of the Wounded Self

But all the power in the world cannot stem the hemorrhaging many of us experience as a result of the traumas we lived as children.[3] The majority of Latino men walk through daily life hiding one or several of the following wounds: sexual abuse, physical or psychological abuse, drug abuse, alcohol abuse, and the trauma of desertion. They cannot possibly heal these wounds while trying to impress women with their superiority as patriarchal males, competing with others for power in the story of capitalism, or trying to be an all-powerful drug lord or gang leader.

Many Latino men live on the edge. Their cultural privilege is eroding at home because of a working wife and children who are forgetting their Spanish and who want the freedom of Anglo kids. Outside the home, the stories of racism and capitalism confront them. Because many cannot cope with the story of capitalism, which tells them they are not important without money and power, they are tempted to romanticize the past by creating a fantasy of male power.[4] Thus Latino men practice the story of the disappointed male in order to compensate for the loss of a past identity. But the problem is that the response to their dilemma, the story of the disappointed male who asserts his masculinity to compensate for his sense of loss, is to view manhood through an old cultural lens, patriarchal machismo.[5] This kind of machismo is an inherited understanding of what it means to be a man, *un hombre muy macho,* who commands a mixture of respect, obedience, loyalty, and fear from other men, women, and children. He is the central figure, the source of protection and of mystery; he is the only one who can be trusted to provide security.

But U.S. society is one based on power, privilege, and prestige; Latino men find it more and more difficult to be a source of security for their families. How do they explain or understand their loss of honor, respect, security, and standing in the community? Too often it is through the old cultural view that cannot help them to respond to fundamentally new kinds of problems. Some have faced for years a more powerful source of masculinity than themselves: the police, the teacher of their children, social workers, and the boss at the plant. The patriarchs in this country are *gabachos, bolillos, los Güeros*—Anglos, intruders, white men; they have everything and Latino men have very little. They know nothing of Latino culture and language and often treat Latinos badly. They do not know how to challenge this new macho; Latino men can't beat up Anglos, can't compete with them, can't resist their power. Even those who have a college degree and a good job, who are considered middle-class, feel vulnerable. This situation leads to anger against one's self and others: "I have to be in charge; I have to take control again; I have to maintain my manhood, my honor, my machismo." How do many Latinos do this? They turn to the worse. As disappointed men they resort to a machismo that deforms life. They abuse and berate women, dominate children, fight with other Latino men, join a gang in search of lost identity—all in search of a substitute community and family.

If men cannot restore their sense of loss with these methods, they can and often do fall into a kind of despair and turn to self-violence, the self-inflicted wounds of an increasingly powerless patriarchy: *"No sirvo para nada,* I am useless; *no soy nadie,* I am nobody." The alleged remedy for this despair can be drugs or a leader or cause to which men give total loyalty as they search for a renewed sense of certainty. No new insights come to them because they are still possessed by the story of the disappointed male in a form of patriarchy in the service of a bankrupt tradition. Yes, it is good to help Latino men who are hurting from encounters with racism and capitalism by providing them with access to health clinics, to open up job opportunities, to obtain an education and other necessary services. But unless these are accompanied by strategies to address what is crippling Latino men at the deeper level of their lives, these efforts will fail. When those in the health-care professions are congratulated for having helped restore a Latino male to good "health," they feel a sense of success and satisfaction. But if he is cured only of a symptom, have they really helped him? Perhaps they are sending home the same domineering Latino male, restored to physical strength in order to give commands once more. In addition, what if he is a man suffering from the humiliation of racism and a feeling of uselessness that led him to batter his wife and children? Is he now better because someone has secured for him a job, set him up with health care, and arranged for him to obtain his high school diploma? We have still not dealt with the causes of his *coraje,* his anger.

Above all what we need to do together as a community is to recognize that the answer is not restoring Latino men so they can reenter the community with the same broken story of patriarchy based on domination. We need a new and better alternative, a deeply caring and loving male who sees the sacredness in his own life and in the lives of others. Such sacredness and its corresponding creativity can only emerge if our personal faces are free to reject inherited stories and ways of life that undermine us and to choose the story of mutuality and transforming love. As Latino men we deserve more than the fruitless return to the stories of uncritical loyalty, patriarchy, racism, capitalism (which often colludes with racism), the wounded self, and the disappointed male, stories that rob us of our capacity. We need our own deeper selfhood, not the caricature of a male who is lost because he cannot possess or dominate.

What radically grounds Latino men is that each has a sacred face rooted in the deepest sacred source of transformation. Latino men need to rid themselves of the stereotypes of the dominant and refuse to act out its view of them. They need to reject the fatalistic expectations of Latino culture as well: that men dominate naturally, that one of the only ways to get back at Anglos is to turn to violence. Once Latino men have refused to assimilate into the power structure, and have ceased to undermine their own confidence by self-inflicted wounds, they are now capable of passing judgment on outmoded cultural stories and on a society that wounds them in the public realm with racism and capitalism.

These stories, together with patriarchy and the stories of the disappointed male, and the *mujeriego,* the womanizer, have been very destructive. They have wounded Latino men to the extent that men cannot confront the issues that face them or the Latino community writ large. These stories from Latino culture and the stories that Latino men experience in U.S. society have disabled the personal, political, historical, and sacred faces of their being. But Latino men are not doomed to be victims of the past. They can participate with the deepest sacred source of transformation in the creation of more loving and just stories as alternatives that restore to them the full capacity of their humanity and manhood.

Looking Deeper Into the Story of Self-Wounding: Drugs, Gangs, and Violence

La comunidad Latina is at risk due to the collusion between the ways of life of incoherence and deformation. Too many young people are being seduced by the power and money involved in the world of drugs. Some Latinos get caught up in their efforts to survive in this country in what begins as the story of capitalism in the service of incoherence and ends in the destructive death of deformation. I am speaking here of underground capitalism, crime, and specifically drug dealing and drug use. There are those in *la comunidad Latina* who see drugs as a business enterprise. They invest in drugs and sell them for a profit. The fact that drugs are addictive and illegal is ignored with such justifications as "Everybody does it so what is the harm? If they don't get it from me, they will get from someone else." Drug dealing is seductive because an incredible amount of money can be made in a matter of days or hours. The drug pimp becomes a quasihero in the community. But violence and death always travel with drugs.

Many Latinas and Latinos cannot get jobs or good-paying jobs and find it increasingly difficult to make it in this country. They see the drug dealers as successful. Many youth enter into relationships of pseudoemanation with the drug lords and make them their heroes. Of course money also provides motivation: If it is necessary to sell drugs to children to keep profits coming, then it will have to be done. Moreover, people who threaten the drug trade by going to the police are often killed.

People battered daily by the inequities of capitalism and racism are vulnerable to all forms of escape. By taking drugs, they mortgage their paychecks and lives to the dealers. Families are driven deeper into poverty and despair. This situation forces others into crime to survive. There is no end to the destruction caused by drugs. They destroy the fabric of the community and take away our humanity. Shattered communities and families mean crime, increased drug use, infected needles that spread the AIDS virus, dropping out of school, early pregnancy, gang violence, and the perpetuation of the cycle of poverty, despair, crime, and more poverty. Drugs and involvement in other forms of organized crime places our communities in the hell of deformation and self-destruction. This is one of the greatest challenges for the Latino community. All efforts need to be made to prevent deformation from becoming our dominant way of life.[6]

The violence that many Latino males have seen and felt in their homes, together with the violence of racism, leaves them with anger. Many feel they cannot count on their Latino heritage to sustain them. At times they identify their culture with poverty, with violence, with being an outsider, with outdated traditions that don't work, and with a mother who speaks Spanish and refuses to learn English as a protest against the way they are treated. We cannot focus our lives; we are lost. The cumulative effect of these negative experiences surrounding Latino culture makes it impossible to romanticize the culture and to remain uncritically loyal. Often men look for a competing emanation without knowing it.

One such emanational source is the gang. At an early age many young men discover a way to express their anger. One way of escaping from the rejection of the dominant culture is assimilation. But you need recognition from the dominant group if you are to assimilate. Many Latinos feel the world's powerful do not care about them. Besides, they see members of the dominant culture as the enemy, the Anglos, *los Americanos,* "white bread" who call Latinos "wetbacks." Because of the lack of money at home, they feel powerless to do anything about basic issues such as food and clothing. Many Latino youth are not interested in money and power; they want to be loved and accepted. But the sense of powerlessness makes them vulnerable to the fantasy for total power. As the connections to our parents and our culture become more tenuous, there is a danger that Latino youth will try to restore the container of emanation without knowing it. Why is this a danger? Because in order to restore a lost security people are vulnerable to those who say: "I have the answer, just follow me." For me and for many Latina and Latino youth the gang became and continues to be a very seductive emanational substitute that could fill the void created by the collapse of one's culture, one's sacred sources, and one's way of life in this country.

The Mexican gang to which my brother belonged offered me the following: a family who could care for me and protect me in a dangerous world, a place where I could begin to define my manhood, participation in a group who could defiantly declare we were Mexicans and proud of it, an emotional setting that helped us to break away from our increasingly single female–headed homes by allowing male bonding, a testing ground for developing our courage and loyalty in difficult circumstances, a territorial imperative to defend as one's home-boy neighborhood, and a vehicle for getting revenge on a society that had rejected us. This was about loyalty to a group invested with emanational power that was stronger, more powerful, and more important than the sum total of the individuals in the gang.

Total obedience and loyalty immersed us in the gang; but this immersion had nothing to do with finding out who we were. My personal face was never further from me as I sought to see my face only in the faces of the most powerful in the gang, those who were the most daring. We erased our own faces as we smashed the face of the outsider. It was a politics of violence and revenge against those who dared make us invisible and inferior. History was now made worse as we repeated the story of racism and tribalism that victimized us. The lord of deformation possessed our sacred faces and reveled in our violence and self-destruction.

The gang is not a return to the world of emanation; the gang is a pseudo-emanation, a fake. We could not return to the seamless container of emanation, the world that our parents had transported here from Mexico and other Latin American nations. We lived in a world of broken connections where people from our own heritage no longer shared the same ideas, emotions, and hopes. We found ourselves in a world of fragmented individuals who pursued self-interest and power and who cared very little for community or shared values. In such a broken world we sought security and even absolute power over our lives and those of others. We had no money or prestige or power as defined by the dominant culture. What we did have was power, not just power but absolute power, the power to end our lives and the lives of others through violence. There was something very nihilistic about our gang. Nothing was important but us and our loyalty to each other. This uncritical loyalty to the gang, especially to the leader, led us to fight, steal, drop out of school, turn to drugs, and escalate the violence. We were not making it in the world of capitalism, and our connections to the tradition inherited from our parents were dissolving. This made us vulnerable to the way of life of deformation.

On one occasion, we went looking for trouble. I was determined to cement my position in the gang by proving that I could be just as bold in my use of violence as the toughest in the gang. We cornered a group of white boys in Clark Park, a recreational center on the west side of Detroit, and began to goad them into a fight. They refused to be provoked. This was my opportunity. I grabbed a boy my size and punched him in the face. He fell to his knees, crying and holding his face. I was overcome with a sense of utter despair. I didn't feel good or tough; I felt sick. But the members of the gang were all pleased. They congratulated me and my brother on what a fighter I was. Ironically, I decided then and there I would never hit someone like that again. But we lived in a violent neighborhood where I was never sure who would come after me. Under these circumstances, I could have learned how to kill feelings of compassion. Between the danger in the hood and the need to express my anger, it could have been only a matter of time before I became a victimizer.[7]

Many Latino men have seen too much chaos in their own homes, either in the United States or in their Latino homelands. As the breaking of traditional connections goes on, there arises in many a nostalgic compulsion to restore the old respect, the old authority, the old family values that were part of the world of emanation. But the way of life of emanation is fragile precisely because it cannot respond to new kinds of problems. So there follows the saddest and most dangerous aspect of a Latino male's efforts to make the past work again. He wants to reestablish old truths that no longer work.

How can he demand that his wife have a hot dinner on the table when she does not get home in time from a job that is necessary to help support the family? To what extent can he force the children to speak to him only in Spanish, to address him with *de usted,* a term of formal respect, to be home from a dance at 9 P.M.—when they are hell-bent on fitting in, belonging, assimilating? His attempts to restore the past lead to more rebellion on the part of wives and children. In order to reassert himself and to prove his manhood, he uses punishment. He may begin with the occasional slap in an attempt to return family members to obedience, docility, and the traditional world of *respeto.* But this is no longer possible; this world has been ruptured forever. Because of their refusal to face the end of traditional stories, too many Latino males turn to violence. Once the logic of rebellion and violence begins, it usually escalates to more force and beatings, which leads to deformation.

But Latino males are not predestined to be victims. They have choices. There are four faces to their being. With their historical faces they can refuse to repeat the stories, intervene against those aspects of the culture that are destructive, and create new stories, turning points that initiate a new tradition, a new history that was not there until they decided to create it. They can find the strength within their personal faces to void themselves of this destruction and within their political faces to practice a politics of compassion in creating a new and more loving society in which sacred faces become a manifestation of the deepest sacred source of transformation. Latino men can choose to be deeply caring and loving human beings at home and to carry the same kind of love and concern with their political faces into the public realm.[8]

The Politics of Sexuality:
Guilt and Power in the Bedroom

Love and sexuality in the midst of the breakdown of emanation as a way of life too often reduce sexual encounters to contests for power. Latina women know that they have rights in the United States. They are able to find work and get an education that for many means a degree of freedom from men that was impossible for their mothers and certainly for their grandmothers. Since many Latina women feel their lover will ultimately disappoint them, they prepare to protect themselves from the fate they inherited from their mothers. This reality profoundly affects their sexual response to men and the sexual reaction of Latino men to their partners. As a result, the encounters between men and women in the Latino community are permeated by covert manipulation on both sides. Latinos and Latinas pretend everything is going well, but in the most intimate aspect of their sexual lives, their dishonesty has a corroding impact.

Latino men and Latina women are still profoundly affected by dying fragments of the way of life of emanation. The old stories of patriarchy, uncritical loyalty, and possessive love in the service of emanation still carry enough emanational power to cause them to hesitate and to be caught between the craving for the old security, even though the price has proved to be too high, and the new world of naked power. Archetypal stories are very powerful because they draw their strength from the sacred sources in the depths. After all, many Latina women and Latino men are disappointed precisely because the world of emanation failed to provide them with a life of security with minimum conflict and change and a maximum of continuity and cooperation. Now that this way of life and the stories lived in its service have failed them, they are not sure what to do. Life in the United States seems to give an answer: Since you cannot count on others or on religion to take care of you, it is up to you to protect yourself by any means necessary. The sacred lords of emanation, incoherence, and deformation compete for individuals' loyalties. To ignore their presence is to continue to place one's life in peril.

Latinas are often caught between ways of life, a desire to be loyal to men and the need for power to protect themselves from men. Latinas who are angry about their lives, living the female version of the story of the disappointed Latino male, are reluctant to show their feelings since it will reveal their unhappiness. Thus they resort to a life of dissimulation. Even if they desire sexual pleasure, they have to be careful not to show it because it would reveal weakness and need on their part. So they try to be indifferent and not to show passion. When they do demonstrate passion, it is often to bargain for something they want from their spouse. A Latino male knows that there is a game going on and is careful not to expose it. Since he is often fearful of intimacy, he is content to have his sexual needs satisfied without too much show of affection or unnecessary passion. In the midst of this subtlety he is conscious that his partner is holding back and that when she is being passionate it might be a show to put him in a weakened bargaining position. Contrary to what some may think, many men are not that interested in bringing about sexual passion in a woman to show their prowess. On the contrary, there is a deep fear that any show of spontaneous passion and sexual pleasure might make him vulnerable, that is, capable of being wounded by a woman if he makes himself defenseless to his or her sexual desire.

The Anger of the Latino Male

For many Latino men, cruel responses to women may be a kind of revenge against their own mothers, who disabled them by breaking their rebelliousness, sidetracking a necessary step toward adulthood and invoking sin, shame, and guilt so that they would not leave their mothers. As adults, these men desert women, ignore them, are unfaithful to them, and use them. Perhaps their involvement with other women is also a search for revenge against the mother, because they can have affairs without feeling any kind of remorse.

One of the most hurtful aspects, for both men and women, of the encounters between a Latina woman and a Latino man is the rendering of the male into a child who is indulged by a possessive mother. This kind of behavior seems to be in the service of emanation, that is, a woman being uncritically loyal to the needs of her *marido,* her husband. But in reality it is a power play in the service of incoherence, which is always in danger of becoming deformational. By relating to her mate as if he were a child, the woman takes away his manhood by becoming his mother. Because of his own concern for his mother (the Latino man often "protects" his mother from his own father), a Latino man frequently accepts this kind of mothering without complaint. But as soon as he realizes, at least on some kind of intuitive level, that he has been had by his wife as mother, he pushes away from her. He is often enraged and feels used. His wife has become a competing emanational force with his mother. Due to his ambivalent feelings toward his own mother, whom he protected when he believed she should have been defending him, he does not know what to do with his mixed emotions: desire, resentment, guilt, need, and anger.

Treating a Latino man as a child, a Latina woman can also excuse his infidelity, behavior she feels is her fate as a Latina woman. Since he is only a foolish child, such wanderings can be dismissed as those of a naughty boy who will eventually see the error of his ways and come home to his forgiving wife. By indulging him in this way, a Latina woman helps to perpetuate the immaturity of the Latino male. Why does he wander? On a deeper level he has been given permission not only by the culture but also by his mate. The culture has prearranged it this way. What is required of him is to undergo the necessary rituals of repentance followed by forgiveness. But many Latinas are not easily won over. They get their revenge by punishing the man as if he were a little boy. In this kind of sadomasochistic dance, a man is not allowed to grow up and a woman does not have to worry about becoming too vulnerable, since she knows he will always return. He is dependent on her for forgiveness, and he needs her to take care of him. In this sad scenario nobody can discover who they are. Both Latina women and Latino men are caught in underlying sacred archetypal stories that possess them and traumatize them.

Many Latino males cannot relate to their wives as equals, which is necessary to develop intimate relationships. These men project their ambivalent feelings toward their mothers onto motherly wives. But mothers are not their sons' equals; sons owe them respect and obedience and protection. A wife who takes the place of a mother cannot be a man's equal either. A Latina wife walks behind him as his support; at other times she is on a pedestal, playing the part of his mother. When he looks for sexual pleasure, pleasure that is more than just sexual indulgence, he seeks passion from a woman who is not a threat, who is not his mother, who is not his wife. Why is a passionate relationship a threat? Many Latino men, and especially men raised in the story of patriarchy, are in full flight from their own selves. Passion toward a woman is dangerous because strong feelings make them feel trapped, beholden, dependent. *Casado,* the word for a married man in Spanish, literally means "housed" or "housebroken," which no patriarchal Latino male wants to be.

And yet men are often trapped, taken over by the archetypes of the *parandero* and the *mujeriego,* men who are womanizers wandering in a rootless manner. So the Latino male is not free. He cannot rid himself of archetypes that send him searching from one woman to another, none of whom is capable of quenching his longing to belong. The patriarchal Latino man is a partial self who is wounded and angry. Since he cannot understand or name his pain, he turns to self-wounding through alcohol, drugs, fighting, and other kinds of self-destructive behavior. Too often he turns the anger outward toward those with whom he lives, his wife and children. Every time he hurts those he loves, he is wracked with guilt and he flees. Soon, he returns home, hoping to be forgiven. Until the next time. And there will always be a next time because nobody has dealt with the deeper underlying cause of this behavior. When he seeks reconciliation from his wife and his children, the patriarchal macho is once again reduced to a child looking for forgiveness. The wife may demonstrate power by withholding her *perdón,* forgiveness, at least for a time. She gains bargaining power in the house and uses her advantage to take revenge for the latest outbreak of humiliation and pain. The whole family is caught in a deformational cycle of abuse, guilt, return, forgiveness, temporary lull, and more abuse.

In this cycle of battering, drinking, withdrawal, and supplication for forgiveness, Latina women and Latino men participate in a mutual dance of wounding. Often a Latina wife or mother will blame herself in order to rationalize taking the man back. Or she might choose to believe that this is her fate, the will of the lord of emanation. She might use these periodic outbreaks as an excuse to gain control of the family and its finances. Eventually, she might have enough power and money to leave him. But many Latinas come to accept this kind of deformation as a punishment for some unknown sin. They see their punishment as justified.

The patriarchal Latino male is aware of these choices available to Latina women: He tries his best to exploit every one of them. He knows, for example, whether his wife is one of those long-suffering women like his own mother. If she is, he will take advantage. A patriarchal male is intuitive enough to know if his spouse accepts the battering and betrayal as her fault; if so, he will co-opt her guilt mercilessly. More difficult for him to address, a woman who takes all his skill, is the Latina woman who establishes her own economic autonomy and who enters into a contest for power with him. Now he must do everything he can to keep the game going. He can no longer blatantly stray; he has to be more circumspect; he needs to appeal to the feelings of guilt and motherliness of their earlier relationship. He may undercut her confidence. And there are the children, pawns of guilt to be used to keep the family together. All of these power plays on the part of the Latino male and the counter power plays on the part of the Latina woman keep the two of them arrested in crumbling stories and relationships.

Neither the Latino man nor the Latina woman is in control: Neither one nor the other is the villain; nobody can possibly win in these situations. Both of them have been taken over by stories from their cultural past, such as the story of patriarchy. Increasingly in U.S. society, Latinas and Latinos live the dominant story of capitalism, which gives them the right to be free, to pursue their own self-interest, to divorce, to seek power. Because all of this takes place in the service of incoherence, it is not helpful to either Latina women or Latino men. They remain partial selves, not knowing who they are, incapable of changing their lives for the better. I emphasize archetypal stories that overwhelm them, but not in an attempt to excuse the Latino male as an innocent victim or to blame his inherited cultural past. Unless he understands the power of these stories and their ability to undo him, he is merely beating the air as he tries to change his life.

Deformation as a way of life threatens to pull men and women into the abyss because they cannot respond to new problems. They cannot connect to others in any kind of loving way. Shows of affection become increasingly ritualistic forms of avoidance of loved ones and often become cynical and dishonest means of manipulation. This kind of ritualized avoidance of one another allows a kind of sex as indulgence. If a male child is hungry, one feeds him. When an adult male needs sex, the Latina woman has been raised to indulge this demand. She of course stays detached as well; she is there but not really present. When he is temporarily satisfied, she is content, not joyful or happy. She has been a dutiful wife once again. To be joyful would mean that she was fulfilled as a woman and a lover. But nothing of the kind has taken place.

The Archetypal Drama of the *Mujeriego*

A *mujeriego,* a womanizer, is a man who lives a Don Juan existence and is condemned to wander from one partner to the next, never able to meet himself or the other in their sexual encounters. All that counts is the momentary rush of passion that accompanies each conquest. He treats women as sexual objects whom he does not want to know for fear he will have to face himself. He has been given the right by society and culture to have as many sexual partners as he can. Women are never given the same privileges. Similar to the story of the disappointed male, this story is a spin-off from a nuclear cluster of archetypal dramas that rotate around patriarchy. In this drama:

- Men are considered by other patriarchal males to be *muy macho,* very masculine, because they can please more than one woman.
- Other men consider *mujeriegos* fortunate and see them as heroes.
- A man has a secure base at home from which to operate, provided by either a mother or a wife.
- The culture expects men to have more than one sexual partner.
- Wealthier men can even have a *"casa chica,"* another family and household that they support.
- Wives and mothers are placed on pedestals, which frees a man to have sex with other women.
- To practice this lifestyle men need docile mothers and wives who collude with the story.

- If they are religious, *mujeriegos* seek forgiveness from "God" (that is, the lord of emanation), knowing that they are not expected to change.
- Sons might be angry because of the cost to their mothers, but they get caught by the story and learn to become the next generation of *mujeriegos*.
- Daughters learn that it is the fate of Latina women to live with the behavior of *mujeriegos*.

Responding to the *Mujeriego* Archetype

The archetypal drama of the *mujeriego* is falling apart. It has always been sustained by violence. Of its very nature this story can never be in the service of transformation because it is grounded on the perpetual violence that neither a woman nor a man will ever be allowed to be or become fully who she is or who he is.

In the service of emanation a woman is required to repress her own personal face by denying all of her needs and desires; her political face cannot mount any resistance to the power of men since she practices a politics of uncritical loyalty; historically her face is determined by the stories of the past that blessed her inferiority based on gender; her sacred face is obscured by the belief that only men were sacred and important. Practicing the stories of uncritical loyalty and patriarchy disarms a woman so that when her husband is unfaithful she sees it as her fate.

Latino men continue to hold on to the story of the *mujeriego*. And what often works is limited forms of freedom. A Latina woman is given more money. The Latino man no longer brazenly pursues other women. He allows his wife or lover to work or perhaps go to school. These are attempts to win her back to normal, to return her to her senses, to keep her sweet and docile, living the stories of her inherited past. He wants her to repress her own desires, to practice loyalty, to reinvigorate the tradition of being his possession. He attempts to reform the story, that is, to modify it from within. He wants to make it more bearable without really changing it.

A Latina woman may rebel, may take her stand. But if she is not fully present and is still fighting battles determined by the stories of the past, her consciousness is still caught by the stories of patriarchy and uncritical loyalty. She may seek power so she is never again vulnerable to a man. She might go to school, get a job, and win a great deal of freedom for herself and her children. Her husband might respond with a sense of inevitability. He does not agree, but there is nothing that he can do. Latino men who give up often get depressed, turn to liquor or drugs. They feel useless. Their children may resent them for all the years of abuse. They recede into the background, asserting themselves on occasion, but they have lost their power. What we do not understand is that these men are not just pouting or licking their wounds. They have lost their way in life. So they remain sleeping volcanoes.

Latina women may indeed gain power but lose their way. They get caught up in exercising freedom previously forbidden to them. They have jobs, lunches with colleagues, even male colleagues, they go to conferences, travel alone to see their parents. They get involved in competition with others on the job and they struggle with their children. But what about their hurt and their anger over having been sexually betrayed? What about their passion, sexuality, and creativity? They find themselves living with a man with whom they no longer know how to relate. Their sexual life has become part of a contract to take care of each other's needs, but there is no passion, love, or spontaneity. Power will never heal the wounds and create a new and better relationship. Unfortunately, sexual relationships are reduced to fulfilling a duty.

Some Latina women live for years trying to get revenge on their partner for his infidelity. She can exercise her newly won freedom by taking a lover herself. Frequently, however, when entering such a relationship, she does not discover herself or reignite her own passion and sexuality; she is absorbed in getting back at her husband, showing him that she can also play the game. She ends by using another person in her story of anger much as her husband has used her. Because her husband has hurt her, she might refuse her husband his marital dues. If she does consent, she is not present. Her detachment from him belittles his sexual prowess and undermines his manhood. She might choose to humiliate him in front of their children, or when they are alone. She tells him that he is living here in this house on borrowed time. If he takes her up on her threats, she might back down. In some distant corner of her heart, she still has feelings for him. She may still be caught by slivers of the stories of uncritical loyalty and patriarchy that continue to make her feel guilty. But she remains caught by her anger, by her desire for revenge.

A Latina who has been betrayed can learn to forgive both her husband or lover and herself only if she is willing to take the risk to love again. This means that she needs to empty herself and to rebel on the deeper level against the stories that both she and her husband inherited from the culture. A Latina woman can come to see that it was the sin, shame, and guilt of the way of life of emanation that held her captive for years as she practiced the stories that violated women: patriarchy, uncritical loyalty, and the *mujeriego*. Furthermore, she comes to recognize that the answer is not power in the service of incoherence that leaves her a partial self, nor is it the obsession for revenge that plunges her and her lover deeper into despair. She can and needs to empty herself of these arrested fragments of the core drama of life (Act II, Scene 2) and move aggressively to create a more loving, passionate, vulnerable, and intimate relationship in which she rediscovers herself.

If she can awaken to the realization that she was a victim of the culture, it is also possible for her to recognize that her husband was hurt in the same way. After all, why did he fall apart? It was more than the loss of his male privilege. He no longer knew who he was outside of the stories sanctioned by their shared culture. He too is lost, confused, and looking for answers. As a man of color in U.S. society, he has been battered by the stories of capitalism and racism. If he is willing to empty himself of those cultural stories that are destructive and those stories that undermine his humanity in the wider society and the ways of life in which they were practiced, then there is hope that together they can create their own marriage, their own sexual relationship, their own family. If either he or she is not willing to take this risk, then a Latino man or a Latina woman has to be ready to go on without the other.

In a student essay a Latina woman described her painful relationship to Latino men:

> All my life since I could remember I have always needed a man to tell me that I am someone special and I thought that the only way I can prove to them that I cared was by having sex with them. Never have I made love to a man. I have always had SEX. . . . I use sex as a form of escape and security. In order to keep the one thing that I have always wanted, the feeling of having someone hold me, and the feeling of knowing that I have made someone else happy . . . even though I do not enjoy sex, I do enjoy seeing their faces full of joy and pleasure when we are done. I like teaching them how to feel pleasure; I like pleasing them because it makes me feel like I have done something useful. I do not love them. I use them and I let them use me. It's a game of who will give in first. By being with me, I feel like they care about me and not the sex. But of course I am wrong.[9]

This is an extraordinarily honest expression by a Latina who has always tried to show how tough she was and that she didn't need men; they needed her. Sex, for her, was about power. She wanted to give pleasure as a form of control, to enjoy seeing their need for her. But she never gave herself, she was not present. She gave only her body for "SEX," which took over her life and obsessed her, symbolized by her capitalizing each letter in the word. In her attempt to remain aloof from men and to inoculate herself from the pain of eventually losing them, she had to repress and suppress her own sexual pleasure. She was not there when engaging in sex; she was hiding her own personal face, exercising a politics of power over men, repeating the stories of other Latina women with her historical face. She felt that her sacred face was obscured and controlled by the lord of incoherence, who inspired her to devise new and more cunning ways to attract men, use them, and then reject them before they had the chance to leave her. She became fully aware that she was living on the edge of sanity and deformation:

> I cannot count on any absolute meaning or the loyalty of anyone. The only certainty now is the insecurity of knowing that nothing is secure and lasting; this I learned when the boys left me and when they left me I felt lonely and worthless.

"Lonely and worthless" indicate the inherent limits of power and the reality of deformation. In order to ask another to love us, we need to take the risk of being fully present to that person, and we cannot take such a risk when we are locked in a contest for power, and when we fear the other will walk away because the relationship is no longer in their self-interest. There is no way out when we get caught in the stories of patriarchy and romantic love that deform our lives. Inevitably we get depressed and feel useless.

But this Latina woman awakened to what she was doing to herself and others:

> I realize that this was not the way to live. I let the boy I was dating go; yes I am alone and scared but I know now that I have no need to repress or to hold someone in order to have him love me. Someone once asked me if I have ever been loved and I said, no, because I never felt that anyone loved me enough or cared enough about me to tell me that sex wasn't everything in a relationship. I always thought that the more sex I had the more love they showed me. I never thought that this could hurt me so much and every time that I repeated the story I

repressed my emotions and thought that it was a fact of life. That everything that happened to me was just part of the territory. I was wrong. I now know that I am someone special and that instead of finding a man who fulfills me I should find the sacred within me. I should learn to find my true inner self, instead of getting caught up in things that are deformational and always end up hurting me and cause me to lose myself.

This is an extraordinary example of a woman awakening in Act I, Scene 2, and listening to her inner voice, an inner voice that had led her to rebel against the man she was dating. But she is not through yet. She is on her way to doing something truly radical. She is getting at the underlying sacred roots of her problem. She is freeing herself on the deeper level in Act II, Scene 2, of the stories and of the ways of life of emanation, incoherence, and deformation that arrested her life as a partial self. She is intent on discovering her own destiny, her own sacred self. She has not resolved everything. She is still very vulnerable to relating to men in the manner with which she learned to protect herself; that kind of behavior she said "was part of the territory." But there is hope, since she sees her current situation as unbearable, unfruitful, and untenable. When I met with her, she assured me that she was not alone. She was confident that she could count on others in her support group to help her complete the task of emptying herself of the stories and the partial ways of life that had wounded her so that she could bring about more loving and just relationships with men and women.

Notes

1. See Ronald Glick and Joan Moore, eds., *Drugs in Hispanic Communities* (New Brunswick, NJ: Rutgers University Press, 1990); and Justin Bachman, "Black and Hispanic Gays Hit Harder by AIDS," *The Star Ledger: The Newspaper for New Jersey,* January 14, 2000, p. 6.

2. Marshall Berman, *The Politics of Authenticity: Radical Individualism and the Rise of Modern Society* (New York: Atheneum Press, 1972).

3. In this regard I have learned so much from my students, who are asked to write papers applying the theory of transformation to their own lives.

4. David T. Abalos, *The Latino Family and the Politics of Transformation* (Westport, CT: Praeger Press, 1993), chapter 4.

5. I have learned a great deal about men in societies dominated by the story of patriarchy in the service of emanation, and of how they react to the collapse of male power, from Hisham Sharabi, *Neopatriarchy: A Theory of Distorted Change in Arab Society* (New York: Oxford University Press, 1988).

6. For a good insight as to how drugs destroy the entire community, see Glick and Moore, *Drugs in Hispanic Communities,* and the brutally honest film *American Me* starring Edward James Olmos.

7. For a very good book that addresses the issue of abusive relationships in the Latino community, see Myrna M. Zambrano, *Mejor Sola Que Mal Acompañada: For the Latina in an Abusive Relationship* (Seattle, WA: Seal Press, 1985).

8. David T. Abalos, *La Comunidad Latina in the United States: Personal and Political Strategies for Transforming Culture* (Westport, CT: Praeger Press, 1998).

9. Student's work used by permission. The paper was written for a course I taught in the spring semester of 1999 at Seton Hall University (Religious Studies 1502—Contemporary Moral Values). Successive excerpts are from this source.

4

~mm~

The Latino Male in
the Service of Transformation

Latina women and Latino men are responding in four fundamentally different ways of life as they confront their relationships to one another. Some pray to the lord of emanation and ask for their husbands or lovers to see the light and to change. In the meantime they believe that daily life is the will of an all-powerful lord who is testing them and who will reward them, if not in this world then surely in the next. Still other Latina women become angry and fight back by ridding themselves of the guilt that repressed them. They seek power so they can protect themselves and their children. Their response is often muted by fragments of emanation that connect them to the past: religious teachings forbidding divorce, the honor of the family, the fear of being the first to break up a marriage, concern for the children, waiting to get enough education or job security to make the move.

In the meantime the relationship becomes contractual; the Latina woman now insists on rights that her mother never would have dreamed of demanding. She has her own car, her job, her money, her friends, and time alone. The third response in the service of deformation leads a woman to look for ways to hurt her mate, to get revenge, to do to him what she has suffered. She becomes a victimizer. But the same story continues to possess her life and that of her husband or lover. Another form of deformation is self-doubt and self-wounding. The Latina woman sees herself as unattractive and so does whatever is necessary to become what she fantasizes her husband is looking for in a woman. She goes on a diet, seriously considers breast implants, liposuction, new wardrobes to make her sexy. When all her efforts fail, she begins to believe that there is no hope and lets herself decline physically and emotionally. She becomes suicidal. What prevents the worst kinds of self-wounding is her love for the children. But at times, even mother love does not work. Her self-confidence has been eroded and perhaps even destroyed.

Responding to New Problems:
But in the Service of What Way of Life?

Latino men in the service of emanation expect a woman to stay in her place as demanded by the culture, by the society, and by the lord of emanation. When she fails to please him, he sees it as his right to make her feel guilty until she returns to normal, that is, until she returns to the container of patriarchy wherein she is only a shadow of her master. In the way of life of incoherence, Latino men realize that they are in a new world and that they cannot undermine their wives with the same old mystique. They give concessions, they provide more freedom as long as they hold the string, they appreciate the higher standard of living enjoyed because of a working wife. But the gain is an economic one; it is not to aid the fulfillment of a partner.

I have come to realize only of late how pervasive and destructive the way of life of deformation is in my own life as well as in the Latino community. For the longest time I thought that physical abuse and only the most virulent kind of psychological abuse were what constituted patriarchy in the way of deformation. Now I realize that ignoring a woman, indifference, acting as if she is not even there, and other such forms of turning a person into a nonperson are acts of violence that are as deadly, if not more so, than actual physical attacks. This kind of silent violence makes Latina women feel like nothing, like *mierda,* crap. Their humanity is completely undercut so that it takes their breath away and incapacitates them. Many are so hurt and made to feel so foolish and so useless that these feelings of inadequacy send them back to the traditional ways of being a woman. They often feel it was their comeuppance for daring to think they could achieve more than their mothers. They become so sad; their spirits are broken. I have seen this happen many times. And I have participated in this kind of wounding.

Those Latino men who are more intellectual and can castrate their feelings before they get out of hand are able to fake it a little bit better. They use academic rationalizations as buffers to hide the real horror of what they are doing. So they manufacture guilt when they hurt or use a woman. They feel bad about what they did, they claim they really do respect women. But they repeat this kind of hurt again and again. They practice being sorry, protesting they will change, when in reality they put off dealing with the underlying stories and ways of life that possess their lives.

I am in no way trying to blame my mother or any mother or woman; my mother was deeply disabled by the culture that made her feel guilty so that even thirty years after the death of my father she could not get to the point of criticizing him without feeling guilty. Because of the stories of patriarchy and uncritical loyalty under which she was raised, my mother felt she was betraying my father by revealing he was more responsive to others, especially his own mother, than he was to her. She was badly hurt. She held this hurt and it sapped her self-confidence for most of her life. I believe my mother never realized the source of her hurt. My mother was disappointed with her life; she only had her children to give her some compensation for the loss of her dreams. Am I angry that my mother did not fight back? That she left me vulnerable to the story of patriarchy as the male representative of another generation? Do I feel anger toward my father?

There is a shared responsibility for the pain and loss but one that goes beyond individual lives to the part played by the culture, the society, the patriarchal Mexican family, the Catholic Church, and by those institutions that legitimized the stories of patriarchy in the service of partial ways of life that doom participants to the perpetuation of a deadly story.[1] Nevertheless, Latinos and Latinas are not victims, powerless men and women who are crippled by the sins of the past. They have choices that I wish my mother and father would have made for their sake and for my siblings and me, their children. The choice for transforming change can never be accomplished by continuing to blame ourselves or others; we have to go beyond the guilt and anger we feel. Unless we get to the deeper underlying forming sources, the stories and partial ways of life, and free ourselves of them, there is little hope. I saw many Latino men try to appease their anger and guilt by drinking, fighting, and other forms of self-wounding. But none of these forms of escape could heal the pain of being only half a man, a partial person. Latinos need now more than ever to be men, aggressive machos who are radicals rooted in their deepest self, revolutionaries who are prepared to step forward urgently to say, *"Presente,* Here I am," fully present for perhaps the first time in their lives with selves who know who they are because they have fought the struggle on the deeper levels of their lives. They are now ready to go to the roots of the system of oppression, to vomit those roots out of their lives and then create a new and more loving alternative. This is the kind of valor, courage, bravery, fortitude, strength, guts, *ganas,* honor, *machismo, huevos,* balls, *cojones,* commitment, and love required of the authentic Latino male.

Emptying the Destructive Stories and Ways of Life

In addition to the truncated ways of life of emanation, incoherence, and deformation, the deepest source offers Latino men a fourth choice, the way of life of transformation. At any moment the spirit of transformation can intervene in Act I, Scene 2, and speak to men from within: They read a book, see a film, meet a person, dream about a grandmother, feel an intense anger. All of these inspirations represent sacred forces breathing within. Men need to test them to see where they guide them. The initial awakening may make them so angry that they want revenge by hurting others; another reaction could be to forget the anger and go back and try harder to be the perfect husband and father as protector and provider but still patriarchal to the core; this would be reform, that is, putting in place a more gentle form of the story of patriarchy, but it is still the same story made more dangerous by the seductive power that threatens to return men to a world that no longer exists. Another inspiration might be to calculate how to pursue their own self-interest and exploit the weaknesses of women; but the inner voice that awakens them can also be one that moves them to create the fundamentally new and better.

What is the process by which Latino men actually go about emptying themselves of destructive stories and ways of life? Having experienced these feelings and inspirations (Act I, Scene 2) they are now moved in the deepest depths of their being to do something about their lives. They begin by getting *angry,* which helps them to generate the necessary energy to *rebel,* to break with those who were holding them (Act II, Scene 1). But now they also realize that it is not enough to simply rebel against individuals who are the concrete manifestations of the underlying, formative sources; they need now *to rebel on the deeper levels* of their lives (Act II, Scene 2) to free themselves from the stories of patriarchy, the disappointed male, matriarchy, possessive love, capitalism, and the ways of life of emanation, incoherence, and deformation, which castrated their capacity and prevented them from creating a new and better life.

At this critical point, lest Latino men turn their anger to the worse, they need *guides,* people who love them for their own self and who above all return them to their inner selves and mystery. Such guides in the service of transformation never possess the men they help. They do not have all the answers. They get those in need through the night as they tell the stories of their lives. They are not judgmental, but they assist others in judging for themselves the destructiveness inherent in their stories. They listen, acknowledge their own pain and hurt; they are wounded healers who know of what others speak because they have experienced in at least one aspect of their lives the fulfillment of transformation. Since these stories and ways of life take on concrete reality by literally feeding on men, they have the capacity, inspired by the deepest sacred source, to *name and expose the stories* so that they clearly realize what they do to us and others. Then men need to *starve the stories to death* by refusing to practice their lives in their service. Finally, Latino men need to begin acting out the particulars of new and better stories. They can begin by relating to women with mutual respect and love.

For example, Latino men should stop this moment speaking and acting as an authoritarian male practicing the story of patriarchy and refuse to act with self-interest by living the story of capitalism when facing a situation in which they are tempted to assert power to cover their sense of insecurity. When we are poisoned, our bodies identify and isolate the invading and harmful microbes; our bodies contract and begin a process that involves the production of digestive juices that nauseate us and bring about a violent wrenching of our stomach muscles that causes us to vomit out the poison. In a similar way Latino men have been made sick with stories and ways of life that have entered into them. It is now time for them to *empty themselves* of the dramas enacted in partial ways of life. Thus to enter into Act II, Scene 2, is literally to experience a death and emptying of the old self. This is perhaps the most difficult part of the process. Men wait and listen, preparing to be filled with a new and better life, a new and more loving way. This period of creative anticipation is perhaps what the great Spanish mystic, John of the Cross, meant by the "dark night of the soul." Participants will have done their part: become angry, taken action, sought out guides, and voided themselves of the poisonous stories and ways of life. This participation has opened their lives, made them vulnerable, receptive, ready to be filled with a new and better alternative. They cannot demand or force this to come; they need to be ready to respond. Waiting is an act of faith that leads participants to hope

that when the deepest source of being reveals itself they will be ready together to create a new and more loving story.

A New Kind of Ministry: The Sacred and the Political

> His inner voice had begun to tell him when and where rebellion is su-
> perior obedience in the service of a direction to be implemented by
> knowledge not yet acquired, by techniques to be learned and opportu-
> nities to be recognized.[2]

Inherited sacred stories and ways of life do not go easily; they have
been so much a part of *la cultura Latina* for centuries that they are often
unconsciously practiced. I have experienced the great power of the
backlash of which these archetypal forces are capable. In these encounters I feel that I am not only facing my own personal demons but that I
am in fact confronting in my own person what the Latino community as
a whole must deal with. I feel a powerful desire to speak, teach, and
write about the process of transformation in *la comunidad Latina*. When
I struggle to free myself from the stories that hurt me I realize that my
confrontation with the culture converges with and responds to the needs
of others in the Latino community.[3] Ever since I was about nine years
old I felt a need to practice a higher obedience by rebelling against aspects of my Mexican culture, especially in regard to the treatment of
women and the culture's insistence on uncritical loyalty. At first I believe that this resistance was related with the temptation to assimilate.
But then as I got older and began to appreciate my Chicano heritage, I
recognized that on some deeper level there were destructive elements in
the culture and in my religious upbringing. My rebellion manifested itself in my disobedience to the demands of an emanational, patriarchal
priesthood that had silenced my inner voice with sin, shame, and guilt.
When my anger expressed itself I was surprised. I knew intuitively in
my bones that there was something very wrong with the parallel demands of my Mexican heritage and the Catholic Church for my total
loyalty. Gradually I came to recognize what this was all about; it was
the beginning of a vocation born from within. I responded to another
voice, which led me into the service of a direction that I came to know
as the politics of transformation. In responding to this inner need I
sensed, but did not yet know how to conceptualize, that I had to free
myself of stories that I was living that blocked the discovery of my
deeper self. When I first heard the terms of the theory of transformation,
I knew that I had found a language, a wisdom, that would allow me to

implement my life's work. As a teacher, both in and outside the classroom, I now had the opportunity to teach, write, discuss, and live a politics of transformation.[4]

This newfound understanding of my identity helped me to reject a philosophy of self-negation that some call self-less service. On the contrary, the more I discovered about myself and my vocation to serve others, the more I realized that this was really self-fulfilling service. The more I became myself, the more I could be of service to others. In my search for identity, I realized the limits of my culture not only in my life but also in the life of my community. If I could transcend the limitations of my own identity and of my cultural heritage, then others would not have to accept the past as a permanent burden.[5] Because of my awareness of the political and historical faces of our being, I am moved by an overwhelming conviction to respond, together with others, to create history by bringing about new turning points, new alterative stories, that will allow us to achieve love and justice wherever we find ourselves. I have found the focus for my life's work in the classroom of the university and the classroom of *la comunidad Latina,* where I am both a student and a teacher. It is this sense of having been called from within that makes it possible to step forward with a sense of urgency to respond to the needs of students and to participate within the Latino community to help change our lives for the better.

Having learned a theory of transformation, discovered so much about my own temperament, developed my intellectual capacities and come home to myself, I was ready to embark on my life's work: a vocation of praxis, applying theory to practice in all aspects of my life. All around me in the university and in the community I saw personal, political, historical, and sacred challenges. I wanted to change for the better the here and now, that is, to discover and uncover the sacred in the ordinary. This kind of service and ministry is inspired by the spirit of transforming love, a spirit that transcends all attempts to institutionalize it.[6]

On many occasions I have been asked after speaking why I use religious language. Many have commented that the sacred permeated my political and historical analysis. They correctly see it is the sacred that gives my words their ultimate and deeper meaning. I am, as all humans are, rooted in the sacred, the deepest ground of our being. This connection to the deepest sacred invites us to participate in fulfilling the work of creation. I no longer pray, as I once did, to the lord of emanation who had promised me the security of the truth given once and for all, who would save me from sin, shame, and guilt; nor do I honor the lord of incoherence, who will give me power and privilege; and I seek no lord of deformation, who would give me absolute power to destroy myself while I diminish others. To create the fundamentally more loving and just means to become a co-creator with the deepest sacred source, the god of transformation, who inspires us to move from being religious knowers to religious innovators, religious cartographers, persons who are not map readers but who journey where no boundaries exist, guides who awaken in others the inner need to make real the passion for justice that we feel in our bones. The challenge of being a religious innovator is to open up new doors and avenues into our creative imagination, from where we draw the visions of how to bring about new and more loving stories that overcome the nihilism of life. I hope to inspire in others, especially my students, a passionate energy that leads them to go beyond mere criticism of patriarchal culture and to claim a shared task that is mutually fruitful: men and women growing their own masculinity and femininity in such a way that they are both male and female, whole human beings.

This capacity to feel, to understand, and to share the process of transformation in teaching, writing, scholarship, speaking, and above all in applying theory to action in the community, allowed me to go beyond my own personal identity and that which I shared as a member of the Chicano/Latino communities to embrace a wider identity, to extend my householdership as teacher and husband and father to the work of transformation. This meant nurturing, fathering, and mothering first of all my own immediate family and community and then all other racial and ethnic groups and indeed all creation.[7] In affirming my Chicano/Latino identity, which was necessary given the shameful neglect of the wider society of my culture, I established the life space within which I could become uniquely and affirmatively who I am.

Paradoxically this struggle to establish an identity in a hostile land provides members of the Latino community the capacity to simultaneously embrace and transcend our uniqueness by way of a more inclusive humanity, a multicultural society. But beyond this affirmation and transcendence of ethnic and cultural identity, Latinos can also affirm and transcend the unique sexual and gender identities of their historical and cultural context. This liberates Latino men to become a new kind of human being, feminist males who are able to disarm ourselves of the power of patriarchy and to pray to the deepest source of transformation to annul in us a kind of manhood that is only a fantasy and a fragment of who we are and that limits us as human beings. Now we are enabled to place upon ourselves a new overarching and inclusive "hood," one that unites us as both masculine and feminine, that of personhood.

Latina women and Latino men who have come into their personhood in this way become utterly revolutionary. Once they have found
their identities and connected them to a commitment to serve others,
they have discovered their destinies. Armed in this nonviolent manner,
they now wield an exceedingly rare capacity that frightens those who
would continue to abuse their humanity and that of others. Many who
felt they were fated to be on the margins were hurt and wounded as children at home and in school. They felt guilty and blamed themselves for
the sexual and physical abuse and the racial taunts. To relieve themselves of this infantile guilt many got involved in rebellious behavior—
promiscuous sex, drinking, fighting, dropping out of school, joining a
gang, taking drugs, and other self-wounding behavior. But with transformation they have the ability to transcend the wounded self and the
scars of racism. In this way they can prepare themselves to be *response-
able*, capable of responding as the nurturing mothers and fathers of their
community as they build and staff day-care centers, senior citizen housing, hostels for the abused and the homeless. Only by creative activity can
they rediscover the personal, political, historical, and sacred faces of their
being. These Latinos and Latinas can discover what it means to be a new
kind of mother and father only in action in the service of others. The
deepest sacred is revealed to us not only in words but through action.

Parents can prepare children to rebel against all forms of injustice
by encouraging their inner need to create something more loving and
just, the best tradition that they can hand on to them. In this way they
assist a most natural aspect of their growth and development: to go beyond mere rebellion for the sake of finding themselves and the discovery of their life's work. Nurturing Latina mothers and Latino fathers
need to keep in mind that all children, their own biological offspring
and children in the community, exist with a unique consciousness and a
responsibility of their own. Each of them has their own center of silent
contemplation that prepares them for participation in transformation.
Many youth get caught at the extremes so that some live empty narcis-
sistic lives of self-indulgence or are absorbed by a deep pessimism and
anger that destroys them. Parents can provide guidance through these
extremes. In the midst of the cacophony of family life, parents respond
to the messages and the visions that move them. In doing so they experience the reality of creating something that was always in them but that
they had not previously recognized.

Latina women have been for generations so undermined by the stories of the past that the community is deeply impoverished by the loss
of a great deal of their creative participation.[8] Too often I have heard

how Latinas kept the family together. The community, however, restricts Latina self-expression in public life. The community has a habit of referring to its mothers as saints because of the suffering they endure from Latino men and from Anglo society. They keep the home fires burning. But because their creative endeavors have been restricted to the home, the community's political and historical fights against racism and capitalism are profoundly weakened. Latinas have been selfless, which means their personal faces and sacredness were celebrated as long as they spent their energies taking care of the family. Many Latino men have long been afraid that if Latina women got involved in the public realm, in which they could enact the political and historical faces of their being, male authority would be diminished. To prevent the collapse of patriarchal authority, Latino men have attempted to force Latina women back into a container that no longer works for anyone.

Women have been gaining some autonomy in the public arena, exposing the vulnerability of men who were excluded for reasons of race and class from their rightful involvement. Many Latino males have become rebels: They have responded to the deformation of racism and classism in the wider society by practicing the deformation of patriarchal violence against themselves and their own families. But there is no excuse for such fear and behavior. Together Latina women can say with Esperanza as she spoke back to her husband in the film *The Salt of the Earth:* "If you do not want the Anglos to control you, then neither do we want our men to control us."9

Latina women have, for the past thirty years, been freeing themselves and helping to liberate Latino men and *la comunidad Latina* from destructive stories. Latinas moving toward transformation have recognized that they were living stories that arrested them in the core drama of life. They know on at least an intuitive level that they have lived dramas that held great power over their lives. Fighting to attend college and to live in dorms, they have helped all of us to free ourselves from the stories of patriarchy and possessive love that have held women and men in the deadly embrace of a partial way of life. As they have made it to college or into the workplace, they have realized that they are not yet free. Once again they have to fight for their selves against their possessive fathers and against the guilt instilled in them by parents for allegedly abandoning the family. Moreover, they have had to fight jealous lovers and professors who doubted their ability to do well. On campus they have faced issues of race, class, and gender that threatened to undo their fragile self-confidence. Having experienced success, many Latinas

fight to include the community in their victory and to resist the temptation to join the powerful in the story of capitalism. Finally, many
women have struggled to avoid feelings and acts of deformational revenge for the hurt they encountered in their relationships with men.

Latinas who were married when they heard from their deepest self
have fought to go to work or to return to school to redeem the dreams
that they had repressed. Many Latino males are deeply threatened by
this rejection of the stories of uncritical loyalty and patriarchy and the
way of life of emanation. Their legitimation of control based on their
manhood has been eroded. They find themselves with broken emanational relationships in the midst of the story of capitalism, where they
were not allowed to compete due to racism and ethnocentrism. Thus
they see their tradition dying and their failure to make it in the United
States as an assault on their identity. The only place where they have
felt they could be in control was in the home.

Latina Women Creating New Forms of Justice
When the Patriarchal Rainbow Is Not Enough

I want to give an example of what Latina women are capable of once the
personal, political, historical, and sacred faces of their being are free from
the stories of romantic love, patriarchy, uncritical loyalty, and the disappointed male. Recently a Latina mother of four, Esperanza, had a bad feeling because Latino and Latina children were being ignored in her local
school system. She wanted to do something but she wasn't sure what to do
or how to go about it. She shied away from any kind of challenge to authority. She felt inadequate and believed she had little credibility with the
teachers and the administrators in the schools since she only had a high
school education. But she remained alert, ready in her not knowing, that is,
in the pregnancy of her silence, to move when the opportunity came.

Soon she met a Latina woman who put her in contact with others
who knew how to help her to respond to the needs of the students. She
called a meeting. People came who had been strangers to each other before the meeting. During the discussion they began a friendship and
formed a community of concern; they pooled their own resources and
those of the networks of people with whom they were connected. Before long the group had an agenda, working committees, fund-raising,
meetings with the school district superintendent, discussions with people in the community, and linkages made to other organizations that

promised assistance. A Latina/Latino youth conference was established with the promise of follow-up sessions to bring the concerns of the students to the faculty and administration of the school district.

But there was more. There were plans to make the conference an annual event. The students requested a Latina/Latino student organization. A proposal was submitted to develop a curriculum that was multicultural and gender-fair and to provide seminars on the Latino culture for faculty and staff. Esperanza and her colleagues were determined that their effort would not be just a one-act show of concern. This Latina woman, appropriately named Esperanza, Hope, called on those of us in the community to protect children outside of our immediate families and to discover a wider understanding of nurturing and parenting. Her dream, which had initially brought her feelings of fear, apprehension, and powerlessness, was realized. People connected to their inner selves took a political risk to create a new turning point in the history of the school district so that Latina and Latino students would no longer be absent from the agenda. The whole endeavor was a sacred task inspired by the deepest source of our being, who reveals to us time and again that each of us is sacred.

By transforming her vision from a mere possibility to actuality, Esperanza realized that when she took a risk she discovered aspects of her own person of which she was only dimly aware. In action she found a new personal face that was no longer repressed, hiding, or canceled by fear; her political face challenged parents, teachers, and the school district to practice and fulfill the story of democracy. With her historical face she sought to change the history of the school district by opening a new story, multicultural education that would allow the district to respond to the diversity of its students. With her sacred face Esperanza brought the light of the deepest source of our being to reveal to everyone involved their own sacredness and that of the students in their care. All of this she accomplished in spite of her fears of failure, her feelings of inadequacy, and her struggles with her family. She took her nurturing face outside of the politics of her own personal home to include the wider political arena of the community.

Esperanza also reveals the poverty of the relationships of emanation, subjection, buffering, and direct bargaining when she faced the issues in the community. Esperanza needed to practice new relationships, isolation from her own family for periods of time, and autonomy as she discovered she had skills that gave her the ability to organize. The introduction of these two relationships brought conflict between herself and her family because she was acting outside the expected patriarchal norm of mother and wife. There were times as well when the family disagreed over what was expected of the rest of them. But there was also transformation as Esperanza and her children and husband realized they had rediscovered Esperanza not only as a mother and wife but also as a woman, a person who had much to offer. By enacting these new relationships, Esperanza was also undermining the story of patriarchy and the way of life of emanation. Her husband went through much turmoil, but he loved her enough to trust her and to move toward letting go the story of patriarchy so that together they could create a new story, that of mutual love, as they supported one another in their life's work.

In the core drama of life, Act I, Scene 2, the emergence of unsettling inspirations can come at any time; we hear a new voice that fills us with new ideas, feelings, or intuitions we cannot ignore or repress. Even in the worst nightmare of deformation, the deepest source of our being intervenes so we are never alone. This source breathes within us new personal, political, historical, and sacred possibilities. When Esperanza listened to her inner voice, she heard the silence of the students shouting out to be heard. She responded as a parent and called upon other parents and teachers to nurture the next generation. This is what politics in the service of transformation is about: always taking the next step, which opens new doors and challenges that in turn invite us to enter into the making of something fundamentally more loving and compassionate out of the silence of a nothingness pregnant with possibility.[10]

A guide in the service of transformation is like a minister who leads persons to find the sacred in the depths of their own lives; he or she is a shaman, a *curandera,* a healer, a medium, a mediator who puts us in touch with the deepest sacred source of our being. To be a guide in the service of transformation means choosing to belong to a new kind of community in which all people can participate. The guide places us in the presence of the sacred, mediates the sacred, and then leads us to the sacred so we can create our own relationship to the deepest source of our being. To know yourself is to know your lord. For each of us to become a self is the desire of the deepest sacred. The Muslim mystic Ibn Arabi teaches that to know and create yourself is to reveal the face of the deepest sacred.[11]

Returning to the theme of growing one's own masculinity and femininity, there is no place for exaggerated maleness or femaleness; each person comes forth in her or his wholeness as human beings who have brought together the masculine and feminine archetypes of our being in a new and marvelous way. In the Latino community, both women and men need a phallic maleness to move aggressively and decisively, to be always on the move. The male side is counterpointed by a corresponding need to be open, to be ready to be moved by a higher inspiration, and thereby to become *qua mulier en actu concepto,* like a woman in the act of conception.[12] In this way individuals become pregnant again and again with the creative imagination that makes us most like the Creator of Genesis. We are made in the image and likeness of this Creator precisely by becoming and being creators ourselves, co-creators, together with our Creator, the deepest source of transformation of the fundamentally more loving and just in all aspects of our life. It is in this way that we can overcome, and indeed redeem, the negative experiences of our own mothers and fathers and, just as importantly, overturn the patriarchal story and ways of life that wounded our forebears so we can give birth to our own humanity by fathering and mothering ourselves.

But it is important to emphasize that men should not be overcome with guilt. Men should not disarm, give up being aggressive, for the sake of some pious passivity or fake sorrow. To do so would be to become once again victims of the past. They need to leave behind the story of patriarchy, not rebel against it by renouncing their masculinity and by demonizing machismo. They need to go beyond sterile self-flagellation and move to reject the story of patriarchy and then move to create a new and better alternative. Latino men are now free to step forward with urgency as new kinds of men using the energy of machismo to protect their authentic humanity and that of all others. The only proper function of aggression is to serve love in the service of transformation.[13]

In my own life and in the lives of my colleagues in *la comunidad Latina,* time and again I see and feel the force of the stories and their possessive power. For example, one day when I was having lunch with my wife, Celia, and mother-in-law, I became annoyed when they both questioned me over a fairly trivial matter. I was angry at seeing them join forces against me so that I actually pounded the table with my finger, not my fist. This is significant because when a person in the Latino community wags an index finger back and forth, it means that there is no longer any discussion, the matter has been closed.

I was acting the patriarchal male without even wanting to do so. I then became embarrassed at my behavior, which made me angry twice over out of pride. So I proceeded to pout, go silent, and then leave the table. I was amazed by my own behavior. But what I have no recollection of at all is pounding the table with my finger. My wife later pointed out my behavior to me. It was so ingrained and second nature to me that I do not even recall it. This is a typical response on the part of Latino men caught in the story of patriarchy with the ever-present overtones and undertones of violence lingering menacingly in the background. It is another example of how violence in the service of deformation always arises in collusion with maintaining the dying way of life of emanation, which reconnects to a life-support system every time men like myself continue to practice it. Latina women sense in their bones when they are in danger of having their personal faces erased by the violence of men who deny to women the right to practice their political face in the home.

To give a similar example, Celia and her mother had gone shopping and were gone for hours. As soon as they returned my mother-in-law came to give me some food and to tell me they had bought me several items. This was a classic performance that is played out countless times in the barrios of our community. Latina women have been trained to be grateful for time off, not to take it for granted. Latina women find it very difficult to give themselves permission to exercise freedom. Many Latinas feel guilty, as if they have done something wrong. I discussed this with my wife and her mother later that same day. My mother-in-law recounted how her father and her husband both became angry if she was not back on time to serve their needs. Out of guilt and to restore her good standing with them, she had to make up to them by cooking or performing some other service for them. Such was her apology for her act of rebellion. We agreed that both men and women have colluded for too long with each other in allowing this game to go on unchallenged. In the kind of dialogue my mother-in-law and I had, Latina women and Latino men can create an opportunity to find the sacred in the ordinary of life. These encounters help us to see how politics is the stuff of everyday life. To be political is to shape a daily environment in which people will either grow as full persons or be stunted and diminished. Politics is often thought of as official contests for power. To practice the politics of the home and family is to restore to each of us the political face of our being. We are always political as we shape daily life. Relationships between men and women, relationships between students and teachers, the acts of voting for a senator or holding a meeting to discuss the plight of the homeless—these things are all political. Politics in the service of transformation always asks the question: "What is it that we can and need to do together to create a more just and compassionate society?"

We need strong, dissenting Latina women who recognize the dilemma of Latino men and refuse to feed the story of patriarchy by placating us, taking revenge on us, or seeking to gain advantage over us, and who insist that we face ourselves. My wife has been a great help to me because she refuses to accept my behavior. But she goes beyond mere criticism. She speaks to me in private and expresses her concern without anger and with great love. But she is determined not to allow me to surrender to the stories of patriarchy and the disappointed male. If I act on patriarchal feelings, she gives me the time and the space to evaluate what has happened. Then we discuss and analyze what has taken place. This allows us to learn from seemingly trivial events that the sacred resides in the ordinary occurrences of everyday life. Alone we cannot defeat these destructive forces from the depths; we need to be grace-full, that is, filled with a relationship to the deepest source of our being, the source of transformation, so that together we can overcome.

The Story of Matriarchy:
A Response to the Story of Patriarchy

There is an urgent need in *la comunidad Latina* to confront the absence of the Latino male and the emergence of a negative form of the story of matriarchy. Increasingly in the community families are headed by Latina women who are single parents, working and raising their children alone. Many Latino men have failed and been failed by the society at large so that they have not taken responsibility for helping in the nurturing of children. Many of the reasons for this failure have been discussed elsewhere in this book, but I want to bring together some of them here. Again, Latino men are experiencing the collapse of the way of life of emanation and the undermining of those stories that largely gave them their power and identity, primarily patriarchy, uncritical loyalty, and the *mujeriego*. Many Latino men, even after generations in this country, find themselves far behind the economic standards of European Americans. Latino cultural heritage with its focus on male privilege is waning. Latinos often can't make it in the world of capitalism and power, which is too often allied with the destructive story of racism. At times they feel uprooted and believe that they can't make it anywhere. Throughout my life I have seen Latino men drink and often cry because of their lost heritage. This sense of loss can and often does lead to conflict in the home, conflict that escalates to domestic abuse, to problems in the workplace, and to children, especially male children, doing poorly in school and dropping out. The lack of schooling leads to poor jobs, high unemployment, no health insurance coverage, and further despair. To compensate for these crushing problems various forms of self-wounding occur: drugs, gangs as substitute families, crime, violence, sexual promiscuity, and the abandonment of responsibility for children. As a result, an alarming number of Latino males get caught in the criminal justice system.

The technology of birth control dramatically altered the relationship between men and women. Men have controlled women's bodies for centuries. More recently they decided when and if they would use condoms. They often refused, not being concerned about the woman's health or the emotional and physical stress brought about by unwanted pregnancies. Now many women have become active participants in preventing pregnancy. In addition, abortion-on-demand means that women can end unwanted pregnancies. All of this technological change has led to great changes in the family and in the relationships between women and men. Throughout the industrialized nations of the world, fully one third of all children born in 2000 were born into single female–headed households.[14] Some of these women are *choosing* to raise children alone. But many children were abandoned due to the desertion or death of their fathers.

This raises many serious questions. How does one bring up a child without the presence of a man as father, parent, guide, or friend? What are the implications for the future of the family? How will the children learn to develop loving and mutual relationships with the opposite sex if their mothers have given up on taking the risk? How will boys and girls learn to be full persons, whole in both the masculine and the feminine aspects of their being, without a father present? Is it enough to have a mother manifesting both her masculine and feminine selves in her relationships to her children? What about children raised by two mothers, a lesbian couple? How will these children relate to men, to the masculine aspect of their beings? Is it necessary for boys to have strong men available to them in order to grow into mature and loving adult males? We do not know the answers to these questions. But we need to find the answers.

La familia Latina has been and continues to be profoundly affected by this technological and cultural upheaval. Latina women, because many fathers, brothers, uncles, and lovers are either absent or in such difficult straits as to render them absent, are under tremendous pressure. As protectors in a dangerous world they become *mamasotas,* super moms who take on archetypal proportions in the lives of children. Mothers become anchors, focal points, heroes, breadwinners, guides, teachers, and fathers too. Latina women are in a bind. For religious and cultural reasons they find it difficult to develop relationships with other men once fathers are gone due to abandonment, domestic violence, divorce, prison, military service, or separation. As a result, many, but certainly not all, turn to their sons, especially the first born, for the kind of attention and love they were denied by their lovers or husbands. They bond in a very deep way. They bond, at times, in an archetypal drama, the story of matriarchy.

Looking Inside the Story of Matriarchy

Some forms of matriarchy are positive, but when matriarchy is a form of rebellion, a compensation for the absence of the male, matriarchy becomes the story of patriarchy with a feminine face.[15] A Latina says: "Your father is gone. Now I am in charge." But ironically the mother is not in charge because she is still enacting the story of patriarchy. Many Latina single mothers continue to give preference to the male children and to raise the girls and young women according to a double standard. Life goes on as if the father were still present. Even when mothers mock men as weak, or when a father is "present" but so disengaged from the family that the mother is forced to take over, she continues to exercise power as a man would; as matriarchs they demand obedience and respect as if they were men.

Matriarchy arrests individuals in the service of emanation, incoherence, or deformation just as patriarchy does:

- The story has not changed, only the gender.
- Matriarchy parallels patriarchy in that its domination still relies on gender.
- A matriarch remains caught by the tradition and practices the story of patriarchy and raises her sons and daughters as if she were the father.
- The story has been reformed, but no new and better story has been created.
- The matriarch becomes a master at using guilt as a form of manipulation.
- The matriarch takes on the mantle of silent martyrdom or of a complaining victim.
- To her children the matriarch is either a negative devouring mother or a saint who deserves the best.
- Matriarchal mothers in rebellion against patriarchy remain fragments of what they could have been.

Many Latino men have had the experience as boys of protecting their mothers from fathers or lovers and from the male authorities of this society. Thus these men discovered that their mothers needed them even though they hoped their mothers would protect them. Becoming men before their time puts boys in danger. On the one hand they have great power, which is impossible for boys to handle responsibly. On the other hand, mothers, feeling guilty for having invaded their sons' childhoods, overindulge them. Conflicted feelings of power, anger, and confusion are all mixed with love and guilt. I became suspicious of my mother's affection because I came to see it as a form of manipulation. It was a reward for protecting her or giving her something. However, there was often genuine passion on her part. This fear of affection influenced my relationship to women for years. As the "little man of the house," Latino boys are given too much power and attention. Sisters are there to serve brothers, especially if the girls are older than the boys. Boys become accustomed to such privilege and see it as their right. But some also have a sense of crushing obligation that does not allow them to play, imagine, and create in the world of the child. They compensate for this loss by accepting the submission of women.

I became aware of my mother's ability to overwhelm me with guilt. I had a corresponding fear of being emotionally abandoned by her. I used to play with her and make fun of Mexico to anger and harass her. That was my way of getting attention and affection. My sisters, especially the youngest, Marge, had the heavy responsibility of being a mother to the three youngest children, all boys. I felt especially close to Marge and looked to her for affection. But she was overburdened; she was only twelve years old and had no life of her own. She had no time to play, to be a young girl discovering the world. So she and I, both with our own needs and our inability to meet them, entered into a strange relationship. I used to get her angry with my needs because she could not even care for her own. I remember one birthday when I asked my sister to pin up the pant legs of my new trousers. I wanted to go to the movies and so I asked my sister to do it. She was angry but she agreed. When I moved too much for her, she struck me several times. I was more hurt by her anger, by her rejection, than I was by the pain of her slaps. I stood there sobbing. I was overcome with sadness as I watched her trying to take care of me. She felt so bad she hugged me, and I felt it was worth the slaps if this was the kind of affection and concern they earned me. There she was, bent over pinning my pants, feeling guilty for her show of impatience. Even at the early age of six I could tell that my sister was being asked to do too much. Yet the two of us bonded. We had deep feelings for each other, even though those feelings were steeped in pain. This story shows how desperate I was to be loved, given attention, and accepted. Soon after this episode I showed signs of a growing independence. Unfortunately, this independence was not based on any inner strength but on the fear that I would need others too much, that in the end they would disappoint me. Looking back, this experience might have had a great deal to do with my fear of intimacy and my identification of love and sex with pain. Neither my sister nor I could grow from such experiences. On the contrary, we both had an overwhelming sense of need, the need for love and affection.

My sister Marge never did have a chance to play, to enjoy her life by discovering who she was. Just six short years after this painful encounter, my sister was married. She had six children, one after the other. She went from mothering us to taking care of her own children; she never had the blessing of being nurtured, of being a child. She left one patriarchal/matriarchal nest in exchange for another.

I hope this description makes clear the heavy price Latinos and Latinas have paid and continue to pay because of the stories of patriarchy and that negative form of matriarchy that is enacted as compensation for patriarchy. These stories have been devastating. My mother could not respond to me and my siblings because she was living a story with my father that made it nearly impossible for her to be fully present to herself and to her children. Then she got caught in the same story by becoming a powerful matriarch in all of our lives.

Freeing Ourselves of the Story of Matriarchal Mothering

When Latina women and other women of color began to get involved in the feminist awakening in the 1970s, many were reluctant to see patriarchy or matriarchy as a deadly story on the same level as racism. Latinas often felt that it was their duty to protect the Latino male, a father or a brother, who was the subject of racism and a debilitating capitalism and who had been given the heavy duty of protecting the family. In addition, they were angry with white feminists who had the luxuries of money and time to attack patriarchy. Latino and Chicano men discouraged Latinas from taking up the issue of patriarchy because it would split the movement, show disloyalty, and take energy away from the fight against racism and the exploitation of capitalism in the community. At the root of this decision was a refusal to challenge *la cultura Latina* in order to fight the wider society's discrimination. Thus the Chicano movement, *la Causa,* and other liberation movements such as the Young Causa Lords in the Puerto Rican community were left for the most part unchallenged from the perspective of sexism as men continued to exercise the decisionmaking. Latinas were there to do the cleanup, the encouraging, the feeding, that is, the mothering.[16]

As a community too many Latino men have failed to recognize that oppression in all of its forms has to be fought simultaneously. Latinos cannot afford to wait to defeat racism before taking on the story of patriarchy and its feminine version of matriarchy; to do so would severely hurt their ability to work with Latina women. Latino men need to aggressively resist the urge to be pampered and nursed. This childishness gets in the way of becoming authentic men who know who they are and who realize that they need Latina women as colleagues. Together they can discover new and more loving ways to express the fullness of the feminine and the masculine aspects of their being.

I want to give an example of nurturing in the service of transformation. One day recently, as Celia was finishing her lunch, she had an intense impulse to save her pasta for me. Her colleague asked her why she was taking part of her lunch home and she answered that it was for me. That afternoon, Celia drove me to the airport and offered me the pasta. I was reluctant to take it, but I did. My plane was delayed and I became quite hungry, but I did not want to leave the gate fearing that we might be recalled for boarding. I remembered the pasta. As I ate it I was glad that Celia had insisted I bring it along. When I called that evening she asked about the pasta and I told her how much I had appreciated her thoughtfulness. She told me that she was afraid I would simply throw it away because I do not like to carry food with me. When I returned home, we talked about why she had given me part of her lunch. Was this another way by which Celia denied her own needs in order to defer to me as she had seen Latina women give preference to men all of her life? Was this a form of mothering, and thus of control, which would make me beholden to her, a way to ingratiate herself? Was this a manifestation of the eternal mother who was required to make sure I eat? She answered that she fought the urge but had an overwhelming sense of concern. She felt that it was the right thing to do. In our discussion I told Celia that I deeply appreciated her concern for me. I also stated that this show of affection on her part had inspired me to be not only a recipient but someone who wanted to be just as sensitive when it came to her needs and the needs of others. Thus the conclusion, to which we mutually arrived, is not to refuse the urge to do something for each other but to respond always in the service of transformation. In this way we free ourselves from cultural stereotypes and from demonizing anything we do for one another; we rescue the act of kindness by subverting it, by freeing kindness from the old cultural stories and ways of life and rediscovering it in the caring and justice of transforming love.

Open and honest conversations are crucial so that men and women together can expose and root out the deadly stories of patriarchy and matriarchy, uncritical loyalty, possessive love, and the disappointed male. Again and again they need to ask themselves, "In the service of what way of life and sacred story am I doing what I am doing?" In the service of the crumbling way of life of emanation, we do things out of guilt and to secure the acceptance of others by putting ourselves last; in the service of incoherence we do "good" deeds to score points on our tally sheet and gain power when negotiating with the other; in the destructive way of life of deformation we assist others in order to make them so dependent that they are crippled and unable to live without us; only in the service of transformation do we critically and creatively and consciously choose to free each other from burdens so that we will be free to do the tasks of transformation. Mutual nurturance means freeing each other to be fully present to each other and the community which we serve. In this way each of us is wholly present as we discover our unique gifts and use them to fulfill the inner need that each of us has to create; this personal emergence gives us the courage to risk ourselves and to discover new ways by which we can become alive and active as we struggle together with others to create a more compassionate and just society.

Neither matriarchy nor patriarchy can be practiced in the service of transformation because both of these stories are based on aspects of guilt, domination, fear, repression, and force. We do not need mothers or fathers who force-feed us with attention and overwhelm us to the point where we cannot walk away from them to discover who we are. What we need are deeply caring and loving mothers and fathers who guide us through the core drama of life so that we can realize our own personhood and rediscover our parents as friends.

Entering Into Act III, Scenes 1 and 2: The Story of Erotic Love

We have never been alone. We have from the very beginning of our journeys had at our side and within us a more powerful sacred force who can help us to undo the bonds of the lesser but destructive lords of emanation, incoherence, and deformation. The sacred source of transformation assists in this battle by inviting us to become co-creators in finishing our journeys and in completing the ongoing creation of the cosmos. Even in the darkest abyss of deformation, the Spirit intervenes and awakens Latinos, inspires them anew to rebel against those who possess them and the stories and ways of life that choke them (Act I, Scene 2). They respond to this call because having said no and rebelled against the partial lords, they are prepared to respond to the fundamentally new and better. The four faces of their being are now ready to say yes to this sacred invitation. The personal face of their being takes the risk of facing its true mystery by emerging out of the cave of the night of the partial self. The Latino man's self-confidence growing, he now stands on firm ground and reaches out to others with his political face so that together they can practice a politics of compassion, love, justice, and inclusion; history ceases to be the mere victimization of the past as they refocus and put into play historical faces to end a historical nightmare and participate in creating a new history, new turning points, new stories. Latino men's sacred faces are now empowered to participate as a bi-unity in the fulfillment of their own and the personal, political, historical, and sacred faces of the deepest source of transformation.

This encounter with the deepest sacred is one based on mutuality, on friendship, on love. The mystics knew the most profound way to describe the relationship between the sacred and the individual was by writing poems of erotic love. That the deepest sacred is closer to humans than their collarbones is a statement about intimacy. The source of transformation participates in our persistent creation of humanity, and we participate in the fulfillment of the deepest sacred source. The sacred source of transformation needs us in order to be concretely present in the world. The deepest source needs us just as we need the deepest source. "Allah is too exalted ever to become the 'father of mankind'; for that is a 'paternalistic' notion alien to all *nuptial mysticism;* the divine image which here invests consciousness and transcends transcendence is not that of the Father, but that of the *Beloved* (as in the Song of Songs)."[17] The relationship between the deepest sacred source and the soul is an erotic encounter that becomes the archetype for our relationship with one another:

> St. John of the Cross, to describe the ecstasy of mystical contact with God, uses images drawn from the joys of love. When he is most personal

and direct, he is most sensuous; thus he implies that the metaphors of sexual love are the best symbols for the deepest relation to God. "In the Song of Songs . . . the language of worship is the language of love, manifestly fleshly love. . . . The sexual mode of intense self giving at all levels is the best means of expression for a constant opening to the penetrating love of God.[18]

The encounter with the deepest source of our being is open, mutual, interconnected, lovingly erotic, and affectionate. That encounter and those characteristics become our guide as we enter deeply caring and loving relationships with others. When a Latino man loves a Latina woman, they mutually reveal their personal faces as the manifestations of their deepest selves. Now they can become truly naked, perhaps for the first time, in each other's presence. With their political faces they free one another to reach out to others in the society around them. Together they respond to fundamentally new kinds of problems and, just as they created a new history in their personal lives by growing their own family and marriage, they can now help to create more open and loving turning points in the wider community. Their sacred faces are connected on the deepest level with the source of all connections, the sacred source of transformation.

Creating New Archetypal Stories:
Transforming the Latino Male

We need to create alternative stories to replace those from which we have emptied ourselves: patriarchy, romantic love, the disappointed male, capitalism, tribalism, the wounded self, and uncritical loyalty. But I am concerned that we not just say no to the inherited stories of the past with nothing to put in their place. I want to begin with the Latino male who makes a decision to free himself from the despairing story of the *mujeriego,* the womanizer, and creates an alternative, the story of the faithful lover.

From Mujeriego *to Faithful Lover*

Creating more loving and compassionate alternatives is the most difficult part of the struggle for transformation. Once a Latino male has emptied himself of the stories of patriarchy, the *mujeriego,* and uncritical loyalty (Act II, Scene 2), then he can count on the deepest source of transformation renewing him with a more loving and just story, that of the faithful lover.

This story offers the following alternatives to the competing stories of the womanizer and of patriarchy:

- Freed from the narcissism of the story of the *mujeriego,* a step-child of the story of patriarchy that kept him a partial self, the Latino male now learns how to love his deeper self and his inner mystery so he can love others as himself.
- A Latino male as a faithful lover is fully present to his wife or lover.
- He shares with his mate a passionate sexual relationship based on mutual pleasure.
- He is both a friend and lover, relating to his mate as a companion in all aspects of their lives.
- In order to heal himself, he becomes vulnerable by revealing his woundedness.
- He encourages his lover to take the necessary risks to discover her own creative imagination.
- He is always open to criticism and dialogue and learning from and with his lover.
- He is a guide to his wife or lover, and he seeks her guidance in all of his decisions.
- A Latino male as a faithful lover never sees himself as the only source of inspiration for his wife.
- He frees his wife through his love and affection to be fully who she is.
- Whenever he or she is away, he trusts himself and her to be faithful.
- Because he cares deeply for his wife, he takes the courage to disagree with whatever she is doing that carries potential harm for her and their relationship.
- No longer doomed by the cultural stories that wounded him, he can be a deeply caring, loving, and compassionate man wherever he finds himself so that he is never insulated from the wider society; on the contrary, his love politicizes him so that he is a source of joy and hope at home as well as in the community.

This is the kind of story that needs to be nurtured and practiced by Latino males. First of all it is essential for them to starve the old stories to death by refusing to feed them with traditional behavior. Latino males need to become the *carne y gueso,* the flesh and bones, of fundamentally more loving stories such as the Latino male as faithful lover.

I want now to explain how in actual practice each of the characteristics of this archetypal drama can be lived today, here and now, with the person with whom a man shares his life.

A man cannot share life or love others unless he has a deeply caring love for his own self and person. It is because he realizes that his life is sacred and valuable that he comes to see the importance of the life of others. If he has experienced the joy of knowing who he is on the deepest level of his being, then he longs to share this with others by guiding them to discover their own deeper mysteries. To love others is never an escape from the self or a desire to lose one's own self in another but the recognition that one can only love others if one has something to give: one's self. For this reason Latino men need to reject the phony selflessness we often hear about. If I am not present, then I can never really share the heart of intimacy, my self.

To be fully present to a lover is to listen, to really listen, to tune in on often hidden messages and to hear, perhaps for the first time, what is being said and, just as importantly, what is not being said. To be fully present is to be sensitive to each other's hurts and desires and to see with seeing eyes. In the beginning, being present takes a great deal of conscious effort. But as the relationship grows, presence, being fully there for the other, becomes filled with grace, a blessing. A man moves and relates to his mate with gracefulness. This kind of presence takes time. Men need to be focused. They must not expend their resources so that they no longer have the energy to respond to those closest to them. To become the light of the world and the darkness of his own home means that a man has failed his family. Having lost his center he also loses his way in the world. Since he cannot do justice to those with whom he lives, he cannot be present to anybody, including his own self.

There is no substitute for being fully present wherever a man is. He needs to be present to himself and to those whom he loves. A Latino male who is not renewed by love and affection at home, because he is not present to his family, too often looks for affirmation, nurturance, and love where he is involved. Rather than facing himself and his family, he tries to escape into old fantasies. For all of our revolutionary talk, too many get lost in the stories of the *mujeriego,* patriarchy, and the disappointed male. I sought help myself with these issues by entering into therapy several years ago so I could free myself of the old stories.

Since so many Latino males were raised to be little *caudillos, caciques, mayordomos,* and *jefes,* bosses and chiefs, they find it very difficult to listen to others, especially women. To be gentle is to allow the others in our life to be there with us with no sense of anxiety. Our wives and lovers have a right to be able to disagree, to voice their own opinions, to state their ideas, to give us directions when we are lost on the road, to offer suggestions with no fear of being ridiculed, to warn us without being concerned that they will be mocked for being overly worried. Most Latino men were not raised to listen but to give orders, especially when they became the heads of their own households. To really listen to their wives is to respect them as people with their own ideas, feelings, and insights.

An affectionate and passionate lover creates an environment that is open and free and therefore erotic. To be an erotic man means to be connected to everything. Erotic men have an awareness and concern for others in the society. They love nature. They are able to take great pleasure from a sunset, a full moon, or a gentle rain. They understand the repair needs of the home. They can touch their lovers with real tenderness and affection. They are glad to be in the presence of their lovers. When the erotic man goes to the store, to the gas station, to the bakery, he is pleased to have his lover at his side. This is the kind of daily activity that prepares men to be erotic lovers in all aspects of their daily lives.

Jealous men are often weak and afraid of life. They use sex to repossess their wives and lovers when they have been away for a few hours at work, especially if they have been collaborating with male colleagues. The love and affection of a man who is a faithful lover, on the contrary, releases his lover from the fear of being tempted by others. Love frees us to be fully present in our wholeness as a person wherever we find ourselves. Yes, there is a risk that a wife will find another man attractive. But it is a risk well worth taking. The alternative story of possessive love that breeds suspicion, fear, lies, holding back, denial, and repression is simply not worth it. Nothing is more attractive and desirable than a woman who is open, honest, intelligent, competent, articulate, sensitive, and gentle, that is, a woman who is herself. And she has all of these qualities because she is free from the stories of patriarchy, possessive love, and uncritical loyalty. She is grounded in the story of the faithful lover with a man who has also freed himself of the old stories and ways of life and who is not obsessed with keeping her for himself. Her real beauty and attractiveness is grounded in her capacity to awaken in others the desire to be selves. Jealousy is never effective with a woman who knows who she is. She is connected to herself and to the deepest sacred source and those with whom she works to make life more loving and just.

I believe that a faithful lover knows in his bones he cannot be everything in his lover's life. The majority of women have spoken loudly about their need for tasks and challenges outside of the home to test their own ideas and intuitions. To confine the creativity of women to the home is to expose women to the dangers of dying of boredom or escaping into fantasies.

Transforming love means being faithful to the truth that a man sees in the life of the person that he loves. A faithful lover is willing to fight and disagree with his lover when he is concerned she is doing something harmful and untruthful with her life. A Latino male needs to bring to his lover's awareness how worried he is that she is risking her life and health by smoking. Under the old regime, he would simply order her as the patriarchal ruler to stop. Now he needs to practice a new kind of domestic politics. He needs to give up the old bossiness and domination. He must act out of concern and love for her and her well-being.

Latino men can as faithful lovers also protest when wives or lovers endanger their relationships. Their protests must, however, not be based on any attempt to control and command but rather on a desire to continue to love. The way to resolve dilemmas in a relationship is through taking the risk of being open and vulnerable. But a Latino man does have the right to speak out honestly, just as his wife does, about the lives that they share. If he withdraws, and neglects to speak out from fear of conflict, he becomes less present. His wife or lover will feel this estrangement. Unless there is good conversation that leads to mutual change, the relationship may begin to drift. I am counting on two mature people to confront together whatever becomes a potential obstacle to sustaining and enriching a life together.

Learning to Love One's Wife or Lover as One's Self

There can be no authentic love by anyone who loves as a disinterested partner, never wishing to be loved in return. This kind of self-less love is just that, a love wherein no self is present, neither one's self nor the other person's self. Latino men need to heed the commandment that urges them to love their neighbors as themselves. But they need to ask, "In the context of what story do I love others?"

If Latino males love Latina women in the story of patriarchy or the story of romantic, possessive love in the service of emanation, neither partner can be fully present. Men cannot love others as themselves because their selves are not available. In the service of emanation men are actively trying to be an extension of the powerful and mysterious others in their lives: parents, teachers, or leaders together with the lord of emanation. Nobody feels valuable or important except to the extent that he pleases others. Even the recipient of the adulation, the patriarchal male, is not present to himself since he sees himself as powerful and valuable only when he himself is linked to mysterious others. Even the most powerful source of emanation, the *patrón, el jefe,* the boss, chief, or the head of the household, cannot count on being the source of inspiration for others because these bosses are always fearful they will lose their magic.

In regards to the four faces of his being, the Latino male in the service of emanation represses his own personal face to please, for example, his father, while his wife represses her own feelings in order to live in accord with her husband's or the society's wishes. So the husband or lover never sees his own face or the face of his wife but only those partial aspects presented in order to meet the expectations of others. Traditionally, neither men nor women have been able to challenge uncritical loyalty and patriarchy. Both men and women have practiced a political face of unquestioning loyalty, not only to a real person but to a story and way of life embodied in a religion and culture that demanded that they be loyal to the status quo. With their personal and political faces disabled in this way, there was no possibility that they could challenge the stories; therefore they repeated the past as inevitable fate. This whole way of life and the stories practiced within it have been blessed by the lord of emanation, who filled the sacred faces of the people with sin, shame, and guilt. In this context, conflict and change are avoided for the sake of continuing and cooperating with the inherited culture. Justice for people who love in the way of life of emanation is not fulfillment, not joy, not wholeness, not passionate sensuality, but security in the belief that they are doing the right thing by staying loyal no matter what, by refusing to see problems, by putting everything in the hands of the lord. This is the kind of repression that puts humans on the road to self-cancellation in the service of deformation.

Latino men living the story of patriarchy or uncritical loyalty in the service of emanation cannot be present to themselves or to their wives and lovers. They cannot truly love others as themselves because nobody is fully present. To claim that they love others as themselves in this fragmented way of life is to say that they can enact a partial love, a sad and lukewarm passion, because the lovers are only fragments of their potential selves.

Whenever men love somebody as themselves in the service of incoherence, it can only be a partial and shallow love. All who live the life of incoherence within the system of capitalism are engaged in the pursuit of self-interest and power. As men and women rebel time and again against the powerful in order to get what the powerful have or rebel against the powerless in order to secure their own power, they are only present as powerful selves, selves who cannot afford to be whole, filled with compassion and a sense of justice. It is necessary that men suppress their personal faces and any desire they may have to share with others. They are forced to hide their emotions and to manifest those fragments of themselves that serve the pursuit of power. One might think, "Since I am consciously hiding my personal face, I assume that you are doing the same, so we play power games and shadowbox with each other and call it love." Again, nobody is at home. For the man engaged in incoherent love, the political face of his being is intent only on increasing power in relationships that enhance his personal aggrandizement. His wife or lover is thus reduced to being an asset or a hindrance as he goes for the golden ring. Time is not for benefiting humanity but for accumulating more fragments of power; time is money, interest earned. Timing is everything in buying and selling on the stock exchange. In this manner a man's historical face is reduced to being a puppet of economic forces rather than an initiator of turning points that make life better. His sacred face is obscured by the lord of incoherence, who tells him that he is one of the chosen only if he gains enough power.

In the service of deformation (at the exit from the core drama of life in Act II, Scene 2), to say that I love my wife or lover when I demand that she does harm to herself is to wound her. As I practice stories like the *mujeriego* or the disappointed male as spin-offs of the destructive story of patriarchy, I erase the face of my lover or wife and therefore my own. My political face practices a politics of total power, that is, the power of life and death over myself and others and lashes out with anger to hurt, to seek revenge, to do physical or psychological violence, to wish to exclude a person from the fullness of her or his life. Time does not heal the wounds but makes them worse. Some men ignore the pain until they become numb in the broken places. Their historical faces condone the presence of violence. History takes a downward turn into the abyss and things get worse. My sacred face is almost totally obscured by the lord of deformation, who sucks me and those I "love" into the abyss of death. This is a destructive love wherein a lover says to his partner, "If you love me, take drugs with me, have unprotected sex with me although there is the danger of infection with AIDS or other sexually transmitted diseases. Stay with me even though you must leave children unattended at home." This is the type of deformed love that leads to battering. This is no longer living together but dying together.

Only in the service of transformation, practicing the stories of the transforming self and of the faithful lover as guide (Act III, Scenes 1 and 2), can a Latino man truly say that he loves his lover as himself. In the last act of the drama Latino men come to find out who they are, to experience the self as a transforming self, a self capable of participating in persistent transformation as we respond to the problems of life. This is because they are fully present as whole human beings. They are not perfect, but they have achieved transformation in at least one aspect or problem of their life. They know and have faith that they can fulfill all aspects of their lives as they bring them to fruition in Act III. They have succeeded in traveling the core drama and have experienced the joy of being who they are. They have an inner need to do this time after time. This process of transformation becomes the focus of life in regards to all aspects of their being. In contrast to emanation, incoherence, and deformation, the personal face is no longer repressed, hidden, or erased but emerges into wholeness as a man declares that he loves and blesses his life. He enacts his political face daily by practicing a politics of compassion, justice, inclusion, and love, which is far different from the politics that lamed him through uncritical loyalty, exploitation of others as a means to gain power, or the politics of death: anger, violence, hatred, and exclusion. His historical face takes responsibility for the stories he has learned so that he can reject those that are harmful and choose with others to refuse to repeat the destructive past so that together we can create more loving and just stories.

Personally, I rediscover daily my sacred face as the connection to the deepest sacred source to whom I am related in a bi-unity. Together, we persistently participate in transforming my personal, political, and historical faces so that I can be fully present to others. Now when I love myself I am loving a mystery within me, the inner self that guides me to realize my own creative imagination. To love others as myself is to love them for who they are as temples of the sacred, of the holy spirit. Each person is a revelation of the deepest source of transformation. When a Latino man loves a Latina woman as himself in the service of transformation, he treats her with love, respect, tenderness, patience, humor, kindness, gentleness, firmness, and honesty precisely because he has learned to relate to himself out of love for his own self with these same attributes, which are concrete manifestations of the deepest sacred.

What does this kind of authentic self-love look like in the daily flow of life? Several years ago, as I was driving down U.S. Route 1 toward Princeton, I found myself feeling very sad; this sadness approached but had not yet developed into depression. During that spring semester I was teaching at Seton Hall and serving as a visiting professor teaching Chicana/Chicano students at Yale and Princeton. I felt I had taken on too much: I was tired feeling overwhelmed and unsure of myself. I remember as if it were yesterday that as I stopped at a light, I actually hugged myself and said, in the midst of my all sadness, tiredness, and problems, "I bless my life." At the time, I had in my car papers I had collected from my weekly seminar at Yale. As I drove home after teaching at Princeton, I asked myself, "Why are you doing what you're doing?" As I sat down that evening to read the Yale papers, I was emotionally shaken by the depth of feelings revealed by the students regarding their own personal, political, historical, and sacred struggles. As tears formed in my eyes, I knew why I was doing what I was doing. In their papers they were looking for love and guidance from people who would be fully present to them as real people. They saw that possibility in me; they wanted me to be real. They blessed me with their trust by asking me to be that kind of person who loved himself and was together enough to help guide them to discover who they were as persons. As a result of this experience, I felt challenged to do all I could to be a better man, person, teacher, husband, and father. In this way all four faces of my being were renewed to move toward transformation. To be and know who one is, to be at peace with one's *self,* to give oneself a hug, is to love oneself in all situations and to love others as oneself, thereby being fully present wherever you find yourself. People calling each other to wholeness is what loving oneself and loving one's neighbor as oneself are all about.

The Story of Creative Isolation
in the Service of Transformation

For most of recorded history our foremothers never had the opportunity to practice the relationship of isolation. Isolation, let us recall, is a relationship in which two parties agree to cooperate in refraining from demanding anything of each other. Both sides agree to avoid conflict and change. Justice means the right to self-determination and the right to be left alone, but at the price of not being able to effect change or to conflict with the other. At first glance this relationship sounds rather negative, a seemingly selfish desire to be alone. Traditionally, Latinas had no right to ask to be left alone. Women left to themselves might harm the honor of the family. In addition, women left to themselves could undermine the belief that the meaning and value of their lives consisted in belonging to a family and being the handmaids of men. They might discover that they are strong enough to be away from the family and actually enjoy being alone, alone with their own self, perhaps for the first time. Such an experience could lead women to believe that there was more to life than the traditional security of their homes and families.

But relationships draw their deeper meaning and value from the service of the way of life in which they are enacted. Isolation in the service of transformation means that two people agree to give each other time to reflect, to write, to study, to read, to travel, to do what is important to renew their lives. A Latino male as a political innovator and faithful lover knows that there are times when both he and his wife need time apart in order to achieve their life's goals. Women were hurt by their inability to go away to re-create their lives. But men were also deprived of creative isolation. Men have always had the right to go away, but they often exercised this isolation as a form of power to do whatever they wanted, regardless of the needs of their wives and families.

The relationship of isolation is not an invitation to be sexually promiscuous; isolation is not at all contrary to a relationship or marriage in the service of transformation. Latino males take their sexual selves wherever they go. Their sexuality is an aspect of the personal face of their being and therefore an attribute of their humanity. It is not possible to leave sexual selves at home or to command them to go into a corner and to behave like a well-trained dog. Latino men cannot live in fear of being their sexual selves outside the home; they should never take their mates along so they will protect them against infidelity. That would be to use them in a childish way as parents and to reduce them to moral police. Latinos do not have to see being alone as a sexual free-for-all. Maturity as an authentic male means that men acknowledge their sexuality and the attraction that they may feel for another woman. But because they have freed themselves from the stories of romantic, possessive love and patriarchy, they no longer need to prove their masculinity by conquering women sexually. They have choices. They can be attracted to women quite naturally and recognize their beauty both intellectually and physically without desiring these women for themselves.

Every person has a personal, a political, a historical, and a sacred face, a story they are living and a journey they are attempting to fulfill. The task of Latino men in the service of transformation is to assist others in that journey, not to take advantage of their vulnerability. To be open, to be inspired by other people, both men and women, is to be ready to risk relationships that will allow Latino men to grow. Every person they meet has the potential to awaken something in them of which they were unaware or to rekindle aspects of their selves with which they have lost contact. When they return home, having reexperienced themselves, having felt old emotions in new ways and developed new ideas, they can now share themselves in a deeper and more fulfilling way with the lover with whom they have chosen to be fully sexual and passionate.

If Latino men have the right to go away alone and practice the relationship of isolation, their wives and lovers need to have the same opportunities. Every right that I accept for myself must be equally available for my partner. She too can meet and be attracted to other men. She has choices to make as she takes the risk of being open to the fundamentally new and more loving source of life. For too long isolation for women was seen as a deviant and dishonorable attempt at freedom. Why only an attempt at freedom, and why dishonorable and deviant? Too often isolation has been considered an act of defiance by the Latino culture. More importantly, Latina women have been taught that a woman alone committed, by being alone, a deviant act, a crime outside the acceptable limits sanctioned by her community. Many Latina women raised in the United States, as well as those Latinas who have recently arrived, find it very difficult to give themselves permission to acknowledge that they enjoy and want to be alone. The emphasis on the woman as the carrier of the family's honor, the constant fear that a woman would be sexually assaulted by men, and the even greater fear that a woman would initiate some kind of sexual involvement on her own have kept women *tapadas,* covered up, hidden, literally under wraps for generations. They were to be chaperoned, to act and dress modestly, and to carry themselves with decorum and high regard for their station in life, that is, as extensions of the men in the family. One of the fears of men, even if women remained completely faithful to them, has been that they would start to imagine a different kind of life. But perhaps the most profound threat faced by Latino men has been the thought that their wives or lovers or daughters might have a sexual life of their own that was not centered on them, secret sexual desires that did not include them. The possibility of such a secret inner garden of sexual desires from which a woman could draw inspiration has kept men on the alert at all times.

Isolation has been considered a sin of rebellion against the stories of patriarchy and possessive love sanctioned by the culture that gave men the right to possess women, a right that was legitimized by an all-powerful sacred lord. Thus a woman was not only contesting the terrain of freedom with one or several men, she was fighting the whole culture, which included the religious institutions that gave men their blessing. Every Latina who resisted found herself locked in a battle that involved the personal, political, historical, and sacred faces of her being as she confronted the society around her and on the deeper levels the stories and ways of life that threatened to drown her in psychological guilt and the overt physical violence of men.

This fear of the freedom of isolation, of the right to be alone, that women experience is wonderfully captured in the thoughts of Mrs. Brown, a character in Michael Cunningham's 1998 novel *The Hours.* Laura Brown is a young mother and wife in the seemingly innocent years of the 1950s. She feels like a drifter flying high over her own life and an outsider observing herself as she slowly descends into depression and possible madness. She wants to step outside of this cartoon existence in which every action and emotion is prescribed for her. She wants to get away, to be alone, if only for a few hours. When she finds herself on the Pasadena Expressway outside of Los Angeles, her act of freedom gives way to panic and indecision: What will she do with this "free" afternoon? Her son is safe, the cake for her husband's birthday is done. Nobody is expecting anything of her for a few sweet hours of isolation, of freedom:

And so she's left for a few hours. She has not acted irresponsibly. She's made sure her son is taken care of. She's baked a new cake,

thawed the steaks, topped the beans. Having done all that, she's per-
mitting herself to leave. She will be home in time to cook the dinner, to
feed Kitty's dog. But now, right now, she is going somewhere
(where?). To be alone, to be free of her child, her house, the small party
she will give tonight. . . . She is clean and well dressed, driving away.[19]

For several hours she is safe in her getaway; after that, alarm bells go
off. The babysitter will expect her and her husband will be coming
home soon. But for now she is alone to go where she wants. She de-
cides to check into a nice and rather expensive hotel. An inexpensive
hotel would cheapen her escape and raise the possibility that her search
for time alone might be mistaken for some tawdry meeting with a
stranger. Freedom is difficult enough: no need to burden it with suspicious fears. She is giddy and as nervous as a girl: such extravagance.
She is worried about how the clerk at the registration desk will react.
But the clerk betrays no suspicion. Having passed through the ritual of
registration, she can hardly believe that she has done it. And then there
follows this painful observation about a woman seeking freedom, a
freedom dripping with guilt and pain:

> She has been nervous for so long, and her nervousness has not dissi-
> pated but its nature seems to have suddenly changed. Her nervousness
> along with her disappointment in herself are all perfectly recognizable
> to her but they now reside elsewhere. The decision to check into this
> hotel, to rise in this elevator, seems to have rescued her the way mor-
> phine rescues a cancer patient, not by eradicating the pain but simply
> by making the pain cease to matter. It's almost as if she's accompanied
> by an invisible sister, a perverse woman full of rage and recrimina-
> tions, a woman humiliated by herself, and it is this woman, this un-
> fortunate sister, and not Laura herself, who needs comfort and silence.
> Laura could be a nurse, ministering to the pain of another.

As she gets deeper into her comfort, Laura does not want to go back and
begins to contemplate going away for good: suicide, the ultimate act of
freedom. But she quickly dismisses these wishes. She loves life, loves it
with such deep hope for her son and husband and unborn child growing within her. This act of freedom and pushing it to the limits have
nevertheless assured her that in the end she is free:

> Still, she is glad to know (for somehow, suddenly, she knows) that it is
> possible to stop living. There is a comfort in facing the full range of
> options; in considering all your choices, fearlessly and without guile.

I have never read a more powerful description of a woman facing the emptiness of her life and then choosing, because she is now free, to live. I have known many Latina women who have experienced similar feelings of loss, depression, and meaninglessness and who have contemplated suicide. But they had very little opportunity to explore or act on these emotions. Thus many Latina women, unable to get away to think and reflect on their lives, are tempted to descend into a kind of fantasy world where they become a mere fragment of who they could have been. Some turned off the volume and accepted their lives as given and went under the fog for good as walking wounded. Others rebelled and went the way of sexual libertinism as a protest against their oppressors, often ending by being oppressed once again. Still others reverted to trying to be ideal wives to silence their doubts. But some Latinas did break through to create their own womanhood. It is these women who set the goal for what all Latinas can strive to accomplish. Latino men need to be dedicated to assisting them in acquiring such freedom, whether the steps be more education, trips taken alone, a room of one's own, special seminars, or simply days off to do whatever one pleases *with no questions asked*. Latino men need to recognize they cannot be everything in the lives of their wives and lovers. Just as Latino men find it helpful to get away so they can experience different aspects of their selves, so Latina women need to have the right to work, study, travel, read, meet other people, and to experiment with fulfillment.

To be alone, to practice creative isolation in the service of transformation, prepares Latinos and Latinas to come together again in a renewed manner. Two people apart do not necessarily withdraw from each other. The purpose in being apart is to allow one another to grow so they will have more to share. But they are never really apart in the sense of having broken with or forgotten the other. In their deepest moments of being alone they remain interconnected. Their temporary isolation leads to a new experience of connection, a way of living that allows each to be with others and also to be with one's self. After all, what gives each of us the strength to spend time alone is the assurance that our lover cares deeply for us and will be there when we return. Thus we go apart only to be able to reconnect in a more loving and fruitful way. To become more deeply caring and connected opens infinite possibilities for responding and caring for others in an interconnected world of mutual love and concern.[20]

Creating One's Own Gayness, Bisexuality, and Transsexuality

Some would say that for Latino males, being gay, transsexual, transvestite, or bisexual is a blessing of the deepest source; others would say it is a curse from which they need to free themselves through a life of abstinence and penance. Some see being gay, transsexual, or bisexual as a choice or a preference; still others see sexual preference as a chemical or biological alignment that moves us to cross-dress, to have same-gender sex, or to have bisexual relationships. Whatever the basis for a Latino male's gayness, bisexuality, transsexuality, or transvestism, like all other Latino men, they need to come to terms with who they are sexually as a fundamental aspect of the personal face of their being. Thus everything I have written regarding the struggle of the heterosexual Latino male to empty himself of destructive cultural stories such as patriarchy, the wandering lover, the *mujeriego,* and the disappointed male, and to create new and better stories, such as the faithful lover, creative isolation, the political innovator, and the story of loving one's own self, apply to gay, transsexual, bisexual, and transvestite Latinos as well.

Latino transvestite, transsexual, gay, or bisexual men need to ask the same question that heterosexual Latino males ask: "In the service of what way of life am I expressing and living my sexuality?" In the service of emanation filled with absolutes regarding the true nature of "man," gays and bisexuals continue to be condemned as unnatural, sinners, abominations bound for hellfire. The Catholic Church remains especially harsh regarding these forms of sexual preference. To be gay, transvestite, transsexual, or bisexual in the world of emanation was to be filled with sin, shame, and guilt. Gays have been forced to repress their own desires and to deny their own sexual expression in order to be politically loyal to the image of man held out to them by the authorities of church and state and thus perpetuate the history of man as a warrior. As men they were blessed by the lord of emanation, who gave them their privilege. It was a sign of being blessed as well as proof of his manhood to sire many children. In the way of life of emanation, gays, transvestites, bisexual, and transsexual men live on the edge of violence by those who consider them to be outside the pale of society and of the church.

These attitudes of hostility have remained prevalent in Latino culture to this day. This is why many Latino gay and bisexual men cannot affirm their own sexuality; they are often filled with fear of discovery and self-hatred. From an early age, because they know that they are different and therefore unaccepted, many become depressed and suicidal. To be gay or bisexual, a transvestite, or a transsexual in the container of emanation was, and continues to be, to live an underground life. These Latino men unconsciously repress themselves and convince themselves that they can overcome the alleged evil in them by being better Christians, sons, brothers, citizens, even husbands and fathers.

The inability to find acceptance in the Latino community and to be filled with self-denial in regards to one's sexual preference has life-or-death consequences when it comes to the current tragedy of AIDS, which is growing among Latino men. The tragedy of HIV infection is devastating for the communities of people of color. The Centers for Disease Control reported recently that 52 percent of the 18,153 gay and bisexual men who were diagnosed with AIDS in 1998 were men of color: 33 percent African American and 18 percent Latino. This contrasts sharply with a report in 1989 that found that of all the new cases of AIDS reported among gay and bisexual men, Latino and African American men were 31 percent of the total. In a ten-year period the number of gays and bisexual Latino and African American men infected with AIDS jumped an alarming 21 percent. In an attempt to determine why the number of men of color infected with AIDS has increased so dramatically, researchers have discovered that one of the reasons is cultural taboos firmly rooted in the family and in religious upbringing. As a result, many gay Latino males are ashamed of their lifestyle, and the fear of being outed leads them to refuse to seek the necessary medical help. In a recent survey of 8,780 HIV-infected men who had sex with other men, 18 percent of the Latino men who were surveyed did not regard themselves as bisexual or homosexual. This kind of denial places them in grave danger. Unless attitudes in the Latino community change, the epidemic of AIDS will continue to get worse.[21]

Some transsexuals, transvestites, gays, and bisexuals in the Latino community have succeeded in freeing themselves from the trinity of repression: sin, guilt, and shame.[22] They awakened and heard their repressed sexuality demanding to express itself. They entered into rebellion against those who would make them deny their sexual identity. But some arrested their lives and turned this defiance into permanent rebellion in the pursuit of self-interest and power. Some took lovers and used them in the same way in which heterosexual Latino males use their wives and lovers. They practiced the story of patriarchy and of possessive love in the way of incoherence: They used others as a means to their own end. Some heterosexual or straight Latino men and women use sex to get ahead. So do gays and bisexuals when their main concern is power. It is ironic that even though many gays rebelled against Latino patriarchal fathers who rejected them, because they have not emptied themselves of the story of patriarchy, they continue to practice that precise story in their own relationships. Just like heterosexual Latinos, transvestites, gays, and bisexuals are taught that in order to survive in a world of power, they need to suppress or hide their personal faces, practice a politics of self-interest, use their historical faces for the accumulation of power and privilege, and deny their sacred faces. Those who seek power in the white, male, and heterosexual world are encouraged to assimilate into the lifestyles of their colleagues. Under the pressure to assimilate, gays may marry, have children, and carry on a "normal" life. The denial of their own sexuality causes them to use others to give them cover. The politics of the bedroom described earlier are just as destructive whether the participants are gay, transsexual, heterosexual, or bisexual.

Gays, transsexuals, and bisexuals who practice their sexuality in such a way that it wounds them and their partners enter into deformation. Those transvestites, gays, or bisexuals who hate themselves and others in the community often engage in destructive behavior: excessive drinking, dangerous and addictive drugs, violent relationships, and reckless sex. Just like the heterosexual Latino male, they can become so angry with their lives as disappointed males that they participate in self-wounding. And they may vent anger at their partner. Practicing this form of self-wounding causes them to erase their own faces and those of their lovers. They engage in a politics of anger, violence, revenge, and exclusion against themselves and their partners. Those Latino men who are in the so-called closet and who hate their lives often express their revulsion of self by bashing members of their own group. In doing so, they join the powerful in their acts of violence against the transsexual, transvestite, gay, and bisexual men in the community.

In the service of transformation Latino gays, transvestites, transsexuals, and bisexuals can practice the stories of transforming love, the political innovator, machismo in the service of transformation, the guide, and the faithful lover with their loved ones. In the third act of the core drama they experience for the first time a true love of self as another manifestation of the deepest sacred source. In their wholeness they are now capable of being fully present to others and to love them as they love their own deepest self. Transsexual, transvestite, homosexual, and bisexual Latino men living in the way of life of transformation have successfully emptied themselves or are moving to void themselves of the stories of patriarchy, the wounded self, the concept of being normal as defined by an orthodox, straight, heterosexual world, the wandering *mujeriego* with the Don Juan complex, and the stories of capitalism that arrested their lives in fragments of the core drama of life wherein they remained partial and angry selves. Freed from these underlying sacred sources, they can come forth without self-hatred, without the sin, shame, and guilt imposed on them for so long. Like Celie in *The Color Purple,* they can shout to the world as their personal faces emerge into wholeness: "I am so happy. I got love, I got work, I got money, friends and time."[23] Now that they are free to love and think and discover their own voices, they can reach out to others with their political and historical faces to help bring about a new and more compassionate world for all those who are oppressed so that together they can renew their historical faces. Each Latino man is sacred: gays, heterosexuals, bisexuals, transsexuals, and transvestites, each in his own unique way manifesting the deepest source of transformation.

What counts ultimately is not whether men are masculine, feminine, heterosexual, gay, bisexual, celibate, or transsexual but that they become selves, persons who are connected on the deepest level of their lives to their own selves and to others as themselves, to the deepest sacred, and to the world around them with love and compassion. In the service of transformation there can never be any stereotyping, labeling, or hatred based on prejudice. In this way of life nobody can be considered evil or deviant simply because they are a particular color, ethnicity, member of a social class, sexual group, or gender. All of us need to ask: "Who is present? What story am I living? What does this archetypal drama do to the four faces of my being? Where am I in the core drama of life, and, most importantly, what sacred source do I incarnate, that is, in the service of what way of life and ultimate sacred source am I enacting the stories and relationships of my life?" Since we are all women and men living in the midst of change, we need to ask these questions of ourselves and others so as not to stereotype people as inanimate puppets.

Looking Inside the Drama of the Political Innovator

There is a danger that as Latinos and Latinas deconstruct the negative machismo and the story of patriarchy in their culture that Latino men might respond by becoming discouraged, passive, cynical, or nihilistic. I would like to offer the Latino male as a political innovator as an archetypal drama that is a creative response to meet the needs of *la comunidad Latina* and Latinos' responsibility to the wider society.[24]

The Latino man as a political innovator is a man who embraces the personal, political, historical, and sacred faces of his being in order to bring to bear the fullness of his humanity on the issues that surround him and *la comunidad Latina*. Here is what this story looks like in daily life:

- A Latino male comes to recognize that there is something profoundly wrong with his life.
- From this awakening, he begins to ask questions: "Why am I so lost? Who am I? Where am I going? What means the most to me?"
- He finds himself arrested in relationships that are patriarchal, competitive, and self-wounding, so he enters into rebellion against those with whom he has been practicing these stories.
- But he knows that the people with whom he related are not the real problem; he discovers deeper underlying reasons for their collective sense of loss.
- He searches out the reasons for his personal and the community's sense of loss, which lead him to the discovery of archetypal stories and ways of life without really being able to name them.
- He begins with his own experience to name and bring to light what was afflicting him and to change his life by refusing to live as he did in the past.
- As he searches for meaning in his life he reads, he discusses with his colleagues, he feels, he intuits, he meditates.
- He becomes pregnant with the fundamentally more loving and just, which is ready to come forth.
- In tune with his creative imagination, that is, with the spirit of his deeper self, which is connected to the deeper source of transformation, he is now ready to do something; the time for hibernation is over; it is time to act.
- Having listened to his personal and sacred faces, he is prepared to make a new history for himself and others by being political.

Politics is what we can and need to do together to respond to the issues in our lives. But the ultimate value and meaning of our politics is grounded in the service of the way of life wherein we practice our political faces. While he was arrested in fragments of the dying way of life of emanation, the Latino male exhausted his political face by trying to make a dying way of life relevant. To accomplish this he practiced the stories of the disappointed male, patriarchy, uncritical loyalty, and possessive, romantic love. These stories in the service of emanation could not respond to his depression. Locked in contests for power in the wider society, the story of capitalism depressed him. His politics were reduced to pursuing his own power and living in fear of the encroachment of others. At home he often tried to compensate for the stress and loss by enacting a politics of revenge and violence that diminished the lives of his wife and children. They were asking new questions that he either could not or refused to answer, the chief of which was: "What about my dreams and desires?"

Politics in the service of transformation means that Latino men hear their own suffering, perhaps for the first time, which awakens them to the pain of others. Now asking the question "What is it that you and I need to do together?" takes on a whole new meaning. The politics of broken ways of life and their stories left them chasing after doomed projects. Transformational politics frees our personal capacity to respond to the creation of new turning points in the community. Therefore we risk ourselves to create an environment in which each person is sacred: this means in everyday life dealing with the building of day-care centers, establishing living networks of tutors and mentors for students, assisting those in need of employment, organizing and setting up hotlines for abused spouses and providing housing for them, acquiring affordable health care, and on and on. There is no limit to the responses necessary in order to build a more just and compassionate society.

To be a Latino male as a political innovator in the service of transformation is not to be hampered by the heritage of the past. To be an innovator is to be open to one's inner voice grounded in the deepest source of our being, which continues to inspire one to take the next step. Having said no to destructive stories and ways of life, we can cooperate in ways that allow us to continue the best in our tradition, such as sharing, but also enter into conflict with and discontinue those aspects of the past, such as male domination, which are destructive for the community. The justice of this openness is fulfilled in the capacity of each person to step forward as a full participant in his or her own personal and political lives so that together they can make a new and better history that ensures the sacredness of each person.

The Story of Democracy
in the Service of Transformation

Perhaps the greatest challenge facing the Latino male as a political innovator is to work aggressively in order to bring about the story of
democracy in its fullness for all citizens. At the present time U.S. society is practicing a limited fragment of the story of democracy. There is
another story, liberal capitalism, that also sets the context in which we
live. This story is at odds with the story of democracy. Liberal capitalism is inherently flawed because it

- Requires everyone to compete with each other, but without
  killing each other.
- Establishes shared rules of the game.
- Agrees on procedures by which to pursue self-interest.
- Ensures that there is a safety net for those who are intended not
  to succeed.
- Guarantees certain inalienable rights such as freedom of assembly, speech, religion, and press so that commerce or the pursuit
  of happiness through unlimited possibilities for acquisition will
  go unhampered.

From the perspective of transformation, the most important criticism of
liberal capitalism is that it is primarily interested in power, not in justice
and compassion. If we reject forms of democracy that are hobbled by
the predominance of liberal capitalism so that democracy becomes "lib-
eralized," that is, becomes a front for the powerful to justify their freedom to enhance their power, then what alternative is there?

Al Farabi in tenth-century Damascus said that democracy is the best
opportunity for people to gain enough freedom and opportunity to move
toward transformation. But we need to go beyond Al Farabi's understanding of democracy. He believed that the common man and woman
could not understand democracy or how to practice transformation. But
we know that we have the freedom of the very nature of our being
human to participate in transformation. With this great freedom we can
redefine politics to be that which we can and need to do together to
achieve love and justice. Each of us, by the very nature of our humanity, is political; each of us has a political face of our being. Each of us
can participate in creating a more compassionate and loving environment for all people. The following characteristics describe how, in the
practice of transformation, we can live the story of democracy:

- Each person is valuable.
- Each of us needs to participate.
- We are free to break unbearable relationships.
- We can practice the four faces of our being in their wholeness.
- The power of the people rests upon conscious critical and creative response to the deepest ground of our being.
- Democracy recognizes an equality of needs and opportunities.
- It makes possible the formation of communities that act with justice and compassion.
- The story of democracy substitutes community for the state and self-interested power for full human capacity for each member of the community.
- Democracy creates an environment that enables each person to travel through the core drama of life again and again so that he or she is free to help others overcome poverty, injustice, and exploitation.
- Both the sacred and we ourselves are transformed by enacting true democracy.
- The power of the people is to enter into dialogue with their own selves, with others, and with the deepest sacred in order to confront problems.
- No person is complete until each of us is free to participate with the deepest sacred source of transformation so that we can co-create responses to injustice.

The story of democracy, together with the stories of the political innovator and machismo in the service of transformation, are especially crucial to responding to the growing reaction of many citizens who are afraid of the demographic changes that threaten their view of the United States. New forms of the story of tribalism are evident as people attempt to cut off the benefits of undocumented immigrants and workers. Whole groups of people are rendered invisible by school systems that refuse to change their curricula or teaching styles. But these times of trouble also provide Latinos and Latinas with the great opportunity to help create for the first time in our history a truly multicultural and multiracial society in which each person is valuable. To this task Latino men need to bring to everything they do the fullness of the personal, political, historical, and sacred faces of their being. Passion, commitment, hope, love, emotion, intimacy, feelings, intuition, and creative imagination arise from the deepest depths of our being—the source from which comes the vision of how to create a more loving, just, and compassionate society.

Personal, Political, Historical, and Sacred Strategies

The four faces of our being are always with us; to deny them or separate them is to disable and take away our birthright.[25] As we learned from the feminist movement, the personal is always political. But what I have come to understand is that the personal is not only always political but also historical and sacred. This realization leads to a fruitful and more enabling understanding of our human capacity.

What is the significance of seeing this new arrangement of the four faces of our being? If indeed the historical is personal, a new way of seeing the historical opens up. Whereas traditional history courses teach students about great events, it is individual people who are the true subjects of history. This approach profoundly impoverishes the power of the historical face of our being, our personal ability to make and remake history.

History is the story of humanity, and it is an ongoing story. To take back our individual historical face restores our personal intervention in the making of history. We do not have to be the victims of the great forces of history. We have been led to believe that only the great, only the powerful, made history. We became the powerless recipients of events. What we failed to understand was that the great became great because they learned how to manipulate people and lead them to believe that they, the king or queen, prime minister, or president, were making history. History was made by the powerful, using the resources of the people, to shape events. So long as we believed we were not important and had no say in our lives, we allowed ourselves to be the objects of history. To reclaim our historical face is to assert that individuals, either alone or together with others, can resist and rebel against the forces of society. As victims of events, we were caught in a story that possessed us until we became its blind followers.

To take responsibility for one's historical being is to accept the challenge of becoming aware of one's personal and collective past and then make decisions as to whether or not this is the path to continue. Latino men inherit from the past archetypal stories and ways of life that have been sanctioned by society as "the" story or stories. The knowledge of their awakening throws their personal faces into bold relief. Once I am awakened to the strengths and the weaknesses of Latino history and culture, and how it shaped me, I can now agree or dissent. History can be made and unmade by people like you and me. "No one can make history who is not willing to risk everything for it . . . to declare that his or her life is not a continuation of the past, but a new beginning."[26]

Latino men's inner voices tell them they are not the final products of history but the agents of its transformation. They need not despair once they discover the extent of their woundedness. Latino men are more than the objects of history. They transcend the case history of the stereotypical male; their conflicts and inner turmoil constitute the mystery of life histories:

> Patients great or small are increasingly debilitated by their inner conflicts, but in historical actuality inner conflict only adds an indispensable momentum to all superhuman effort.[27]

The painful past can become a great source of strength. Latino men need to struggle with the stories of their heritage and reconnect to aspects of their own personal lives: the right to play, to experiment, to discover, to create, to love and be loved. As a Latino male this view of history has great significance for me. I can be skeptical, critical, and subversive. I don't have to believe that men are superior. My personal pain of living this story undermines its validity. I can dare to question and even to reject an inherited past. But the most important task remains: to create a new and more loving history.

Creating new and better stories demonstrates that the historical is always political. History was not made by chance; history was made through the acts of the powerful and the powerless practicing a particular kind of politics. The powerful made decisions in the service of the politics of fixed truths, in the service of self-interest and power, or in the service of absolute power over life and death. But this has not happened in the service of compassion and justice. This awareness takes the mystification, the obfuscation, out of history. Latino men can end the oppressiveness of a relentless repetition of history by being political now. They can transform their lives, relationships, families, and communities. Transformational politics opens history to the excluded and the injured.

The historical is always sacred. The stories of the conquering hero, the nation-state, patriarchy, capitalism, war and violence, church and state, that have formed human history have always been enacted in the service of a particular sacred source. The lords of emanation, incoherence, and deformation inspired much of history. Those sacred sources arrested Latino men and held them in the core drama of life as fragments, partial selves. When they free themselves from the deep freeze of history as inevitable, from a history made by the powerful, they are inspired by the deepest source of transformation to make history in their homes, the streets of their communities, and the cities of the world.

They can make the everyday events of life fundamentally new and better. They can create a new turning point, opening a new history for everyone. Each woman, each man, can make history by ensuring that our encounters really matter, that we liberate the sacred in all things, small or large.

Conversely, the sacred is always historical. The deepest source of our being is found and engaged in the daily stuff of life, the making of history. The deepest source of transformation is never outside history, outside the world of human events, but is ever present to us in the deepest depths of our being, inspiring our sacred faces to create a new turning point, a watershed experience based on a passionate love for mercy and justice. In this way we come to know the sacred through the concrete events of history. In this way the sacred becomes real, becomes present to us in our daily lives.

The sacred finds its greatest expression in the personal faces of our being. Human beings are the only creation that can critically and creatively participate in the ongoing creation of the cosmos. The deepest source of our being, and the lesser, jealous lords of emanation, incoherence, and deformation, need our participation in order to be concretely present in history and politics. Our personal faces carry and manifest the sacred in our daily lives through the stories and ways of life we enact. The source of transformation manifests itself through our personal faces so that when we come to know who we are, we also reveal the face of this deepest of all sources. To know myself is to know my sacred source. This source renews me and inspires me anew. If we get lost on the journey through the core drama of life, our personal faces will manifest the lord who has taken us over and holds us in a fragment of the core drama of life. But when I know my authentic self, I also reveal in my face the face of the deepest sacred. The ultimate ground of our being cannot know itself without us; we are necessary to the deepest source:

> And when we look for the existential foundation of this experience of the Divine as an unknown God seeking to become known to Himself in and through the creatures which know Him, do we not find it typified in the wish (whether cry or sigh) . . . "Oh to be known as one is!" Such is the sigh of God in the solitude of His unknownness, from which He is delivered by the beings to whom He is revealed and through whom He exists.[28]

But if we fail to discover our deeper selves and become arrested as disciples of the lesser lords and their stories and ways of life, the source of transformation will not come to know itself through our unique and personal faces.

When Latino males practice patriarchy in the service of emanation, incoherence, or deformation, they become the concrete expression of that sacred source who inspires them to live and act. When men dominate women as the will of an all-powerful lord in the container of emanation, they become living, concrete manifestations of a patriarch fated to control and overpower as his sacred birthright. When Latino males exercise power over women and use them as means to their own ends, they become living exemplars of the lord of incoherence, who inspires them to pursue their self-interest and power; these men become actual patriarchs, possessed by this variation of the archetypal story of patriarchy. If they become abusive men who diminish women, they practice the story of patriarchy in its most violent expression and follow the lord of deformation, who offers them absolute power, absolute because these men are given as their right power over the lives and deaths of women, not to mention their own. The beings of abusive men are taken over by the archetype of the man who batters. They become death. But when men become merciful, loving, compassionate, and just, they incarnate those archetypes, and those archetypes are fulfilled through them: They become mercy, love, compassion, and justice.

The sacred is always political. To be political is to ask what it is that you and I need to do together to achieve a particular goal in love and justice. The sacred is a mystery that moves our lives decisively from the depths. But archetypal analysis reveals this mystery. We can come to know the underlying workings of the mystery of the sacred by analyzing its expressions, its stories, and its ways of life. But only in the service of the deepest source of transformation are we called on to critically, creatively, and intimately participate in the creation of the sacred. Through participation Latino men can free themselves of destructive archetypal stories and create new and more loving alternatives that enable them to respond to the continuous need to transform their lives.

Notes

1. David T. Abalos, *La Comunidad Latina in the United States: Personal and Political Strategies for Transforming Culture* (Westport, CT: Praeger Press, 1998), chapter 1, pp. 63–68.
2. Erik Erikson, *Ghandi's Truth: On the Origins of Militant Non-Violence* (New York: W. W. Norton, 1969), p. 141.
3. Ibid., p. 397.

4. See in this regard David T. Abalos, *Strategies of Transformation Toward a Multicultural Society: Fulfilling the Story of Democracy* (Westport, CT: Praeger Press, 1996), chapter 5.

5. Erikson, *Ghandi's Truth,* p. 162.

6. Ibid., pp. 168–169, 253.

7. Ibid., p. 399.

8. Abalos, *La Comunidad Latina,* pp. 66–67.

9. *The Salt of the Earth,* a film directed by Herbert Biberman, produced by Independent Productions Corporation and the International union of Mine, Mill, and Smelter Workers (1953).

10. This awakening of a Latina woman to the needs of the Latina and Latino youth in her community took place in New Jersey.

11. Henri Corbin, *Creative Imagination in the Sufism of Ibn Arabi,* translated by Ralph Manheim (Princeton, NJ: Princeton University Press, 1969), p. 95.

12. Erikson, *Ghandi's Truth,* p. 402.

13. Ann Belford Ulanov, *The Feminine in Jungian Psychology and in Christian Theology* (Evanston, IL: Northwestern University Press, 1971), p. 313.

14. Lionel Tiger, *The Decline of Males* (New York: Golden Books Publishing, 1999).

15. Abalos, *La Comunidad Latina,* chapter 3, p. 100.

16. Elizabeth Martínez, "Chingón Politics Die Hard: Reflections on the First Chicano Activist Reunion," in *De Colores Means All of Us: Latina Views for a Multi-Colored Century* (Cambridge, MA: South End Press, 1998), pp. 172–181; also in Carla Trujillo, ed., *Living Chicana Theory* (Berkeley: Third Woman Press, 1998), pp. 123–135. In this regard see also the works of other Chicana/Latina feminists cited in Chapter 1 of this volume especially pp. 8–9 and p. 42, note 2.

17. Corbin, *Creative Imagination,* p. 289.

18. Ulanov, *The Feminine,* p. 307.

19. This and the excerpts that follow are from Michael Cunningham, *The Hours* (New York: Farrar, Straus, and Giroux, 1998), pp. 142, 148–149, 152.

20. For an excellent discussion of the need to care for and to be connected to each other, see Carol Gilligan, *In a Different Voice: Psychological Theory and Women's Development* (Cambridge: Harvard University Press, 1982), especially chapters 2 and 6.

21. Justin Bachman, "Black and Hispanic Gays Hit Harder by AIDS," *The Star Ledger: The Newspaper for New Jersey,* January 14, 2000, p. 6.

22. In this regard I have learned much from my colleague at Seton Hall, Carlos Rodríguez Matos, and the wonderful book he edited, *Poesída: An Anthology of AIDS Poetry from the United States, Latin America and Spain* (Jackson Heights, NY: Ollantay Press, 1995). See also the following works, which have pioneered much of the work now being done on homosexuality, bisexuality, transvestism, and transsexuality among Latino men: Tomás Amalguer, "Chicano Men: A Cartography of Homosexual Identity and Behavior," *Differences* 3, no. 2 (1991): 75–100; José Joaquín Blanco, "Ojos que da Panico Sonar," in *Función de Medianoche* (Mexico City: Era, 1981); Rafael Carrasco,

Inquisición y Represión Sexual en Valencia: Historía de los Sodomitas (1565 1785) (Barcelona: Laertes, 1986); Joseph Carrier, *De Los Otros: Intimacy and Homosexuality Among Mexican Men* (New York: Columbia University Press, 1995); David William Foster, *Sexual Textualities: Essays on Queer/ing Latin American Writing* (Austin: University of Texas Press, 1997); Oscar Guash, *La Sociedad Rosa* (Barcelona: Anagrama, 1991); Philip Kayal, *Bearing Witness: Gay Men's Health Crisis and the Politics of Aids* (Boulder, CO: Westview Press, 1993); Marvin Leiner, *Sexual Politics in Cuba: Machismo, Homosexuality, and AIDS* (Boulder, CO: Westview Press, 1994); Ian Lumsden, *Homosexualidad, Sociedad, y Estado en México* (Mexico City: Solediciones, 1991); Ian Lumsden, *Machos, Maricones, and Gays: Cuba and Homosexuality* (Philadelphia: Temple University Press, 1996); Rafael L. Ramírez, *Dime Capitán: Reflexiones Sobre la Masculinidad* (Rio Piedras, PR: Huracán, 1993); Rafael L. Ramírez, *What It Means to Be a Man: Reflections on Puerto Rican Masculinity,* translated by Rosa E. Casper (New Brunswick, NJ: Rutgers University Press, 1999); Jacobo Schifter Sikora, *De Ranas a Princesas: Sufridas, Atrevidas, y Travestidas* (San José, Costa Rica: ILPES, 1998); Jacobo Schifter Sikora, *La Casa de Lila: Un Estudio de la Prostitución Masculina* (San José, Costa Rica: ILPES, 1997); Jacobo Schifter Sikora, *Amor de Macho: Lo Que Nuestra Abuelita Núnca Nos Contó, Sobre las Carceles* (San José, Costa Rica: ILPES, 1997); Jacobo Schifter Sikora and Johnny Madrigal, *Hombres Que Aman Hombres* (San José, Costa Rica: ILPES-SIDA, 1997); and Helio R.S. Silva, *Travesti: A Inverçao de Femenino* (Rio de Janeiro: ISER, 1993). Alberto Sandoval-Sánchez has written a brilliant book in which he argues in part that the tragedy of AIDS and HIV in the Latino community especially among gay men has led to an extraordinary outburst of creativity in Latino theater through which playwrights and actors seek not only to educate the community but also to heal and to redefine the direction of Latino culture in the United States: *José, Can You See? Latinos On and Off Broadway* (Madison: University of Wisconsin Press, 1999).

23. Alice Walker, *The Color Purple* (New York: Pocket Books/Washington Square Press, 1985), p. 222.

24. I first learned about the political innovator from Manfred Halpern many years ago. For the first time, as I thought about alternative stories to replace those Latino men need to discard, I came to understand how this archetype could serve as a story that I and other Latinos can practice.

25. I owe a great debt to Manfred Halpern, who opened up to me a rich vein of understanding and wisdom when he taught me about the four faces of our being. See his "Knowing, Interconnecting, and Fulfilling the Four Faces and the Source of Our Being," *Journal of Religion and Health* 34, no. 2 (summer 1995): 105–119.

26. Ulanov, *The Feminine,* p. 267.

27. Erikson, *Ghandi's Truth,* p. 363.

28. Corbin, *Creative Imagination,* p. 293.

5

~~~

A New Latino Male
and *La Familia Latina*

The family is the context within which Latinas and Latinos can struggle against the destructive aspects of their cultural past and an often hostile society. Together they can create and put into practice fundamentally more loving and compassionate alternatives. Because their personal and sacred faces are always political and historical, their story is not about one or several Latino couples but is rather the story of an entire society and culture seeking to give birth to new and more just relationships between men and women.[1] Only relationships enacted within a creative drama of loving mutuality between Latino men and Latina women, examples of which I gave in Chapters 1 and 4, will be able to create the kind of family necessary to meet the challenges of the twenty-first century.

Female-Male Relationships in *La Comunidad Latina*

What will the Latino family look like when it has been freed of the deadly stories of the past? Then men and women will be free to create alternative stories such as that of the faithful partner. Radical change is taking place in the Latino community, a change especially evident in families. A revolution is happening, not only in the concrete manifestations of male-female relationships but also in the underlying sources of Latinos and Latinas. They are struggling with archetypal relationships and dramas, especially patriarchy, possessive love, uncritical loyalty, and the disappointed male. Many find their relationships and the stories of their lives unbearable, untenable, and unfruitful. In response to the

155

pain of daily life, they have, as earlier described, four radical choices by which to respond. Let me briefly summarize the theoretical perspective with which they can re-vision their relationships as men and women, as lovers and companions.

For all of recorded history, according to the theory of transformation, humans have nine archetypal relationships that occur simultaneously with the five issues of performance encountered in daily living: continuity, change, cooperation, conflict, and justice. I shall give examples from the daily lives of the Latino family to explain the dynamics of these relationships. I would like to stress that these patterns of encounter are not static concepts or categories but relationships in motion. The nine archetypal relationships described in Chapter 2, emanation, subjection, buffering, direct bargaining, isolation, autonomy, incoherence, deformation, and transformation, are responses to the tensions of everyday life. These archetypal relationships are practiced within the archetypal stories of Latinos' and Latinas' lives. All of their stories, such as matriarchy, the conquering hero, patriarchy, democracy, capitalism, the drama of the faithful lover, the political innovator, and machismo, along with the nine archetypal relationships and the four faces of their being, are practiced in the service of a larger context—the overarching ways of life of emanation, incoherence, transformation, and deformation. Thus the struggles that Latinos and Latinas experience in daily life are actually symptoms or concrete manifestations of a deeper contest in their sacred selves. What this means is that the choices they make in daily life have a concrete and an underlying sacred significance.

Too often in the Latino community the sacred is used to legitimize and preserve inherited, concrete manifestations of the nine archetypal relationships and the inherited archetypal stories enacted in the service of a partial way of life. In the midst of daily life Latinos and Latinas are actually inspired by four different underlying sacred sources. In other words, there are competing archetypal dramas, ways of life, and sacred sources that are *inspiring* them, or breathing within them.

I hope to open new doors by which Latinos and Latinas can relate to the sacred. We need to keep in mind that the indigenous communities in Latin America were aware that the sacred permeated our lives.[2] They believed there was a sacred source, a god or goddess, as the underlying cause and companion for water, the sun and moon, death, sex and love, rain and fire, all the aspects of life and creation. But I would argue that they were often unaware of their capacity to participate with the deepest sacred source of transformation to bring about the fundamentally new and more loving. They were often taken over by lesser sacred sources, the lords of emanation, incoherence, and deformation, which they mistakenly believed were "the" god. We can see from the Popol Vuh, the Mayan account of creation, that the indigenous branch of the Latino heritage understood there were destructive, petty, and jealous gods who sought to blind them so that human beings would always depend on the partial lesser lords of emanation, incoherence, and deformation.[3] Latinos and Latinas have seldom if ever been told that there are four fundamentally different underlying sacred sources, or gods, and that they are free to choose among them. For generations they got caught repeating stories blessed by lesser sacred sources that arrested their lives in fragments of the core drama of life. As a result they could not exercise their rights as human beings to cooperate with the deepest sacred source of transformation in the work of bringing about the fundamentally more just and loving in all aspects of life.[4]

When they pray to "God," Latinos and Latinas need to ask, "Which of the four sacred source am I invoking?" The lord of emanation will always be there to arrest life by helping them to justify all that happens with prayers like *"Es la voluntad de Dios,* It is the will of God," when in fact it is the will of a jealous and possessive sacred source who wishes to keep from men and women their capacity to participate in the creation of something new and better. This lord of emanation, who hides under the label of *Dios Todopoderoso,* God the Almighty, does not want them to discover that there is another sacred source, the deepest sacred source, who invites them again and again to become co-creators in the task of continuing the creation of the world. For centuries, the lesser lord of emanation inspired Latino men and Latina women to follow his will as they colluded in maintaining relationships of dependency that sustained the stories of patriarchy and uncritical loyalty in the service of emanation. What should have been a merciful container that nurtured them until they were ready to leave to continue the journey through the core drama of life instead became a permanent *jaula,* a cage, that clipped the wings of their lives.

Relationships of Dependency in the Service of Emanation

The specific, inherited manifestations of the nine archetypal relations blessed by the sacred source of emanation and therefore legitimately practiced by Latina women living within the way of life of emanation are emanation, subjection, buffering, direct bargaining, deformation, and sometimes, as will be explained below, isolation. When any of the nine relationships, with the exception of transformation, are practiced, they are enacted with an eye to strengthening the web guaranteed by the way of life of emanation. Deformation continues to be used as a means of preventing people from leaving the container of emanation. This relationship, which often takes the form of psychological and physical violence, is intended to cripple the capacity of a person, thus making her or his rebellion against authority almost impossible.

But ways of life are vulnerable. Emanation as a way of life inspired by a sacred, underlying source is shaken to the roots when it can no longer convince its followers that suffering and misfortune are the inevitable will of a sacred source, when it can no longer provide security for believers, and when it cannot cope with new problems that create profound doubts.

When this crumbling of the foundations takes place, people can unconsciously repress their doubts by renewing their loyalty to emanation as a way of life. Or having been awakened, they can consciously suppress their new insights. But they can also choose to see the dying of the way of life of emanation as a call from their deepest sacred source to begin a dangerous but necessary journey toward wholeness and transformation. It is necessary to "sin," to rebel against the cultural codes of society, to break with those individuals and institutions that maintain relationships of dependency.

Relationships That Limit the
Capacity of Latino Men and Latina Women

Emanation is a relationship in which those involved are extensions of a mysterious other such as a mother, leader, or lover who prevents change and conflict but who demands unyielding loyalty. The reward of such enchantment is security; the cost is one's selfhood. In an emanational relationship, a Latino man might say to his wife: "You are my woman; you belong only to me."

In contrast, the relationship of subjection is one in which a Latina woman is no longer denied a separate existence. However, in this situation, she very clearly fears retaliation by a man if she dares to threaten his authority. She cannot create conflict or change and is committed to continue to collaborate with him in order to survive: "He says I can't work; he is the boss."

In the relationship of buffering, meanwhile, participants seek some elasticity, some elbow room, as a respite from the unyielding domination of emanation and subjection by looking to a third party to intervene. This third party improves the situation of one partner by creating conflict and change so as to gain a better deal from the powerful other. In this relationship a woman asks her friends or mother-in-law to speak to her husband, or she prays to the Virgin Mary for help with her depression: "Please speak to him on my behalf," she might say.

In direct bargaining, a Latina enters into conflict in order to achieve change through her own efforts; she dares to speak to her father or husband and asks for a favor or benefit that will help her to remain loyal to him. Very often this opportunity arises when a man becomes affectionate or sexually playful. Thus Latinas, along with women in all patriarchal societies, have been taught by their mothers and the culture to use covert manipulation to achieve changes: "I would like to ask you a favor," a woman might say before indulging her husband's request for sex.

But Latino men continue to be careful not to weaken the inherent control of the relationships of emanation and subjection by allowing buffering and direct bargaining. These two latter relationships actually provide the elasticity, the steam valve for the dominant relationships of emanation and subjection; they are intended to head off real changes, or rebellion, by reducing the anger of the woman to a commodity that will purchase some change and conflict only so that she will return to normal, her obedient and docile self, and become even more loyal and compliant. Thus a Latino lover gives a woman a beautiful ring: She is happy but also embarrassed that she could have ever doubted his love. She then gratefully returns to normal, that is, back to emanation and subjection, until the next depression comes and needs to be buffered and bargained away.

Many Latino men refuse to allow their wives or lovers to see their friends so that they can isolate and control them. They fear the meddling of others who might put ideas in their wives' heads. Traditional Latino men use the relationship of emanation to possess their wives. In addition, they do not allow women to ask more than once for a favor that has been denied. The door of subjection closes the attempt to bargain, putting more pressure on women to rebel.

Isolation is a relationship in which two people mutually agree to leave each other alone; they thereby cooperate in avoiding any conflict or change in order to continue the relationship. This relationship is *psychologically* available to Latina women, that is, Latinas are allowed to withdraw into themselves, into a moody silence or pensive state, but they are not allowed *physically* to leave the house or be alone for any extended period of time without permission. To this day many men do not allow women to leave the house while they are away. They usually will not allow wives and daughters to work. But even psychological isolation is often denied to Latinas. I have seen and heard Latino men complain when their wives or daughters withdraw for a time to read a book or the newspaper. Latino men become offended by this silence and withdrawal, which means that women are not available to take care of their needs. So these men do whatever they can to end even this psychological isolation, which they suspect could lead to something more serious, perhaps physical withdrawal.

Deformation is a relationship used to punish women for rebelling. This relationship is intended to preserve the dying way of life of emanation by attempting to force women back into the container of the final truth. It can take the form of physical or psychological violence intended to bring a woman to her knees so that she will never be able to challenge male authority again. This relationship always puts participants on the road to destruction by removing them from the core drama of life and placing them into a physical and psychological abyss that can lead to death.

Patriarchy and Matriarchy:
The Dominant Archetypal Drama in the Latino Family

At one time, it may have been necessary for women to be perpetually pregnant and to nurture children for the sake of the survival of the human race. The conditions that made this drama necessary changed long ago. But people were not allowed to be historical, that is, to create a new history, but only to repeat the past, which removed their responsibility; thus they became ahistorical. They repeat the past as a given reality that cannot be altered. The repetition of the past deprives them of the ability to exercise the historical faces of their being in a new way. They have been denied the right to participate in bringing about new turning points by creating new responses to new problems. Thus patriarchy became a frozen moment, which all future generations have been condemned to live. So men and women remain objects shaped by the past rather than asserting themselves as subjects who could act on and create history.[5]

In most cases, the situation does not get better when mothers are the heads of households. Many, but certainly not all, single-parent mothers are dominated by the stories of the past. It is as if fathers had never left;

mothers nurtured us on the milk of the same patriarchal story practiced by their husbands, lovers, and fathers. Too often mothers continue to say: *"Ya que se fué tu papá, yo mando en esta casa; yo soy tu papá y mamá,* Now that your father is gone, I am the boss in this house; I am your father and mother."* As a result children see enacted the story of matriarchy, which is really the mother's version of the story of patriarchy with a feminine face.[6] For this reason mothers continue the privileges of the males and refuse to grant the same rights to the girls and women in the family. Even given the opportunity of ostensible control, many Latina women are not able to create a new turning point and so create a new and open history for the Latino family. It is not possible while the matriarchs remain caught by inherited stories. The power of the sacred stories and the partial way of life of emanation to possess lives and disable them remains strong. The personal, political, and sacred faces of our mothers are filled with loyalty to male patriarchy. This commitment undermines the capacity of their historical faces to open new doors.

Politically, both men and women have remained uncritically loyal, regardless of their social standing, to males as heads of the church, the state, and the family. The underlying source that has guaranteed this way of life is the lord of emanation, who granted security for society by providing legitimacy and unity. Life was given meaning by truths that were considered ultimate, and although the source of these truths was mysterious, everyone knew their places. Whenever the way of life of emanation was threatened by those who raised new questions, emanation entered into collusion with deformation, that is, the use of violence, to silence the opposition.

The way of life of emanation, in alliance with the way of life of deformation, is the way of life within which most archetypal stories of male-female relationships have been lived for centuries in *la comunidad Latina*. Moreover, of the nine relationships listed at the beginning of the chapter, women usually have been limited to four or five. Even when Latina women have learned how to dominate men, they continue to practice relationships of dependency—dependency because women are forbidden to create other relationships. In this way Latinas can become manly women in a power struggle with men. But the struggle has served only to perpetuate a way of life that grievously hurts both men and women.

Once again, this theory does not allow us to stereotype. All four ultimate ways of life have always been available to individuals and to the entire community. For this reason I do not equate premodern times with the way of life of emanation. People have always had the capacity to break with inherited archetypal dramas, relationships, and ways of life and to enact something radically different. There have always been people who practiced stories and ways of life that put them at odds with their society.

My task in this book has been not only to do empirical analysis but also to provide normative values by going beyond the concrete factual in order to determine the quality of the stories enacted in the service of underlying ways of life practiced by Latinos and Latinas. To determine the ultimate meaning, structure, and value of life is the task and benefit of archetypal analysis. Therefore, practitioners need ever to ask anew, "What way of life is involved? What drama is being played out? Who are the actors on stage? Where are they in the core drama of life? How do the stories they practice affect the four faces of their being? What aspects of their personalities are being repressed or enacted? Which relationships are they forbidden to use?" To ask these questions means to view the cosmos of human relations as a process of continuous creation.

Creating New, Forbidden Relationships

Autonomy is a relationship not permitted for women in patriarchal societies. But American society actually legitimizes autonomy for Latina women. This relationship allows autonomy for self and other. Individuals can accrue skills and an area of competence that allow them to establish economic independence. Managerial autonomy is the essence of bureaucracy wherein people divide jobs along areas of skill or expertise and maintain zones of autonomy. The U.S. Constitution is set up as a series of checks and balances among autonomous zones of jurisdiction: the executive, judiciary, and legislative branches of government. The impeachment of President Bill Clinton in 1999 gave rise to disputes over areas of autonomy controlled by the executive and legislative branches of government. The relationship of autonomy also has a potentially revolutionary aspect. On the group level, autonomy makes it possible for people to organize themselves together around a common issue such as the formation of a day-care center by parents or the organization of a union to protect workers, to sustain each other over a period of time in pursuit of specific goals leading to justice. The relationship of autonomy can be created, and it can help sustain, the way of life of transformation.

Those interested in promoting autonomy might, for example, invite the previously excluded to participate in a new venture on the basis of shared principles, such as the right of each worker to have a living wage. This work is needed because established bureaucracies exclude people from the benefits of their labor and the decisionmaking process.

Many Latino men, who ironically may have benefited from a union in the world of work, continue to see the relationship of autonomy as a threat to their wish to have a docile, dependent woman or lover. In fact, they can be very rigid, not even allowing the use of the relationships of buffering or direct bargaining or psychological isolation to ease the harshness of emanation and subjection. Some Latino men know that if they allow their wives to work, it would be beneficial because it would mean two paychecks to meet high costs of living. But the fear of independence and autonomy is very great. When Latina women do work, they are often required to hand over their paychecks and are not allowed to spend money without permission. In other words, the use of the relationship of autonomy is forbidden.

Isolation, the right to be left alone through mutual agreement, has been and remains a forbidden relationship between Latina women and Latino men. Latino men simply do not allow this relationship to be enacted by their wives and daughters. It is presumed that if a woman wants to be alone, she has some kind of sexual escapade in mind. In addition, since Latino men want to maintain their power by possessing and dominating the women in their household, they cannot allow women to be free to be alone outside the home, indeed even in the house.

Incoherence is a relationship in which two persons stand in the presence of each other and cannot agree on how to relate. The five inherited concrete manifestations of the nine archetypal relationships, emanation, subjection, buffering, direct bargaining, and deformation enacted in the way of life of emanation, which have shaped male-female relationships in *la comunidad Latina,* are all breaking. Everything is conflict and change; there is no continuity or cooperation and no justice. When Latinas are told they cannot work and therefore are denied their right to the enjoyment of autonomy, they can turn to fantasy, sexual play, and teasing their husbands as a kind of buffering to compensate for their disappointment and to hide their growing anger. Latino men know how to make women feel guilty, vulnerable, or ungrateful. They are able to seduce women to return to their duty as faithful wives. Men are constantly dealing with their insecurity as they strive to be the source of mystery in emanation for wives and lovers, to dominate them in subjection if they show disrespect, to refuse to allow buffers to intervene on their behalf, and to reject their use of sexuality as a form of direct bargaining to loosen the reins of control. And if these relationships are questioned, then the relationship of deformation is used to force women violently back into the container of emanation.[7]

What is at stake in all of these encounters is that a whole way of life, emanation, is dying. Latino men know that women are no longer blindly loyal to them and that times have changed. But too many men and the women to whom they relate are still dominated by the archetypal stories of uncritical loyalty and patriarchy. Both Latino men and Latina women feel in their bones that this way of life is dying, but they are not sure what to do. Many Latino men spend more and more energy rebuilding the belief in the mind of Latinas that their manhood is the emanational source of security in their lives.

But women's skepticism can turn the repression into a new consciousness; many Latinas are listening to their own inner desires. Still other Latinas are reluctant to enter into open rebellion against their fathers, brothers, and husbands. At times they become defensive and claim there is nothing they can do to change the situation.

As long as men and women repress the pain and hide the doubts of their inner conflicts, their doubt cannot become critical or creative consciousness. Transformation is forbidden and impossible whenever we refuse to admit the problem. We remain incapacitated and cut off from our deepest source. We cannot create new linkages to others or to a shared justice. We are unable to see ourselves as capable of entering into rebellion and freeing ourselves from destructive stories. As a consequence, we deprive ourselves of the possibility of transforming our lives.

Transformation is a way of life in which eight of the nine relationships are rediscovered (the ninth, deformation, is always destructive) and reconstituted so they are not repetitions of the past. Latino men and Latina women may be tempted not to create anything new but rather to return to the past. Latina women and Latino men need guides who can break through their protestations and buffers to tell them, "A woman is not her husband's property; she belongs to her self." With this kind of assurance and the continuous presence of a support group, Latinas and Latinos are encouraged to create incoherence by entering into open rebellion. For Latina women, the desire to go back to work, to continue their education, to volunteer, or to travel are all attempts to end dependence and to exercise the forbidden relationships of autonomy and isolation in the midst of a patriarchal marriage. These new relationships threaten the foundations of such a patriarchal marriage. In the past Latina women were not able to overcome tradition and a man's use of the relationships of subjection and deformation. Sadly, those responses are the only ones that many Latino men know. Their fathers had done the same to their wives. Both men and women will simply repeat the archetypal stories, including the worship of the lord of emanation, until they consciously decide to break the established way of relating by open rebellion. Then, more importantly, they must empty themselves of the stories that possess mysterious power over them.

Emanation Gives Way to Deformation

Latinas have become angry and have entered into a defiance so deep that their anger now threatens the whole system of male oppression and the underlying sacred roots of patriarchal power. All are victims of the story of patriarchy; neither Latinas nor Latinos are in control of their own lives. For Latinas to give in and to return to patriarchy at this point of their journey would be a loss of the self.[8] They have become fully awakened to who they are, women who have the right by the very nature of their humanity to live their own dreams.

Some Latino men attempt to force Latinas to come back home. Men insist that women must obey because that is what wives should do. But many Latinas have broken with their men. Now the greatest risk arises. Latina women are still vulnerable on the deeper levels to the stories of patriarchy and uncritical loyalty in the service of emanation. The power of sacred stories is compelling. At this point in the core drama of life, Latino men are not the deeper source of the problem; it is the story of patriarchy and its derivative, the disappointed male, that continue to possess both Latinas and Latinos. Unless Latinas sustain their journeys and successfully empty themselves, not only of the stories of their particular lover, husband, or father but also of the story of patriarchy and the ways of life of emanation and deformation that gave men power over them, they will repeat the story with other men.

The risk is that Latinas will abort their journeys to find themselves by using their separation as a bargaining tool or perhaps to revenge themselves on men. When Latinas "return," Latino men are relieved that they have come home and assume that they have given in to the men's wishes and that they are now ready to return to normal. If a woman responds that she is returning on her own terms, which cannot be bought off by the usual bargaining, a Latino man might be adamant. Unless the woman returns to the way things used to be, then she cannot come back. Often the man is bluffing, hoping that the woman will give in to his tactics. But if a woman holds her ground, he needs to decide what to do next. Latinas on the whole do not want to go back to the old stories and ways of life. They want to be somebody; they need to be in the world as well as at home.

Often Latino men suffer from a loss of courage. They have lived for so long practicing the story of patriarchy in the service of emanation in collusion with deformation that they live in a male fantasy, and, as long as they preserve this fantasy, they will not be able to create a new relationship with a woman who is radically new and better. Many Latinas do not want to leave or divorce. But they are refusing to live in marriages and families permeated by the story of patriarchy. Men can no longer assume that because their wives love them they have agreed to return to the inherited relationships of dependence.

Many women in the Latino community are looking for a marriage in which they can grow their own personhood, not a marriage that possesses them. What Latinas want is to participate with men in a truly imaginative revolution by emptying themselves of the stories of uncritical loyalty and of patriarchy and inviting men to participate together with them in creating a new archetypal drama, the story of the faithful lover within which men and women can come forth as whole human beings.

The Relationship of Incoherence in the Service of Transformation

The use of the relationship of incoherence, the breaking of connections that initiate rebellion, can lead to true revolution. On a deeper level men and women can break with inherited relationships of dependency, the stories of patriarchy, uncritical loyalty, the wounded self, and the disappointed male as well as with the lords and ways of life of emanation, incoherence, and deformation, which give the stories their power. For Latino men and Latina women, cultural literacy needs to become not only learning how to read the culture but also how to transform it through acts of liberation. In finding their own voices and desires, they can be firmly grounded in their own authenticity. It is important to note here that the emergence of their personal faces as Latino men and Latina women simultaneously affects the political, historical, and sacred faces of their being. This is a turning point in the lives of all who realize that history need not be an endless cycle of deadly repetition; the life of each person is valuable and therefore sacred.

Transforming Male-Female Relationships

Participants in transformation begin by taking their selves back. They reacquire themselves as sacred beings by practicing the relationship of transformation as the initial experience of their still unrealized inner selves. With their personal faces they need to take on the prophetic gift that allows them to hear the sacred. As philosophers, they need to distinguish between the sacred sources that are destructive and the deepest sacred source of transformation. Then these men and women need to fulfill the prophetic and philosophical tasks by becoming true practitioners of transformation, political innovators.

Our sacred guide, the deepest source of transformation, needs us to finish creation. Men and women can create mutually more loving relationships and stories that heal the wounds and release the repressed energies within. And finally, they become whole—not perfect or finished but whole. They have rediscovered the repressed, suppressed, and oppressed aspects of their being. But the process of transformation is never final. It is a testimony, an act of faith. If men and women have successfully found wholeness in one realm of their lives, they can practice transformation again and again in all aspects of life to solve any and all problems.

In male-female relationships the personal is always also political, historical, and sacred. When Latino men and Latina women discover the uniqueness of the personal faces of their being, they enter into conflict with the political, historical, and sacred forces that had repressed them. For this reason I can say that the struggle to bring about more loving and mutual relationships between men and women holds the key to creating a more human world. When women and men in *la comunidad Latina* refuse to honor the destructive stories and ways of life of their cultural past, they are not just shaking their fists at one particular person with whom they were previously linked in the relationship of emanation; the revolution is greater than that. They are rejecting the legitimacy of the archetypal stories of patriarchy, uncritical loyalty, possessive love, tribalism, and capitalism enacted in fragmented ways of life that for generations wounded our capacity and took away our true inheritance as co-creators of the world.

The Ongoing Struggle of Transformation

Latino men and Latina women hope they will be successful in transforming their lives and marriages; they know they have never had a better opportunity than now to realize that patriarchal and matriarchal marriages and families are unbearable. The liberation of Latina women and men symbolizes the return of the archetype of the feminine in both men and women. The archetype of the feminine can help humans resist the wounded, flawed, and one-dimensional masculine passion of possessive sexuality.

Latina women represent the lost personal, political, historical, and sacred potential that women achieving their selfhoods represent for *la comunidad Latina*. They carry within them the feminine that has been underground for most of history. Yet they are unable to contribute and fully participate in the wider society because it practices stories that favor men. The violence inherent in the sexism of patriarchy cripples the whole society, both men and women. The tragedy is still with us. Many Latino men not only keep alive, but continue to reinforce, the archetypal story of the male as the conquering hero that reinforces the story of patriarchy.[9]

The struggle is ongoing. The revolution both in the depths and in the daily lives of Latinas and Latinos must be a permanent, continuous creation. Latina women are telling their own sacred stories that were filtered out by the patriarchal drama. The web of emanation is now dying, but the ways of life of incoherence and deformation as truncated failures and incomplete fragments of the core drama of life remain tempting choices. Latina women are redefining who they are and Latino men need to respond. In some cases, these redefinitions will lead to divorce, separation, and much suffering. Others will grow marriages and families in the service of transformation.

Latino men ask Latina women to love them, because to love men is to insist on creating new and better relationships with them. Latinas for the most part are not rejecting Latinos as persons. But they are refusing to relate to Latinos in relationships of dependence, the archetypal drama of patriarchy, and the ways of life of emanation, incoherence, and deformation, all of which destroy families and marriages. Latino men and Latina women intuitively understand they have to end this nightmare. Marriage is not the problem; marriage in the service of emanation, incoherence, and deformation is the enemy. The old marriages are bankrupt. But there are other choices. Men and women can create marriages and families in which Latino men nurture the feminine and masculine in themselves and Latina women nurture their masculinity and femininity as coequal dimensions of their humanity.

In the way of life of transformation, Latina women and Latino men have the assistance of the deepest sacred source of transformation. What can they create? They can choose from the eight archetypal relationships (any excepting deformation) and create new forms of them to deal with problems. These eight relationships can be re-created again and again to face new issues within the service of transformation. For example, the relationship of emanation, which seems to be so negative since it is usually enacted to hold us permanently in a childish state, can now be reconstituted as a temporary relationship that is used to prepare us for the journey of life. To daily hug and caress a child because we love her for herself is to nurture her and to prepare her for her life's work. To hold and kiss one's son who is discouraged is to let him take strength from you so that he can return to his journey. In both cases parents emanate their love and affection not to possess, not to dominate, not to render children incapable of living without us. Instead, they reach out to them as children who have sacred missions to find the meaning of their lives. Children become extensions of parents for the moment, and parents lovingly protect them from conflict and change by giving them the continuity and cooperation they need. Eventually, they can experience the justice of this love, namely, to become strong enough to face the tasks of their lives. In this kind of encounter, parents have completely changed the deeper meaning of the relationship of emanation by practicing it in the service of transformation. This is what it means to persistently ask the question, "In the service of what way of life will I love others?" Transformation allows us to take relationships that are often used to arrest our lives and to subvert them so they become the means of opening new avenues to life.

Within the freedom and capacity of transformation the family ceases to be a fortress and becomes the physical and psychic space wherein each member is guided to his or her own sources within, encouraged to enrich his or her consciousness of the world, and urged to create relationships to others, develop creativity, and join together in the struggle for shared goals to achieve justice. Each person is free to create conflict and change in order to make common cause in the persistent shaping of the family. As mothers and fathers struggle to create new relationships and more loving stories, they model for their children the process of making history. In such an environment, children can grow up to see that each person is sacred, men and women alike, that the world is shaped by people asking what politics are needed both at home and in the wider society to create a more just and open history in which the deepest sacred continues to inspire.

The new and better archetypal stories that Latino men can create (described in Chapters 1 and 4)—machismo in the service of transformation, the political innovator, participatory democracy, the faithful lover, creative isolation, loving himself as he loves others—can dramatically help transform the family for the good of the next generation. Let us now consider how children can go home to their own inner sacredness once they are provided with a caring and nurturing home and family wherein both father and mother are attuned to children's needs.

The Inalienable Rights of Children:
The Fulfillment of the Personal, Political,
Historical, and Sacred Faces of Their Being

Children in *la familia Latina* in the service of transformation can be raised and nurtured in a more loving and just environment. Their inalienable rights as children include a home filled with the spirit of two parents struggling with and for each other as they overcome the destructive cultural stories of their past and move aggressively to create fundamentally better and more just stories and relationships. Such a home provides for children a context, a loving, although temporary, enclosure that prepares them to go on their own journey through the core drama of life. The home is the physical and psychic space within which the personal, political, historical, and sacred faces of children are shaped. I see many articles on child abuse and the need to nurture children but none that explain their personal, political, historical, and sacred rights, which parents must not neglect.

What will a home look like in which husband and wife empty themselves of stories in the service of emanation in collusion with deformation and choose instead the service of transformation? What is it like to live in a home in which the Latino male as father and husband practices the stories of the faithful lover and loves his wife and children as he loves himself? Let us turn to literature to give us some hints as to what kind of home nurtures the four faces of children.

The House on Mango Street

Sandra Cisneros's *The House on Mango Street* tells the story of Esperanza, a young Mexican American girl growing up in a working-class neighborhood in Chicago.[10] In this novel, which consists of a series of vignettes that give us insight into Esperanza's world, readers find themes such as a class-based sense of shame at one's rickety home, the search for security, the importance of family, and the need for space both within one's interior self and outside of one's self. Cisneros describes the daily life that goes on in a home, the role of siblings in that life, the pain of domestic violence, and the love of children for parents who sacrifice daily for them. Through the eyes of Esperanza, readers see how the home culture clashes with school and its cultural demands as Esperanza struggles to live in two worlds. As Esperanza looks out on the wide world of her neighborhood, she experiences demographic change that affects her sense of self and security. In the midst of change her home, as poor as it is, becomes a source of roots, a context wherein to discover her sexuality. With the keen insight of a child, Esperanza is conscious that for some of her neighbors the home is a prison. These unhappy people live their lives with their elbows leaning out the window wondering what could have been if their houses had become homes that encouraged love. Like many children, Esperanza believed education was a means to get a new and more attractive house. But she did not yet understand that each person carries a home within: a home in which love puts persons in touch with their deeper homes, their creative selves. This is a home in the heart from which nobody can be evicted. As Esperanza discovers, writing in the privacy of one's home keeps one free. This is the home that strangers, who drive by and lock their doors for reasons of race and class, never see. Esperanza comes to recognize that her home provided her with a window to see the wider world as her neighborhood became more diversified. Her house in this section of town became a home in a deeper sense: The experiences she lived there will forever be a part of her. Even if she moved, she would take the people she has come to know with her. In the midst of poverty and deprivation, Esperanza teaches readers that they become who they are because of what they do during encounters with others. And always there is hope, hope, and more hope (the meaning of the word *Esperanza*). Each individual is someone special; each person's experiences are unique. Each of us is free to respond to life's events by becoming a writer, a poet, an artist, a doctor, an engineer, a teacher. We achieve our life's vocation not in spite of but because of the rickety house, the house that became a home because of loving parents, together with the neighbors who saw something special in us, who nurtured a deeper home in the children, who will never forget who they are and where they came from.

These marvelous insights into the deeper and wider meaning of a house as a home remind me of Gertrude Stein, who taught me that between the paper and the pen one discovers creativity, which is grounded in the internal home of feelings, ideas, and insights, the stories garnered through experience.[11] A child needs space, time, and a sense of self and adventure, a room of one's own, which Virginia Woolf fought for on behalf of all women and for men as brothers and fellow pilgrims.[12] All children need such a space wherein they can meditate and express the wonders of their lives. Michael Cunningham drew in *The Hours* a sad but hopeful portrait of women, young and old, struggling to give themselves permission to be alone to create the world within so that they might better understand and re-create the world surrounding them.[13]

The Wizard of Oz

While we need a physical and psychological refuge, we also need the space to take psychological journeys. In Frank Baum's *The Wizard of Oz*, Dorothy sails through space, hurled out of Kansas, the traditional world of emanation.[14] That world seeks to keep under wraps her budding sexuality and her sense of rebellion and experimentation represented by her dog, Toto.[15] Ms. Gulch, the dry and passionless neighbor, calls on the law of society, represented by the dog catcher, to contain the threat that Toto represents. Dorothy grows despondent and dreams of a place over the rainbow where she can be safe in her awakening self. As Dorothy is hurled through space by the tornado, she is in her home, which represents her psyche and the containment and protection of her vulnerable self. In Munchkinland, she opens the door and is introduced to a whole new world of extraordinary color and amazing little people. She is truly in a new world. But she is rudely made aware of danger. She needs to explore this different world before she can get back to Kansas. She is horrified to find out that she has inadvertently killed the Wicked Witch of the North. From her accidental slaying of the witch, Dorothy learns that freedom means making choices to overcome her internal inhibitions to develop her psychological space, her interior self.

Ms. Gulch, representing the containment of patriarchal law, endangers Dorothy's journey from adolescence into womanhood. Dorothy needs to hang on to Toto, who symbolizes her own instincts, her awakening sexuality. In the Land of Oz she needs a guide. She finds one in the guise of Glinda, the good witch. Now what is required of Dorothy, in the midst of all her fears, is to go on the journey of transformation, to follow the Yellow Brick Road to Crystal City, to seek the pearl of great price, the enlarged possibilities of her own deeper home within the greater city of the self, within which we can encounter the celestial city of salvation, not in heaven, but in our own deeper selves.

On the journey Dorothy meets three male characters: the Scarecrow, who has no brains, the Tin Man, who has no heart, and the Lion, who has no courage. Throughout her journey, Dorothy is watched and harassed by the Wicked Witch of the West, who is angry that her sister has been killed and seeks revenge. At one point Dorothy loses her way and gets lost in the poppy fields and falls into a deep and deadly slumber. Her slumber symbolizes what happens when we lose control of our lives and are taken over by stories that arrest our lives in a fragment of the core drama of life. Through the power of her internal strength, Dorothy frees herself and her companions.

She faces a more serious threat in the very person who is supposed to assist her, the wizard. Like all good but patriarchal males, he is supposed to have the answers. It is Toto, Dorothy's dog, who uncovers the scam and reveals that, when it comes to helping Dorothy discover who she is on the deeper level, masculine power is powerless. Dorothy is furious because the man in whom she placed her hopes is a fake. But he points her in the right direction and tells Dorothy that if she wants to get home to Kansas, she will have to get the broom of the wicked witch of the west. There is no other way. Dorothy needs to face her own internal demons, that is, partial and destructive stories and ways of life.

In the process of getting the broom, Dorothy's male companions discover their own missing pearl. The scarecrow, under the pressure of having to help Dorothy, focuses his energy and finds that he can think and make a plan; the lion gains the courage to protect Dorothy, and the tin man discovers that he has feelings, emotions, a heart after all. Now that Dorothy has been able to gather all of her strength, she defeats the witch and wins the prize, the broom. The power that the bewitching stories held over her have been broken and Dorothy is now prepared to make her greatest discovery.

Dorothy faces one last test, the final leg of the journey: getting back to Kansas. Her last temptation is to let somebody else, a strong man, a conquering hero, take her home. The wizard offers to fly her back home. Dorothy is relieved that she does not have to make this last choice and effort. But just as she is ready to fly off with the wizard in his patriarchal gondola, which symbolizes his male ego or psychological house, her feminine instincts, as represented by Toto, once more come to the rescue. Toto jumps out of the gondola and chases after a cat, a symbol of the feminine for thousands of years. Dorothy, who intuitively fears being deprived of her own instinctual energy, which is the heart of creativity, leaps out of the gondola to rescue Toto. In the chaos that ensues, the wizard flies off. The patriarch is unable to save Dorothy from taking responsibility for her own journey.

Dorothy needed to get back to firm ground, the reliance on her deeper self, home to Kansas, the reality of the world. Now as a young woman firmly rooted in the world, she can help to nurture a new and better world. But she is afraid to take the last step into womanhood that will end her dependence on heroes, warriors, patriarchs, and other male figures. Dorothy is bereft; Glinda, her guide, representing her own inner self, appears and consoles Dorothy, telling her that she has always had the answers within her, her red ruby slippers. All that she has to do is click them three times. Dorothy takes the risk and does as she is told and she finds herself back in Kansas.

Dorothy, in the language of the theory of transformation, has created a new and more loving alternative in the third act of the core drama of life, the story of the transforming self. She comes forth in a new way; she is back in Kansas, but Kansas is no longer the same because Dorothy has ceased to be the little girl getting lost in the fantasy of living over the rainbow, intimidated by patriarchal rules and male authority figures. She has a new attitude toward herself, that of the transforming self and the realization that one's deepest desires are within one's self. As the story ends Dorothy is about twelve or thirteen, which means that she will be facing many more challenges on the journey of life. But now that she has experienced transformation in at least one aspect of her life by enacting the story of the transforming self, she is prepared to reach out to others with the historical and sacred faces of her being to help make real for them what she has experienced; she is now ready to serve as a guide for others as they journey together through the core drama of life.

It has often struck me as I have watched this movie over the years that there is no mention of Dorothy's parents. She lives on a farm with her aunt and uncle and the hired help, the three companions who traveled with her in the Land of Oz. Dorothy can be said to be at home perhaps for the first time in her life because her house and home are now situated in the depths of her own interior home, where she has also succeeded in becoming her own mother and father, having given birth to her own self-hood. In addition her three male friends are now fully integrated within her own psyche as the masculine aspects that complement her femininity and thereby fulfill Dorothy as a person, a whole human being.

These two examples taken from literature brilliantly reveal the kind of interior journey that goes on within all children. It is the sacred task of parents to provide the nurturing context of the home within which this kind of internal growth can take place in a counterpoint relationship to the world around them. Both Baum and Cisneros describe the stories of the wounded self, destructive and creative sacred sources, patriarchy, capitalism, tribalism, the transforming self, diversity within democracy, the guide of transformation, and the healer. All children are raised in the midst of these stories practiced in different ways of life that can either free them for the journey through the core drama of life or arrest them as partial selves in one of its acts and scenes before they reach the fulfillment of finding the self.

A caring and loving home provides the physical necessities of life as well as the guidance and love that will sustain the children through their journey. A wise, deeply caring and loving Latino father and Latina mother support this search for a home both on the deeper level of assisting their children to find the secret to the inner self within one's own home of the heart and in the search for a physical home wherein children are given the actual space to explore and find themselves as persons on a journey. Children, raised with this kind of love, affection, and understanding, are prepared to practice the same kind of love in the wider society and in the context of their own families. As they travel away from home they will never really be away from home; once you know who you are, wherever you find yourself is your home, a home in motion.

In regards to the raising and nurturing of children, their home together with the extended homes of their classrooms, their schools, and their communities are dwelling spaces that profoundly shape the personal, political, historical, and sacred faces of their being.[16] In the service of what way of life do parents relate to their children as they enact stories and relationships? The answer to this question will determine the wounding or the fulfillment of the four faces of their being and those of the parents. If parents bring up children living the stories of patriarchy, matriarchy, uncritical loyalty, or possessive love in the service of emanation, they arrest their lives as permanent children. Such children are asked to persistently repress their own desires and to defer to those who are in authority; they learn a politics of unquestioning obedience, which makes them guardians of the status quo as they seek to be loyal to the powerful; history is repeated because they have no reason to exercise their historical faces except to honor the past; their sacred faces are obscured by the lord of emanation, who inspires them to see the sacred in all authority figures but never in themselves.

Homes and classrooms that prepare children for power and the pursuit of self-interest teach them to enact the stories of competence and capitalism for the sake of domination. The children brought up in the way of life of incoherence are taught to suppress their personal faces lest they reveal a weakness that will endanger them in an environment in which everyone seeks to get an edge in the competition for power. In contrast to emanation, wherein children are brought up to unconsciously repress any hint of personal desire or rebellion, in this way of life they are brought up to consciously hide their personal faces lest they become vulnerable. Parents tell them: "Don't reveal your business to anybody. Be careful not to discuss your weaknesses with anybody. At home we care about you, but out there you can't trust anybody." The only politics that counts is power, so the young are urged to get to know who is influential, to network with powerful people, to join a fraternity or sorority so that they can make connections. They need to learn who can help them and who can hurt them. History is time, and time in a capitalist society is money. "Map out your life," parents say to their children. By the time you are a particular age, you will have a BA, the following year you will have an MA. By the time that you are thirty-five you want to be making a certain amount of money. All of history and the children's historical faces are reduced to accumulating fragments of power over time. Their sacred faces are further obscured by the lord of incoherence, who inspires them to believe there is no deeper meaning to life than self-interest and power. All that counts is power to dominate and to accumulate.

More and more children are being exposed to the stories of racism, the wounded self, and poverty. In this way society hurts children and erases their personal faces by practicing a politics of violence against them that prepares them to enact their own political faces through violence. Life is made worse for them because they experience with their historical faces that life becomes worse as time passes. Their sacred faces are possessed by the lord of deformation.

But I also want to consider how parents victimize children in another way, that is, how they prepare children from privileged backgrounds to become the practitioners of deformation. Children learn that parents do not like the personal faces of dark people or gays or people from other ethnic groups because they never see them in their homes and they are spoken of with contempt or never mentioned. This means we raise children to believe that their personal faces can be superior to others, thus wounding them by preparing them to erase the faces of others and thereby their own. With their political faces they are led to practice a politics of violence, revenge, and exclusion. Children of the powerful believe that they make history and that other people are powerless because "they don't have what it takes." They are taught to believe they are superior to others. Children who are trained in the way of life of deformation are just as much victims as those children who are abused in the home. These children are taught how to become victimizers and predators. Either way, parents can hurt children so badly they can't begin to think about who they are. In contrast, in deeply caring, loving homes, classrooms, schools, and communities love is given to children in order to free them so that they can discover with guidance their own inner mysteries as their homes on the journey of life.

Parents and teachers become guides of transformation, leading children back to their own selves. In the way of life of transformation, children learn the stories of the transforming self, transforming love, participatory democracy, the political innovator, the guide, and the faithful lover. Nobody sits them down and reads to them a list of characteristics or prescriptions. They learn these stories because those who love them practice the dramas in relationship to them. Children blessed in this kind of environment learn through their own experience that their personal faces are unique and valuable. Their feelings, ideas, emotions, and intuitions are taken seriously. They are welcomed into the dialogue of the family as they develop. In this kind of home their personal faces emerge into wholeness. Patriarchy and other deadly stories can only be defeated by actual men and women relating to children within more loving stories that create new turning points that turn the spiral of history upward. The sacred face of each child is an incarnation of the deepest source of transformation; each child is a name of the deepest sacred source that longs to be known.[17] Thus when children know themselves in their wholeness, they reveal and makes known the deepest sacred source in a unique way.

And how will the child pronounce the name of the deepest sacred source, how will the child make real and reveal the face of the deepest sacred in the world? How will the child answer the questions, "Are you the one? Are you the one who will live your life so that you are fully present to fulfill the task that only you as this unique person can fulfill?"[18] These questions can only be answered through love and creative work that fully expresses the personal face of the child's being as she or he helps to reveal the personal face of others as well as the deepest sacred. By their political involvement in the family home and their home as the wide world, children release and bring to fruition in new ways the political face of the deepest source of transformation by making concrete in the world names that long to be pronounced, among them compassion, justice, mercy, and love, by actually nurturing the excluded and the injured. With their historical faces they are now free to go beyond being the recipients of the past and are filled with the spirit that opens up new horizons and new vistas in which together with the deepest sacred they can create more loving responses to the issues that lie ahead of them. This is what bi-unity is all about: Together with the deepest sacred source, which is grounded in love, people can find the fulfillment of their personal, political, historical, and sacred faces as friends, lovers, and companions on the journey through the core drama of life that leads homeward to the depths within self and the deepest sacred source.

The verdict is never final. *La familia Latina* needs to continue to reject those inherited stories that wound it by redeeming its past. Latinas and Latinos will only be condemned to repeat the past if they remain ignorant of or refuse to heed the call that comes from within: Each woman and man alike is sacred and each has the right to live out her or his unique sacred journey. To struggle together as men and women to fulfill each other's destiny is to mutually assist one another in the creation of new and more compassionate archetypal dramas, the sacred stories of our lives. What better way is there to prepare children for life in the service of transformation than to be nurtured by parents who dare to love and care deeply about each other?

> But to resolve even our first problem through transformation requires us to become aware of all of the sources of our being that previously bound us, and helped to create this particular problem, and to reject these sources, even our previous way of life, and to look for help in the deepest depths. Though we have resolved only one problem, we now possess ineradicable theoretical knowledge: no concrete problem is concrete only or exists in isolation. It is always rooted in the archetypal cosmos. No problem can be resolved unless we journey to confront its roots in that cosmos. Unless we learn how to uproot our connections even to the most embracing story of which any problem is a part, we shall not experience transformation. Every specific experience of transformation releases new energies earlier repressed and nourishes and enhances our capacity and desire to transform again. Every such experience, beginning with the first, enlarges our theoretical understanding of what we need to practice in every instance.[19]

Notes

1. See David T. Abalos for other examples of applying a theory of transformation to the Latino family and male-female relationships: *Latinos in the United States: The Sacred and the Political* (Notre Dame, IN: University of Notre Dame Press, 1986), chapter 3; *The Latino Family and the Politics of Transformation* (Westport, CT: Praeger Press, 1993), chapter 5; and *La Comunidad Latina in the United States: Personal and Political Strategies for Transforming Culture* (Westport, CT: Praeger Press, 1998), chapter 3.

2. For further explanation of the sacred and its many forms, see David Miller, *The New Polytheism: Rebirth of the Gods and Goddesses* (New York: Harper and Row, 1974).

3. In order to understand the importance of the sacred in the lives of Latinas and Latinos, see chapters 5 and 6 in Abalos, *Latinos in the United States.*

4. Manfred Halpern, "Transformation and the Source of the Fundamentally New," a paper presented at a conference at Hofstra University on "C. G. Jung and the Humanities." See also chapter 5 in Manfred Halpern, *Transforming Our Personal, Political, Historical, and Sacred Being in Contrast to Our Other Three Choices in Theory and Practice* (forthcoming).

5. For an excellent analysis of patriarchy, see Gerda Lerner, *The Creation of Patriarchy* (New York: Oxford University Press, 1986).

6. Abalos, *La Comunidad Latina,* chapter 3, pp. 93–100.

7. A Latina woman, Gladys Ricart, was murdered on her wedding day by her former lover, Augustín García, who apparently believed that she belonged

to him and if she did not then it was better for her to be dead. Matthew Futterman, *The Star Ledger,* October 26, 1999, pp. 13, 17.

8. Marshall Berman uses this phrase in his analysis of Rousseau's protagonist Julie in *La Nouvelle Eloise* as she rejects her authenticity. See Berman, *The Politics of Authenticity: Radical Individualism and the Rise of Modern Society* (New York: Atheneum Press, 1972), especially pp. 241–257.

9. One of the best and most penetrating analyses I have read regarding the relationship between patriarchy and the male as warrior living in the service of incoherence and deformation is Manfred Halpern, "The Archetypal Drama of the Conquering Hero," paper presented at the annual meeting of the American Political Science Association, San Francisco, September 1, 1990.

10. Sandra Cisneros, *The House on Mango Street* (New York: Vintage Books, 1984). Many other Latino novels, short stories, and films give us an insight into the Latino family and male-female relationships that can be fruitfully analyzed from the perspective of the theory of transformation. For example, by the Puerto Rican essayist and playwright René Marqués, *La Carreta* (Rio Piedras, PR: Editorial Cultural, 1971); Sandra Cisneros, *Woman Hollering Creek and Other Stories* (New York: Random House, 1991); *The Salt of the Earth,* a film directed by Herbert Biberman regarding Chicanos in the United States (1953); Demetria Martínez, *Mother Tongue* (New York: Ballantine Books, 1994); Rosa Martha Villareal, *Doctor Magdalena* (Berkeley: TQS Publications, 1995); *A Portrait of Teresa,* a film directed by Pastor Vega, Cuba (1979); *Camila,* a film directed by María Luisa Bemberg, Argentina (1984); Laura Esquivel, *Like Water for Chocolate* (New York: Doubleday, 1992); and Alice Walker's *The Color Purple* (New York: Washington Square Press, 1982), the novel that has taught me so much about male-female relationships in the African American community and in other communities of color surrounded by networks of racism, classism, and sexism.

11. As quoted in John Hyde Preston, "A Conversation with Gertrude Stein," in Brewster Ghiselin, ed., *The Creative Process* (New York: Mentor, 1963), p. 159.

12. Virginia Woolf, *A Room of One's Own* (New York: Harcourt, Brace, 1929).

13. Michael Cunningham, *The Hours* (New York: Farrar, Straus, and Giroux, 1998).

14. L. Frank Baum, *The Wizard of Oz* (New York: Torch Books, 1993).

15. In the writing of this section I am heavily endebted to Ann Belford Ulanov's interpretation in *The Feminine in Jungian Psychology and in Christian Theology* (Evanston, IL: Northwestern University Press, 1971), pp. 277–285. See also Gail B. Griffin, *The Season of the Witch* (Pasadena, CA: Triology Books, 1995).

16. Too see how the classroom can become a home within which the young can bring to fruition their own unique creativity, see "Teaching and Practicing Multicultural and Gender Fair Education from the Perspective of Transformational Politics," chapter 5 in David T. Abalos, *Strategies of Transformation Toward a Multicultural Society: Fulfilling the Story of Democracy* (Westport, CT: Praeger Press, 1996), pp. 97–126.

17. See Henri Corbin, *Creative Imagination in the Sufism of Ibn Arabi,* translated by Ralph Manheim (Princeton, NJ: Princeton University Press, 1969), especially pages 114–116, 120–123, 191–193, 201–202, 213–214, 307–308.

18. Cicely Tyson, the African American actress, quoted the line "Are you the one?" from her lead role in the film *The Autobiography of Miss Jane Pitman* at the graduation ceremony for Seton Hall University, May 8, 2000. She answered her own question by saying, "Each of you is the one."

19. Halpern, *Transforming,* chapter 4 (forthcoming).

6

—*ww*—

Men in the
Service of Transformation

It is crucial for Latino men as men of color and men from all ethnic and racial backgrounds to rediscover and reclaim their manhood and responsibilities in their communities and in the society at large by telling their stories. I would like to set the tone of this chapter by quoting James Baldwin:

> Let us begin by saying that we are living through a very dangerous time. Everyone in this room is in one way or another aware of that. We are in a revolutionary situation, no matter how unpopular that word has become in this country. The society in which we live is desperately menaced; not only by right wing terrorists but also from within. So any citizen of this country who figures himself or herself as responsible, and particularly those who deal with the minds and hearts of young people, must be prepared to go for broke. Or to put it another way, you must understand that in the attempt to correct so many generations of bad faith and cruelty, when it is operating not only in the classroom, but in society, you will meet the most fantastic, the most brutal and the most determined resistance, there is no point in pretending that this won't happen.[1]

During this difficult time of redefinition and re-visioning, what Latino men need to emphasize is their presence as men of color, *hombres de color,* together with all men who belong to the full spectrum of humanity. Men of color are not "minority" males; indeed, 75 percent of the world consists of people of color and demographic studies reveal that people of color already constitute one-third of the U.S. population. The term *minority* no longer serves us well, if it ever did. No one is a minority or a majority; we are together, the United States, alongside our

European American brothers and sisters. I would like to reiterate what Malcolm X said regarding the issue of being white. Following his extraordinary journey of transformation to Mecca, he realized that it was not the pigmentation of a person's skin but the person's consciousness that made the difference.[2] For Malcolm it was not "white" people who were the issue but rather white attitudes grounded in the story of tribalism in the service of deformation. It is an attitude based on an alleged superiority. The question then becomes one not so much of the color of our skin but of how men answer the question, "In the service of what ultimate way of life do we practice our ethnic and racial heritage, our manhood, the stories and relationships of our lives?" In the final analysis, the terms *majority* and *minority* betray an obsession with power relations. Both of these terms are abstractions that turn all men into faceless stereotypes that deny their humanity as real persons.

When General Dwight D. Eisenhower became the president of Columbia University, he spoke with the faculty about what the university could do for them. He was shocked when the faculty shouted him down and said, "We are the university."[3] Similarly, men of color must not allow themselves to be defined as culturally deprived, disadvantaged, marginal, or underclass; together with other ethnic groups, men and women of color are this country. Too many of us have been socialized to accept marginality and powerlessness as outsiders. Our responsibility is to create new and more loving alternatives and to reject the sickness that there is nothing that we can do.

All men of color and of all ethnic groups have experienced the story of tribalism in the service of deformation. During a period lasting over 200 years, African peoples were brought to this country in the hulls of slave ships. As many as twenty to thirty million African men, women, and children lost their lives. We also know that in 1519, when Cortes arrived in Mexico, it is estimated that there was an indigenous population of fifteen million people there. Fifty years later, there were five million; in fifty years, ten million people were gone due to disease, exploitation, and war. In the U.S. version of ethnic cleansing, Native Americans were consciously displaced from the land, many were killed, and their cultures were decimated by the greed of invaders. The Chinese Exclusion Act was passed by Congress in 1882. In 1908, a so-called Gentlemen's Agreement, restricting Japanese migration to the United States, was passed by the U.S. Congress. The only atomic bomb ever dropped was used against Asian people, the Japanese. In Vietnam over two million

Vietnamese lost their lives, and hundreds of thousands died in the morally dubious war in Korea. With their historical and political faces, U.S. citizens need to put an end to the stories of deformation that have been practiced against men and women from all groups.

The Politics of Miseducation: The Loss of Our Stories

History, the curriculum, and education are political statements. They are political statements by which primarily European American men, who practiced the stories of capitalism in the service of incoherence allied with the story of tribalism in the service of deformation, shaped U.S. national culture for the sake of the powerful. The greatest lie of history is what the history books left out. What was omitted were the stories of the excluded groups: the Irish, the Italians, the Poles, the Jews, and other ethnic groups usually called "white" as well as the stories of women and people of color.[4] In my teaching I share with my students that socialization is a process by which a person becomes a member of a society. That sounds very neutral. But we can also define socialization as a process by which the dominant society convinces one to want what it desires. This understanding of socialization dramatically changes its meaning; in this latter sense education becomes training in repression. The consciousness of Latinos, their whole view of life, is shaped by someone who does not know Latino culture. So what Latino men can and need to do together is step forward and tell the history that is missing.

Elaine Pagels, in *The Gnostic Gospels,* quotes from the Gospel of Saint Thomas the words of Jesus: "If you discover what is within you, what you discover will save you; if you do not discover what is within you, what you do not discover will destroy you."[5] Another author, Leslie Marmon Silko, represents the heart of the *mestizaje,* the coming together of different cultures, world civilizations, and religions. Silko is Chicana, Laguna Pueblo Indian, and white. She wrote a brilliant novel, *Ceremony,* about a young man named Tayo, who is half Native American and half white. Upon his return from World War II he is deeply depressed and lost because he experienced so much death, including that of his cousin Rocky, whom he deeply loved. He has come home but he cannot figure out who he is. He is surrounded by stories of death and destruction symbolized by a six-year drought. But from the beginning of the novel, Silko writes that it is the confrontation of stories and the ways of life in which one practices them that will determine one's capacity to transform his or her life:

> I will tell you something about stories. They aren't just entertainment; don't be fooled. They are all we have, you see, all we have to fight off illness and death. You don't have anything if you don't have the stories. Their evil is mighty; but it can't stand up to our stories, and so they try to destroy the stories and let the stories be confused or forgotten. They would like that; they would be happy because we would be defenseless then. He rubbed his belly. I keep them here he said. Here, put your hand on it, see it is moving. There is life here for the people and in the belly of this story, the rituals and ceremony are still growing.[6]

This is a beautiful statement about how necessary it is that men from all backgrounds become pregnant with their own selves. It is precisely the story of tribalism and the institutionalized violence of society that causes men from different backgrounds to turn against each other, and that has made it almost impossible for all of us as Americans to give birth to the stories, the life, and the sacredness dedicated to the service of transformation that lies within each person. Alejo Carpentier, a Guatemalan writer, wrote of the lost Latino heritage in *Los Pasos Perdidos, The Lost Footsteps.*[7] Plato taught us that we preexisted before we were born and that we carried the truth within us.[8] But somehow many men have lost contact with the truth through repression. They are born into the stories of tribalism, patriarchy, uncritical loyalty, and capitalism in the service of partial ways of life that prevent them from being fully present as men, as persons. They have forgotten the Muslim mystical tradition that taught us that each of us is another face of the sacred.[9]

The Temptation to Lose the Self: Assimilation

In Ralph Ellison's *Invisible Man,* the protagonist comes to New York City and begins working at a paint factory called Liberty Paints.[10] The specialty of the factory was that it made the whitest paint in America. The company had a special way of making white paint with a simple process: a little bit of black paint is mixed within the white batch, and the white paint becomes whiter. The protagonist could not understand the chemistry involved. What he failed to see was the enactment of the story of tribalism in which assimilation plays a prominent part. When Latino men and other men of color are convinced that they are not as good as white men, they try to assimilate (which comes from the Latin *simulo, simulare,* to become like the other). Assimilation convinces the white culture, the powerful, that they are superior to all others since others make themselves over in their image and likeness. In this way a little bit of dark paint makes them whiter than white. Ellison's hero kept adding black paint, but it continued to come out gray. Every time it came out gray he thought he was failing; it should be whiter than before. Ellison's message was that no matter how hard people may try to destroy the authenticity of their selves, nothing can ultimately take away from their sacredness, which comes from the deepest source of transformation. Men of color must affirm who they are continuously. To assimilate is to forget their story; they need to persist in coming out gray because it is their way of showing resistance. Too often men of color are taken over by racism, a concrete expression of the story of tribalism. Some in the Latino community use a term of affection, *güerito, güerita,* little white one, for children who are light-skinned with straight hair. Likewise, *pelo bueno,* good hair, allows them to pass because they are closer to the powerful, light-skinned European Americans. In the African American community some are proud to be called "high yellow," that is, closer to white.

Tribalism in the Service of Deformation

The emphasis on alleged superiority is a justification, a rationalization, as to why the powerful should rule the so-called underclass. These attitudes of white superiority gave rise to the archetypal drama of tribalism. I am not using the concept of tribalism here in an anthropological sense but as a descriptive term that means separating people into superior and inferior groups. Tribalism is a story in which one group takes a fragment of life such as skin color, ethnicity, national origin, religion, or gender and turns it into a fantasy that dominates the whole of life. The group that possesses this fragment believes that it is better than those others, the outsiders. To Latinos' great loss this story of tribalism has been used since the coming of the first Europeans. An inherited drama of the United States, tribalism has scarred all Americans, people of color and European Americans alike.

There are five ways to relate to people outside of the dominant group. The deviants, the outsiders, are first of all turned into *invisible* people whose existence is not even acknowledged. If there are many of "those people" and if there is a need for cheap labor, then the second way of relating takes place: Society allows them to participate if they admit their *inferiority* by accepting inferior wages, housing, education, and medical care. The third way of relating is to allow those who are most like the dominant group to *assimilate:* "You are so much like one of us that we are going to accept you; you are one of the better Mexicans." The fourth way to relate is to *excommunicate or exile* those who become disloyal to their patrons; they have either refused to reject who they are, or worst of all, they have begun to make common purpose with the community from which they were "saved." The fifth and final way of relating in the drama of tribalism is *extermination.* These days this fifth way is more subtle than in the past when, for example, the United States went to war against Mexico because some wanted to expand slavery while others saw Mexicans (whom they considered inferior) as an obstacle to expand the blessings of Anglo-Saxon civilization from sea to shining sea. Today, people of color continue to go to jail in greater numbers, have less access to health care, have less income, have a higher infant mortality rate, and suffer from police brutality at a greater rate than their white counterparts. But the danger is also one of cultural extermination. To undermine a culture is to assault the selfhood of a people. The archetypal drama of tribalism is the basis for the stories of violent exclusion: racism, ethnocentrism, sexism, classism, religious bigotry, and all other forms of fanaticism that elevate one people over another in order to exploit them.

I would like to give an example of tribalism and its effects on one community of color, the Mexican-Chicano community. Prior to 1940 only 1 percent of Mexican children in the Southwest were in school.[11] Some have said that the lack of attendance in school was the fault of a culture that did not value education. Others claim the parents were to blame. These are arguments that prevent participants from seeing the deformation of tribalism at work. The powerful in the Anglo community were involved in making a decision, a political decision, that ensured that the only work that Mexicans were capable of was work in the fields. The intent of this decision was to provide the growers with a plentiful supply of perpetually cheap labor. This was a conscious decision, based on the racism of tribalism, to cripple a whole generation. It is for this reason that there are very few doctors, lawyers, engineers, and other professionals from the generation that grew up in the 1940s and 1950s. Many never had the opportunity to go to school because powerful others concluded they could not learn. When schools were made available, they were inferior. They were intended to provide just enough education so that students would leave with the bare rudiments to do their jobs well. There were scholarships from the Lions Clubs for the more "aggressive" Mejicanos, that is, those who were deemed worthy of assimilating into the dominant group. "Uppity" Mexicans, that is, those who resisted, were run out of Texas by a law enforcement agency, the Texas Rangers, specifically created in the nineteenth century to handle the "Mexican problem."[12] The struggle over bilingual education, the underfunding of schools in the barrios, the political control of the curriculum that prevented Mexicans from knowing their own history, all of these are indicators of cultural extermination that also became political and economic extermination. As a result the personal, political, historical, and sacred faces of the people were erased as they experienced a politics of violence and exclusion that made their history a nightmare and denied their sacred faces. But men from all ethnic backgrounds have suffered because of ethnocentrism, another virulent concrete expression of the story of tribalism. The Irish, who are now considered "white," were pictured as people with black faces in the vicious cartoons published in newspapers in the 1840s and 1850s. They were hated and persecuted by the dominant white group of the time, the white Anglo Saxon Protestants (WASPs).[13] But even the descendants of the so-called WASPs are here because they were persecuted for religious and political reasons and thus came to the New World. The problem is that each group that experienced the pain of tribalism after rebelling against those who wounded them failed to empty themselves of the story of tribalism. They carried this story like a virus to which they believed they had become immune. And so they practiced the story of tribalism against others, the most recent group of arrivals. The new insiders now became the victimizers of the new outsiders. For this reason the Irish excluded the Italians for years from civil service jobs, especially police and firefighting. The Italians, in turn, were just as cruel with the Eastern Europeans.[14] And so, because the power of these archetypal stories remains hidden, one generation of newcomers continues to wound the next.

Just like men of color, white males cannot live authentic lives by forgetting who they are, because they know, deep down, that there is an unrealized self ready to be born. As a result there is always the possibility that they will resist the attempt to go under the fog for good as Big Chief was tempted to do in *One Flew Over the Cuckoo's Nest*.[15]

The threat to all men is that they will allow their manhood to be corrupted and co-opted by the powerful through assimilation. The powerful want to co-opt the creativity and skills of the less powerful for their benefit. It is important to remember that like Malcolm X, men of color and ethnic males for long periods in American history wanted to assimilate.[16] Malcolm wrote about how he "fried" his hair with lye in order to conk it, to straighten it.[17] Many men from different heritages have spent a great deal of time trying to be handsome by the prevailing "white" standards, that is, the norms set down by men in power. So much was done in the hope that the powerful men they wanted to be like would accept them. But men of color and of the first generation of many ethnic groups have been considered outsiders because of their accents, religious beliefs, educational backgrounds, language, cultural habits, and dress. When Malcolm X went to speak to Mr. Ostrowsky, his school counselor, Mr. Ostrowsky told him to forget about wanting to be a lawyer, to be more realistic, to become a carpenter.[18] Like Malcolm, all men of color want to belong; they long to be a part of the American dream. Nobody can claim that they are disloyal Americans, that they don't want to take advantage of opportunities. Those opportunities have not yet been offered in their fullness to people of color and to some ethnic groups.

Richard Rodríguez in his book *Hunger of Memory* writes about being so dark-skinned that his mother used to rub his face with egg white and lemon juice concentrate to see if she could make his skin lighter.[19] This is a form of self-denial and even self-hatred. But in her defense, many people of color have felt that they had to be more like the others, the powerful people, the lighter-skinned. In the process many lost contact with their sacred source, with their stories of transformation.

Ethnic groups who later became "white" also suffered initially from the tribalism of American nativism; but they were able to assimilate much more effectively because of the color of their skin. They suffered initially because of ethnocentric attitudes. For example, the Slavic people were ridiculed as "Hunkies." The Italians were also discriminated against, as were the Irish, who were stereotyped as Papists and whose churches were attacked. Jews were anxious to assimilate so that they could escape the anti-Semitism and the violence of the pogroms that drove many of them from Eastern Europe. But in the end, these groups were able to make it because they were light-skinned. People of color would not be able to assimilate quite so easily. They could not simply change their family names to fit in; there was always the issue of skin color.

Much of the reason for the antagonism whites felt toward people of color served as a cover for deep fear. White ethnic groups were deeply affected by the story of capitalism as the official story of U.S. society. They were afraid of competition and saw each new wave of immigrants as a threat to their newly won status. When it came to people of color, many whites enacted the story of capitalism in alliance with the story of tribalism in the service of deformation to keep out these allegedly inferior people in order to protect their own jobs.

Ralph Ellison did not title his book *"The" Invisible Man;* he called it *Invisible Man.* It seems fair to say that he titled it as he did because he was attempting to say that all people in this country, both whites and those of color, have been taken over by the story of capitalism. The greatest preoccupation of most Americans is power. The only way to make it is to assimilate, that is, join the powerful in the pursuit of self-interest and privilege. All Americans are caught in a systematic process through which bureaucracies turn them into abstractions and put them through an impersonal system without ever knowing any individual in his or her wholeness. They are only allowed to know themselves and others as fragments. All are violated by being turned into objects to be processed. As a result, not even European Americans are making it in the U.S. system; they, too, are living actual stories enacted in ways of life that keep them out of their deepest being. Nobody makes it in this system. The system does not care about human beings; what it cares about is power.

Going Home to the Sources Within

Latino men, together with African American, Native American, Asian American, and European American men, carry within themselves thousands of years of a haunting past beating in their blood. The drum, which is so important in American music, is the heartbeat of the deepest sacred source of transformation. It is the beat or rhythm of the universe, it is the heart pulse of their ancestors, and it is the reminder that sacredness pulsates within each person. They come into contact with this sacredness, with their stories of transformation, by going home. This does not necessarily mean physically going to Africa, Mexico, Ireland, Puerto Rico, China, Italy, Albania, or India but rather going deep within themselves. Men have to dive deeply within themselves and resurface with the creativity to respond to the deformation that surrounds them.

La Carreta by René Marques tells the story of Puerto Ricans coming to the U.S. mainland. The main character, Luís, wanted to find the mystery of life by obtaining what the system promised: *los chavos,* money. Finally, when he arrives in the Bronx, the system literally rips him to pieces. Luís has an accident at work in which he is devoured by a machine, *la máquina lo tragó.* Sadly but ironically his sister, Juanita, says that Luís finally discovered the mystery of the machine, which cannot give life because it is barren.[20] Marques implies that when one loses oneself, there is nothing left; the machine that allegedly brings life is a lie; it did not bring life but death. Luís had lost his self by leaving the land that was sacred to him. We cannot enact in their fullness the political, historical, and sacred faces of our being if we lose our personal faces. The future is up to us. We are the ones who have to give direction to our lives by returning home to our own, inner sources, symbolized by the fertility of the red earth as our mother, the deepest source of our being. And so the feminine, which has been repressed, suppressed, and oppressed in all of our cultures for so long, comes forth as the principle of liberation. This is why men will never be truly men until they rediscover the feminine within themselves. They can and need to rediscover what it means to nurture, to love, to be compassionate, to take care of children, and to participate in a new and better story of mutuality with women.

It is essential for men to understand that each of them has four faces to their being. Each of them, by the very nature of their humanity, has a personal, a political, a historical, and a sacred face. Nobody gives them permission to be political; they are political as a natural right. Each is a historical being and each is a sacred being. For most of U.S. history, the personal faces of men of color have been either hidden so that they could protect themselves. In U.S. society it is the dominant way of life of incoherence that arrests lives as fragments of what is possible. The system values only the pursuit of self-interest and power. What men are required to do by a system in the service of incoherence is to suppress who they are. They are forced to become cagey to hide their personal faces. At times they reveal their inner selves to others and then regret it, saying, "I should never have said anything like that about myself." Why? Because it made them vulnerable. It made them weak in a situation in which they must compete for power. Across the United States, one can walk into any grade school or high school and say, "It's not what you know, . . . " and all of the students will complete the phrase: "It's who you know." This is about power and being connected to people with power; this is not advancement based on merit. Thus, the political face of being is reduced to searching for power and domination. In a world of power, what drives history forward is competition. The entrepreneurs are always running to stay ahead. But they live with the constant anxiety that they are falling behind. The ultimate sacred force in such a society is the lord of incoherence, who inspires humans to practice the story of capitalism for the sake of joining the powerful.

Historically, when people of color and other immigrants arrived in this country, they were not allowed to prepare themselves to compete on a fair level with the dominant group. Yet it was worse than that; not only were many people of color denied education and the right to enter into society as full members, their identity was put at risk. Toni Morrison said it well when she wrote in her novel *Beloved:*

> That anybody white, could take your whole self for anything that came to mind. Not just work, kill, or to maim you, but dirty you. Dirty you so bad you couldn't like yourself anymore. Dirty you so bad you forgot who you were and couldn't think it up.[21]

This is the real tragedy. When the self is undermined, when individual sacredness is denied, the self is dirtied; the sacred face of being is turned opaque, and the person is cut adrift from the deepest sacred source. As a result persons begin to hate themselves; they look to others to tell them who they are because they have no basis to define themselves. It is the powerful and the dominant who now tell ethnic men and men of color who they are. The dominant group, due to the very logic of power, had to define people of color and ethnicity as inferior. Power is power because it is scarce and therefore cannot be shared but instead increasingly leads to the use of deformational violence to preserve it for the dominant class.

To go home to the deepest source within, therefore, is an act of resistance. The spirit speaks to each man. A new feeling, an intuition, comes to them and they rebel against the powerful. Since it is not enough to rebel only against the practitioners of destructive stories and ways of life, they need to be radical and turn their attention to the underlying roots and causes, to the sacred forces in the depths that gripped them in a death hold. By the deepest source of transformation they are inspired to reject the stories of capitalism and tribalism together with the ways of life of incoherence and deformation in which they practice these stories. Men need to exercise their manhood by developing strategies for sending destructive stories—not their lives and the lives of others—into the abyss. Men in the service of transformation grow their own identities. Then they can serve as guides to the wider society. But first they need to expose the deformation in their midst.

Strategies of Deformation

The story of tribalism is still very much alive in our nation. My greatest concern is that it will become worse as the demographic changes eventually turn people of color, taken together, into the largest group in the United States. Estimates are that by the year 2050, Latinas and Latinos will make up fully 25 percent of the U.S. population.[22] In such dangerous times men of goodwill from all backgrounds need to take a stand and break the cycle of discrimination and prejudice by refusing to practice the story of tribalism as victims or perpetrators. The racism and classism to which we have been exposed for generations have bred a deformational behavior in many men that also profoundly affects women. Patriarchal sexism, which often turns violent when men are under stress, is too often a form of rebellion against powerlessness. This kind of rebellion means that men's consciousness is being manipulated by the oppressor; they do not want people to see that racism, ethnocentrism, anti-Semitism, sexism, and classism are all cut from the same cloth. These stories of deformation arise out of the desire to cripple so that the powerful can hang on to power. Thus if men fight racism they must also oppose patriarchy and the stories of capitalism, sexism, and classism in their own communities. In addition to being prophetic, that is, discerning the signs of the time by listening to their deepest voices, men of color need also to be philosophers who can analyze what is being done to them in order to participate as political innovators. At this point it is necessary for men to draw a clear distinction between two fundamentally different ways by which to shape their daily lives and environment: the strategies of deformation and the strategies of transformation.

First, let us consider the strategies of deformation. How did men get to be where they are? Men have an obligation to educate themselves as to what has been happening to them. The first strategy of deformation is that men of color allow themselves to be defined by other people as inferior based on race, ethnicity, or class. When others can tell us who we are, the politics of power corrupts and kills.

Secondly, men from diverse cultures are encouraged to distrust each other and diminish each other as they become locked in contests for power. They have always been told that competition is natural. The very word *competition* indicates its underlying meaning: The root word for *competition* comes from the Latin *peto, petere,* to assault the other. Thus society as it practices the story of capitalism in collusion with the story of tribalism gives men permission to fight with each other and to believe that this is what life is all about. Thus white middle-class men are led to believe that they are losing their jobs because of affirmative action and not because corporations have decided they need to reengineer to maximize their profits. This false consciousness encourages racial anger and turns men of color into enemies who are then berated as being qualified for jobs only because of the color of their skin.

The third strategy is to co-opt anger. The anger of men is manipulated by others and used for the benefit of the powerful. Rather than using the anger to figure out what is being done, many men fight among themselves for resources that are made scarce by the powerful.

The fourth strategy of deformation teaches men that there is nothing they can do when confronting the power of the system. They begin to accept the lie that they are powerless victims. Apathy soon follows, conjoined with fantasies of power fed by drugs, alcohol, gambling, violence, and other escapes. Too many men become passive recipients as permanent puppets of an inevitable fate.

The fifth strategy is one in which the powerful encourage racism and turn exploited groups into mere interest groups. If Latino students get consideration from the school system because of language needs, too often other people of color and whites feel that the Latino community is being favored. Many people have said, "My parents never got bilingual education, so why should those people?" Members of other communities of color feel that *la comunidad Latina* is given preference because it is "closer" to white than they are. This racial infighting prevents a unified politics from demanding the rights of all people.

The sixth strategy is that men of color and of some ethnic groups begin to fulfill the view that the dominant society has of them. They do this whenever they participate in forms of rebellion against whites that lead to excessive drinking, abusing drugs, acts of violence, and other kinds of self-diminishment. Some in the community begin to believe that maybe the dominant class is right. Whites then say, "I told you so. They are all violent."

The final strategy used by those who wish to hurt men of color is to cause men to become so desperate as disappointed males that they begin to exercise their masculinity by abusing women and children. People need to learn to recognize these strategies of deformation as Tayo did in

Ceremony. Because he was betrayed Tayo wanted to kill Emo, a fellow Native American. What held Tayo back was the recognition that this act of deformation would perpetuate not only his own destruction but that of his people:

> The moon was lost in a cloud bank. He moved back into the boulders; it had been a close call. The witchery had almost ended the story according to its plan. Tayo had almost jammed the screwdriver into Emo's skull; the way the witchery had wanted, severing the yielding bone and membrane, as the steel ruptured the brain. Their deadly ritual for the autumn solstice would have been completed by him. He would have been another victim, a drunken Indian war veteran settling an old feud; and the Army doctors would say that the indications had been there all along since his release from the mental ward at the Veterans Hospital in Los Angeles. The White people would shake their heads, more proud than sad that it took a White man to survive in their world and that these Indians couldn't seem to make it.[23]

Silko's point is clear: We need to stop letting others write the scenarios for our lives; we must not fulfill the stereotypes that the dominant culture has of us.

Strategies of Transformation

Now let us turn to the creation of new and more loving alternatives, to strategies of transformation. What are the stories of transformation in our cultural heritages? What are some of the ways that will enable people to reject the stories of deformation and empower them to choose the fundamentally new and compassionate stories of transformation?

The first strategy, which constitutes the heart of any revolution, is to rediscover and reclaim the sacredness of the self. Any society that prevents a person from becoming who they are practices deformation. Ken Kesey's *One Flew Over the Cuckoo's Nest* is one of the best political novels in American literature. Big Chief, the narrator and the main character in the novel, wonders how anybody can pull off anything as big as being who he is, a self.[24] History indicates that the end of a social system begins with the self-lessness of its people.

The second strategy is to analyze the system, that is, the stories and the ways of life that are daily practiced. All men need to figure out what is being done to them. They have to educate themselves to the trickery of deformation and be able to expose it. By doing archetypal analysis they can name the story of tribalism in the service of deformation and the story of capitalism in the service of incoherence and how these two stories and ways of life turn people into partial selves who are incapacitated in their ability to respond creatively to problems. Then, once men have identified these stories, they need to know that they have the freedom to empty themselves of them and to create more loving and just alternatives in the service of transformation.

For men to cooperate in organizing across gender, race, religious, cultural, ethnic, and class lines is the third strategy. There is no hope if they do not do this. The powerful know how to divide men of color from white men and to turn them into special interest groups who are reduced to competing with each other. Men need to build coalitions that liberate the personal, political, historical, and sacred faces of their being. Once they are free in this way they can together practice a politics in which each is valuable in order to build a more loving and open future that will affirm the sacredness of each individual.[25]

The fourth strategy is for men to redefine and reeducate themselves so that they can legitimize and give themselves permission to enact the four faces of their being in response to the needs of others. Men need to stop asking the powerful to tell them who they are and reject the dominant definition of what it means to be a man. Those in power will no doubt respond, "When you can compete with us and show us that you are as good as we are at making money, at moving aggressively to protect your assets, at denying yourself for the sake of the future, at being unemotional and detached so that you can make decisions based on facts arrived at in a scientific and neutral manner, at turning the laid-off worker into an invisible person, at proving you are not a bleeding heart who worries about the poor, then you are men." No. Self-definition, the discovery of men's unique personal, political, historical, and sacred faces and those of their neighbors, is a process of awakening and of taking action; it is excavating and uncovering the capacity within men's selves, discovering their own voices.

To redefine politics is the fifth strategy. Politics for too many has come to mean only participation in official contests for power, such as voting for a senator. For others politics is being uncritically loyal to others, abdicating responsibility so that they are free to pursue their own economic self-interest, or practicing a politics that excludes others from participation. Politics in the service of transformation asks a new question: What is it that you and I need to do together here and now, today, to protect and enhance justice and compassion for all of our citizens?

Since all persons are political by the very nature of being human, they enact a political face precisely by becoming participants in the fulfillment of the story of democracy.

The sixth strategy is for men to reject guilt and self-recrimination and refuse to give loyalty to those who demand disloyalty to oneself and to others. To cancel the guilt means to stop reliving the mistakes of the past, declaring how bad or angry they feel. Men of color in the service of transformation do not want white European American men to feel guilty; no, they want European American men to join them in change, to be ready to become colleagues in the work of transformation.

The seventh strategy is for men to reject and struggle, with all the means at their disposal, against the story of self-wounding, the escape into drugs and alcohol that often leads to crime, AIDS, and the mistreatment of children and women. When men of color get involved in drugs, it is partially because of racism, because these men are used as instruments for the advancement of others in the story of capitalism. But the escape into fantasy is not the answer. Let me recall Tayo's struggle. Tayo wanted to kill Emo. But then Tayo said no, that is what they are expecting me to do. They want me to do that because I would be fulfilling their views of what it is that I should be. Men of color cannot allow themselves to fulfill the prophecies that the dominant culture has determined for them. On the contrary, it is important for men of color to rediscover themselves and women as mutual guides on the journey of transformation and to rediscover their children as gifts from the deepest sacred source of transformation.

To refuse to accept the argument, that men and women have to settle for less by continuing the power struggles and patriarchal relationships that permeate U.S. society is the eighth strategy. Sandra Cisneros, Rosa Martha Villareal, Alice Walker, and Demetria Martínez have done pioneering work by creating models of strong and transforming women in their novels. Chicana and Latina feminist writers, through their scholarship, have not only exposed the subordination inherent in patriarchal power but have also opened up new alternatives for *la comunidad Latina.*[26] They have done readers a great service by going beyond the sterile drama of the reversal of power roles to develop credible and evocative portraits of both women and men transforming their lives.

Alice Walker has also shown the way to go beyond the stereotyping of men. For example, in *The Color Purple,* Albert, Celie's previously abusive husband, begins a whole new life, not only by recognizing and accepting Celie's freedom and creativity but also by growing in himself what he now admires in Celie. Albert, like Celie, begins to sew, which represents the nurturing of others. His shirts are like Celie's sewing of pants: They are weaved in such a way that they respect the uniqueness of each person's body and thus each person's sense of self.[27] Walker gives to both men and women the same right to do away with fixed patterns and set roles and to use their freedom to develop their own patterns, that is, to become persons still growing their own lives.

As the ninth strategy men need to redefine aggressiveness. They know the terms *macho* and *aggressive*. What is creative in this context is to redefine macho or masculine energy to mean the rejection of the use of aggressive behavior against others, especially women and children, to prove manhood. That is not what being a man is all about. To be a macho, aggressive man in the service of transformation, as described in Chapter 2, is to move decisively together with women to protect their humanity while at the same time struggling for justice. The term *aggressive* comes from the Latin word *gredio, gredere,* which means "to step forward with urgency." What the dominant in American society want men to say when they step forward is, "I got mine." This is to be caught by the story of capitalism in the service of incoherence, which arrests lives and wounds people as partial selves. Men have another choice. They can choose to take their machismo and move forward with a sense of urgency to build a fundamentally more loving and inclusive society.

The tenth, and final, strategy is to create new and loving concrete incarnations of archetypal stories that enable each person to travel the core drama of life to its fulfillment in transformation. This search for new and better alternatives to meet the challenge of the times in which we live frees us from old and tired archetypes and dramas. Men need no longer be possessed by the archetypes of the conquering hero, the warrior, the entrepreneur, the hunter, the expert, and the bureaucrat, all of which are practiced in the truncated ways of life of emanation, incoherence, and deformation. Rather these times demand the creation of new, concrete manifestations of the archetypal stories of the wounded healer, nurturer, faithful lover, father, companion, brother, political innovator, guide, colleague, friend, and the man who enacts the story of self-love, which enables him to love others, all in the service of transformation. Men must also exercise manhood and machismo, working aggressively to bring about the fulfillment of the story of democracy so that each of our citizens is valued.

These kinds of creation will dramatically change for the better men's relationship to women, enabling them to create loving families wherein a child can be raised as a person with her or his own unique personal, political, historical, and sacred face, which will prepare her or him for the journey of transformation.

I hope to encounter men and women like those described in a poem by Teresíta Fernández-Viña, that is, people who love themselves and who, because they love themselves, will continue to struggle until all people have given up the stories of patriarchy, homophobia, possessive love, and uncritical loyalty that lead to desertion, abuse, and domination.

> What is love? It is the victory over mediocrity. It's the success of re-building; it's achieving liberation; it's freedom; it's pure, merciful, compassionate protection. A mixture of the human and the divine, it's tolerance, it's creation of the best, over and over again. I am the sea, gentle and forceful. I am the mountain, strong and proud. I am the tone, eloquent and beautiful. I am hoping that you will look at me while thanking all the sacred and mysterious sources of the universe, for having the opportunity to have found each other in our lives.[28]

This is a poem that was written as a relationship was ending. When the two lovers walked away they were not shattered; they had given each other a gift, each of them had found their own self in the relationship. In every relationship, we have a right to come away with a new and better understanding of who we are. Men need to continue to remind them-selves that their lovers and partners are not their possessions and that they are a face of the deepest sacred. Men need lovers to become who they are; and lovers need men to become who *they* are. The greatest task of men in the service of transformation is to establish relationships of mu-tuality, filled with the intimacy of a man who has learned to practice the stories of the guide, whose self-love allows him to love others as himself, and the stories of the faithful lover, who has redefined his machismo as stepping forward urgently only for the sake of transforming love.

Conclusion

We live in dangerous times, as James Baldwin has written. Like Casey, the preacher in John Steinbeck's *The Grapes of Wrath*,[29] and Baby Suggs, in *Beloved*,[30] who both lost and then regained the spirit and the calling to witness, men need to reclaim the spirit. Like Ghandi, César Chávez, Malcolm X, and Martin Luther King Jr., men and women to-gether need to create a new and more loving history as the legacy for children. Each man is in the process of discovering, unearthing, giving shape to his manhood, his selfhood, and yes, his ministry. When a man in the process of searching for his identity and vocation recognizes that his own quest intersects with the needs of his community, he comes to realize that his personal face also has a political and a historical face that link him to the sacred task of building a community of justice. When men undergo this kind of conversion, they know what their life task is about; this is the moment of their ordination as guides to one another. In this way, in the very process of becoming men in the service of transformation, all men can work together to move their community toward becoming fundamentally more just and loving.

To find the calling means to draw on those underlying, formative sacred sources in the service of transformation that are within each of us. Ellison once again serves as our guide in this matter. In *Invisible Man,* the young protagonist tried to understand what his grandfather meant when he said "to agree them to death and destruction."[31] That sounded too much like cynicism: Beat the white man at his own game, tell him whatever he wants to hear, get what you can from him, manipulate him to get ahead. Too often many men of color have done just that. But then the protagonist realized what his grandfather really meant to signify was, "to affirm the principle on which the country was built and not the men, or at least not the men who did the violence."[32] What principle? That all of us are born equal and that each of us is valuable as a person. If men of color lose this reality, the value of each person, then the United States will have lost its deepest meaning. We are all inextricably linked together; in order to save ourselves and our humanity, we need to reach out to one another and help liberate each other from the deadly stories of deformation. Finally, like the protagonist in *Invisible Man,* all men from all cultures and racial heritages have to come out of hibernation precisely by refusing to remain invisible; they need to experience resurrection. This is the true meaning of the Easter that takes place daily in our lives, a new *amanecer,* the dawning of a new day. It is not just on Easter Sunday once a year, and it is not only Jesus who rose from the dead, who defeated the forces of deformation; it is also all persons who decide to rise up and become Christs in their own lives. Ellison ends his novel by saying, "Who knows, but that on the lower frequencies, I speak for you."[33] In the final analysis, when we are in trouble and cry out for love and justice, we speak for all of our brothers and sisters who represent the different racial, religious, ethnic, and sexual orientations in order to affirm our common humanity.

Notes

1. James Baldwin, "A Talk to Teachers," in *Collected Essays of James Baldwin,* edited by Toni Morrison (New York: Library of America, 1998), pp. 678–686. See also James Baldwin, *The Price of the Ticket: Collected Non-Fiction, 1948–1985* (New York: St. Martin's Press, 1985).

2. Malcolm X, *The Autobiography of Malcolm X* (New York: Grove Press, 1966), pp. 362–363, 374–377.

3. As reported in a conversation with Manfred Halpern.

4. David T. Abalos, *Strategies of Transformation Toward a Multicultural Society: Fulfilling the Story of Democracy* (Westport, CT: Praeger Press, 1996), chapter 5.

5. Elaine Pagels, *The Gnostic Gospels* (New York: Random House, 1979), p. xv.

6. Leslie Marmon Silko, *Ceremony* (New York: Penguin Books, 1977), p. 2.

7. Alejo Carpentier, *Los Pasos Perdidos* (New York: Viking Penguin, 1998).

8. Plato, *The Republic,* edited by Betty Radice, translated by Desmond Lee (New York: Penguin Books, 1976).

9. Attributed to Al-Ghazzali as quoted in Manfred Halpern, *Transforming Our Personal, Political, Historical, and Being in Contrast to Our Other Three Choices in Theory and Practice,* chapter 13 (forthcoming).

10. Ralph Ellison, *Invisible Man* (New York: Vintage Books, 1972), pp. 193–214.

11. Alan Pifer, "The Annual Report of the President," in *Bilingual Education and the Hispanic Challenge* (New York: Carnegie Corporation of New York, 1979), p. 16.

12. Julian Samora, Joe Bernal, and Albert Peña, *Gunpowder Justice: A Reassessment of the Texas Rangers* (Notre Dame, IN: University of Notre Dame Press, 1979); and Alfredo Mirandé, *Gringo Justice* (Notre Dame, IN: University of Notre Dame Press, 1987), pp. 65–72.

13. Ronald Takaki, *A Different Mirror: A History of Multicultural America* (Boston: Little, Brown, 1993), pp. 139–165.

14. This repetition of the story of tribalism by different ethnic groups is brilliantly told by William Attaway, *Blood on the Forge* (New York: Monthly Review Press, 1987).

15. Ken Kesey, *One Flew Over the Cuckoo's Nest* (New York: New American library, 1962), pp. 114–128.

16. In regards to my own struggle with assimilation, see *La Comunidad Latina in the United States: Personal and Political Strategies for Transforming Culture* (Westport, CT: Praeger Press, 1998), pp. 38–68.

17. Malcolm X, *The Autobiography of Malcolm X,* pp. 52–55.

18. Ibid., p. 36.

19. Richard Rodríguez, *Hunger of Memory: The Education of Richard Rodríguez* (New York: Bantam Books, 1983), p. 116.

20. René Marqués, *La Carreta* (Rio Piedras, PR: Editorial Cultural, 1971), pp. 168–170.

21. Toni Morrison, *Beloved* (New York: New American Library, 1987), p. 251.

22. Juan Andrade and Andrew Hernández, *The Almanac of Latino Politics 2000* (Chicago: U.S. Hispanic Leadership Institute, 1999), pp. 1–2.

23. Silko, *Ceremony,* p. 253.

24. Kesey, *One Flew Over the Cuckoo's Nest,* pp. 140, 184–190.

25. In this regard I would like to make reference to the work of Chicana and Latina feminists who have been writing about the need to see any oppression as always in collusion with all other forms of subordination. This is why the oppressed in different yet similar situations, made similar by the diminishment of their humanity, need to make common cause with one another. Please see authors and works cited in Chapter 1 of this volume. See also Abalos, *La Comunidad Latina,* chapter 5.

26. Sandra Cisneros, *The House on Mango Street* (New York: Vintage Books, 1984) and *Woman Hollering Creek and Other Stories* (New York: Random House, 1991); Demetria Martínez, *Mother Tongue* (New York: Ballantine Books, 1994); Rosa Martha Villareal, *Doctor Magdalena* (Berkeley: TQS Publications, 1995); Alice Walker, *The Color Purple* (New York: Washington Square Press, 1982). See also the works of Chicana and Latina authors cited in Chapter 1 of this volume.

27. Walker, *The Color Purple,* pp. 279, 290.

28. Teresíta Fernández-Viña, photocopy.

29. John Steinbeck, *The Grapes of Wrath* (New York: Penguin Books, 1989).

30. Morrison, *Beloved.*

31. Ellison, *Invisible Man,* p. 16.

32. Ibid., p. 561.

33. Ibid., pp. 567–568.

Selected Bibliography

Abalos, David T. *La Comunidad Latina in the United States: Personal and Political Strategies for Transforming Culture.* Westport, CT: Praeger Press, 1998.

———. *The Latino Family and The Politics of Transformation.* Westport, CT: Praeger Press, 1993.

———. "Latino Female/Male Relationships: Strategies for Creating New Archetypal Dramas." *The Latino Studies Journal* 1, no. 1 (January 1990): 48–69.

———. *Latinos in the United States: The Sacred and the Political.* Notre Dame, IN: University of Notre Dame Press, 1986.

———. "Rediscovering the Sacred Among Latinos." *The Latino Studies Journal* 3, no. 3 (May 1992): 1–25.

———. "Some Reflections on the Creation of a Latino Culture in the United States from the Perspective of a Theory of Transformation." In *Old Masks, New Faces: Religion and Latino Identities,* edited by Anthony S. Arroyo and Gilbert Cadena. New York: Bildner Center, CUNY, 1995.

———. "Strategies of Transformation in the Health Delivery System." *The Nursing Forum* 17, no. 3 (1978): 284–316.

———. *Strategies of Transformation Toward a Multicultural Society: Fulfilling the Story of Democracy.* Westport, CT: Praeger Press, 1996.

Acosta, Oscar Zeta. *The Revolt of the Cockroach People.* San Francisco: Straight Arrow, 1973.

Acuña, Rodolfo. *Occupied America: The Chicano's Struggle for Liberation.* San Francisco: Canfield Press, 1972.

Alarcón, Norma. "Chicana's Feminist Literature: A Re-Vision Through Malintzin, or Malintzin: Putting Flesh Back on the Object." In *This Bridge Called My Back: Writings by Radical Women of Color,* edited by Cherríe Moraga and Gloria Anzaldúa. Watertown, MA: Persephone Press, 1981.

Amalguer, Tomás. "Chicano Men: A Cartography of Homosexual Identity and Behavior." *Differences* 3, no. 2 (1991): 75–100.

Andrade, Juan, and Andrew Hernández, with Jacqueline Campbell. *The Almanac of Latino Politics 2000.* Chicago: Hispanic Leadership Institute, 1999.

Anzaldúa, Gloria. *Borderlands, La Frontera: The New Mestiza.* San Francisco: Aunt Lute Books, 1987.

————, ed. *Making Face, Making Soul, Haciendo Caras: Creative and Critical Perspectives by Women of Color.* San Francisco: Aunt Lute Books, 1990.

Anzaldúa, Gloria, and Cherríe Moraga, eds. *This Bridge Called My Back.* Watertown, MA: Persephone Press, 1981.

Asturias, Miguel Angel. *Men of Maize.* New York: Verso, 1988.

Attaway, William. *Blood on the Forge.* New York: Monthly Review Press, 1987.

Avineri, Shlomo. "Marx's Vision of Future Society." *Dissent* 20 (summer 1973): 323–331.

Bachman, Justin. "Black and Hispanic Gays Hit Harder by AIDS." *The Star Ledger: The Newspaper for New Jersey,* January 14, 2000.

Baldwin, James. *The Price of the Ticket: Collected Non-Fiction, 1948–1985.* New York: St. Martin's Press, 1985.

Berman, Marshall. *The Politics of Authenticity: Radical Individualism and the Rise of Modern Society.* New York: Atheneum Press, 1972.

Biberman, Herbert. *The Salt of the Earth.* Produced by Independent Productions Corporation and the International Union of Mine, Mill, and Smelter Workers, 1953. Film.

Blake, William. *The Complete Poetry and Prose of William Blake.* Edited by David V. Erdman, with commentary by Harold Bloom. New York: Anchor Books, Doubleday, 1988.

————. *The Early Illuminated Books,* vol. III. Edited by Morris Eaves, Robert N. Essick, and Joseph Viscomi. Princeton, NJ: Princeton University Press, 1993.

Blanco, José Joaquín. "Ojos que da Panico Sonar." In *Función de Medianoche.* Mexico City: Era, 1981.

Branch, Taylor. *Parting the Waters: America in the King Years, 1954–63.* New York: Simon and Schuster, 1988.

————. *Pillar of Fire: America in the King Years, 1963–65.* New York: Simon and Schuster, 1998.

Burckhardt, Titus. *Alchemy.* Baltimore: Penguin Books, 1971.

Campbell, Howard, Leigh Binford, Miguel Bartolomé, and Alicia Barabas, eds. *Zapotec Struggles: Histories, Politics, and Representation from Juchitán, Oaxaca.* Washington, DC: Smithsonian Institution Press, 1993.

Carpentier, Alejo. *Los Pasos Perdidos.* New York: Viking Penguin, 1998.

————. *The Lost Steps.* Translated by Harriet DeOnis. New York: Farrar, Straus, and Giroux, 1989.

Carrasco, Rafael. *Inquisición y Represión Sexual en Valencia: Historía de los Sodomitas (1565–1785).* Barcelona: Laertes, 1986.

Carrier, Joseph. *De Los Otros: Intimacy and Homosexuality Among Mexican Men.* New York: Columbia University Press, 1995.

Castañeda, Antonia I. "History and the Politics of Violence Against Women." In *Living Chicana Theory,* edited by Carla Trujillo. Berkeley: Third Woman Press, 1998.

Castro, Américo. *The Spaniards.* Translated by Willard King and Selma Margarettem. Berkeley: University of California Press, 1971.

Cisneros, Sandra. *The House on Mango Street.* Houston: Arte Público Press, 1987.

————. *Woman Hollering Creek and Other Stories.* New York: Random House, 1991.

Cooke, Michael. *Afro-American Literature in the Twentieth Century: The Achievement of Intimacy.* New Haven, CT: Yale University Press, 1984.

Corbin, Henri. *Creative Imagination in the Sufism of Ibn Arabi.* Translated by Ralph Manheim. Princeton, NJ: Princeton University Press, 1969.

Córdova, Teresa, et al., eds. *Chicana Voices: The Intersections of Class, Race and Gender.* Austin: University of Texas Press, 1990.

Cunningham, Michael. *The Hours.* New York: Farrar, Straus, and Giroux, 1998.

Cypess, Sandra Messinger. *La Malinche in Mexican Literature: From History to Myth.* Austin: University of Texas Press, 1991.

De la Torre, Adela, and Beatríz Pesquera, eds. *Building with Our Hands: New Directions in Chicana Studies.* Berkeley: University of California Press, 1993.

De las Casas, Bartolomé. *In Defense of the Indians.* Translated by Stafford Poole. Dekalb: Northern Illinois University Press, 1992.

De Valdés, María Elena. "Verbal and Visual Representation of Women: Como Agua Para Chocolate/Like Water for Chocolate." *World Literature Today* 69 (winter 1995): 78–82.

Delgado, Richard, and Jean Stefancic, eds. *The Latino/Latina Condition: A Critical Reader.* New York: New York University Press, 1998.

Dillard, Heath. *Daughters of the Reconquest: Women in Castilian Town Society 1100–1300.* Cambridge: Cambridge University Press, 1984.

Ellison, Ralph. *Invisible Man.* New York: Vintage Books, 1972.

Erdman, David V. *Blake: Prophet Against Empire.* New York: Dover Publications, 1991.

———, ed. *The Complete Poetry and Prose of William Blake.* Commentary by Harold Bloom. New York: Anchor Books, 1988.

Erikson, Erik. *Ghandi's Truth: On the Origins of Militant Non-Violence.* New York: W. W. Norton, 1969.

Esquivel, Laura. *Like Water for Chocolate.* New York: Doubleday, 1992.

Flores, William V., and Rina Benmayor, eds. *Latino Cultural Citizenship: Claiming Identity, Space and Rights.* Boston: Beacon Press, 1997.

Foster, David William. *Sexual Textualities: Essays on Queer/ing Latin American Writing.* Austin: University of Texas Press, 1997.

Freire, Paulo. *Pedagogy of the Oppressed.* New York: Continuum Books, 1970.

Fuentes, Rev. Ferdinand. "An Overview of the Hispanic Context in the United States." Working paper for a United Church of Christ Latina and Latino Leadership Summit, Cleveland, 1994.

Galán, Hector. *Los Mineros.* Telescript by Paul Espinosa and Hector Galán, narrated by Luís Valdéz for the American Experience, PBS, 1990. Film.

García, Alma M., and Mario T. García. *Chicana Feminist Thought: The Basic Writings.* New York: Routledge, 1997.

García, Cristina. *Dreaming in Cuban.* New York: Alfred A. Knopf, 1992.

García, Mario T. *Mexican Americans.* New Haven, CT: Yale University Press, 1991.

Ghiselin, Brewster. *The Creative Process.* New York: New American Library, 1963.

Gilligan, Carol. *In a Different Voice: Psychological Theory and Women's Development.* Cambridge: Harvard University Press, 1982.

Glick, Ronald, and Joan Moore, eds. *Drugs in Hispanic Communities.* New Brunswick, NJ: Rutgers University Press, 1990.

Gómez-Quiñones, Juan. *Chicano Politics: Reality and Promise, 1940–1990.* Albuquerque: University of New Mexico Press, 1991.

———. *On Culture.* Los Angeles: UCLA, Chicano Studies Center Publications, 1986.

———. *The Roots of Chicano Politics, 1600–1940.* Albuquerque: University of New Mexico Press, 1994.

González, Juan. *A History of Latinos in America: Harvest of Empire.* New York: Penguin Books, 2000.

González, Ray, ed. *Muy Macho: Latino Men Confront Their Manhood.* New York: Doubleday, 1996.

Griffin, Gail B. *The Season of the Witch.* Pasadena: Trilogy Books, 1995.

Guash, Oscar. *La Sociedad Rosa.* Barcelona: Anagrama, 1991.

Gutiérrez, Ramón. *When Jesus Came, the Corn Mothers Went Away.* Stanford: Stanford University Press, 1991.

Gutmann, Matthew C. *The Meanings of Macho: Being a Man in Mexico City.* Los Angeles: University of California Press, 1996.

Halpern, Manfred. "The Archetypal Drama of the Conquering Hero." Paper delivered at the annual meeting of the American Political Science Association, San Francisco, September 1, 1990.

———. "The Archetype of Capitalism: A Critical Analysis in the Light of a Theory of Transformation." Paper delivered at the annual meeting of the American Political Science Association, San Francisco, 1996.

———. "Choosing Between Ways of Life and Death and Between Forms of Democracy." *Alternatives* (January 1987).

———. "Four Contrasting Repertories of Human Relations in Islam: Two Pre-Modern and Two Modern Ways of Dealing with Continuity and Change, Collaboration and Conflict, and Achieving Justice." In *Psychological Dimensions of Near Eastern Studies,* edited by L. Carl Brown and Norman Itzkowitz. Princeton, NJ: Darwin Press, 1977.

———. "How Can We Re-Discover Wisdom and Love?" Lecture presented to the Princeton Faculty Forum and to the Princeton Graduate School Colloquium, Princeton University, New Jersey, 1998.

———. "Knowing, Interconnecting, and Fulfilling the Four Faces and the Source of Our Being." *Journal of Religion and Health* 34, no. 2 (summer 1995): 105–119.

———. "A Theory for Transforming the Self: Moving Beyond the Nation State." In *Transformational Politics: Theory, Study, and Practice,* edited by Edwin Schwerin, Christa Daryl Slaton, and Stephen Woolpert. Albany, NY: SUNY Press, 1998.

———. *Transforming Our Personal, Political, Historical, and Sacred Being in Contrast to Our Other Three Choices in Theory and Practice.* Forthcoming.

———. "Transforming Ourselves Beyond Present Theory and Practice: For Example Beyond the Nation State." Paper delivered for the national symposium "Beyond the Nation State: Transforming Visions of Human Society," College of William and Mary, September 24–27, 1993.

———. "Underlying Forces Shaping the Fundamental Differences Between Incremental and Transforming Change." Paper delivered at the annual meeting of the American Political Science Association, Washington, DC, 1997.

———. "Why Are Most of Us Partial Selves? Why Do Partial Selves Enter the Road to Deformation?" Paper delivered at the annual meeting of the American Political Science Association, Washington, DC, August 29, 1991.

Hesse, Hermann. *Siddhartha.* New York: Bantam Books, 1971.

Hijuelos, Oscar. *The Mambo Kings Play Songs of Love.* New York: Harper and Row, 1990.

Horno-Delgado, Asunción, et al., eds. *Breaking Boundaries: Latina Writings and Critical Readings.* Amherst: University of Massachusetts Press, 1988.

Idrogo, Curt. "Hispanic Americans." In *A Guide to Multicultural Resources, 1997–1998,* edited by Alex Boyd. Fort Atkinson, WI: High Smith Publications, 1997.

Isasi-Díaz, Ada María. "Ethnicity in Mujerista Theology." Paper delivered at a national conference on "Religion and Latinos in the United States," Princeton University, New Jersey, April 16–19, 1993.

Jannuzi, Marisa. "Like Water for Chocolate." *The Review of Contemporary Fiction* 13 (summer 1993): 245–246.

Jung, C.G. *The Collected Works of C. G. Jung,* vol. 9, *The Archetypes and the Collective Unconscious.* Edited by Michael Fordham and translated by R. F. Hull. Princeton, NJ: Princeton University Press, 1980.

———. *Man and His Symbols.* New York: Dell, 1970.

Kayal, Philip. *Bearing Witness: Gay Men's Health Crisis and the Politics of AIDS.* Boulder, CO: Westview Press, 1993.

Kesey, Ken. *One Flew Over the Cuckoo's Nest.* New York: New American Library, 1962.

King, Martin Luther, Jr. *Why We Can't Wait.* New York: Signet Books, 1964.

Kuhn, Thomas. *The Structure of Scientific Revolutions.* Chicago: University of Chicago Press, 1969.

Lawrence, D. H. *The Plumed Serpent.* New York: Vintage Books, 1954.

Leiner, Marvin. *Sexual Politics in Cuba: Machismo, Homosexuality, and AIDS.* Boulder, CO: Westview Press, 1994.

Lerner, Gerda. *The Creation of Patriarchy.* New York: Oxford University Press, 1986.

Lewis, Oscar. *Five Families.* New York: New American Library, 1959.

Lumsden, Ian. *Machos, Maricones, and Gays: Cuba and Homosexuality.* Philadelphia: Temple University Press, 1996.

Marqués, René. *La Carreta.* Rio Piedras, PR: Editorial Cultural, 1971.

Martínez, Demetria. *Mother Tongue.* New York: Ballantine Books, 1994.

Martínez, Elizabeth. *De Colores Means All of Us: Latina Views for a Multi-Colored Century.* Cambridge, MA: South End Press, 1998.

Matos, Carlos A. Rodríguez, ed. *Poesída: An Anthology of AIDS Poetry from the United States, Latin America and Spain.* Jackson Heights, NY: Ollantay Press, 1995.

Matthiessen, Peter. *Sal Si Puedes: César Chávez and the New American Revolution.* New York: Random House, 1969.

Miller, David. *The New Polytheism: Rebirth of the Gods and Goddesses.* New York: Harper and Row, 1974.

Mirandé, Alfredo. *Hombres y Machos: Masculinity and Latino Culture.* Boulder, CO: Westview Press, 1997.

Morrison, Toni. *Beloved.* New York: New American Library, 1987.

———, ed. *Collected Essays of James Baldwin.* New York: Library of America, 1998.

Murray, Stephen O. *Latin American Homosexuality.* Albuquerque: University of New Mexico Press, 1995.

Najera, Rick. *The Pain of the Macho and Other Plays.* Houston: Arte Público Press, 1997.

Padilla, Félix M. *The Struggle of Latina/Latino University Students: In Search of a Liberating Education.* New York: Routledge, 1997.

Paz, Octavio. *The Other Mexico: Critique of the Pyramid.* Translated by Lysander Kemp. New York: Grove Press, 1972.

————. "Reflections: Mexico and the United States." *The New Yorker,* September 7, 1979.

————. "The Sons of La Malinche." In *Introduction to Chicano Studies: A Reader,* edited by Livia Isaura Durán and H. Russell Bernard. New York: Macmillan, 1973.

————. *Sor Juana.* Cambridge: Harvard University Press, 1988.

Peristiany, J. G., ed. *Honor and Shame: The Values of Mediterranean Society.* Chicago: University of Chicago Press, 1966.

Perwin, Cynthia L. *The Ego, the Self, and the Structure of Political Authority.* Ph.D. diss., Department of Politics, Princeton University, New Jersey, 1973.

Pifer, Alan. *Bilingual Education and the Hispanic Challenge.* New York: Carnegie Corporation New York, 1979.

Portilla, Miguel León, ed. *Native Mesoamerican Spirituality.* New York: Ramsey, Toronto, 1980.

Preston, John Hyde. "A Conversation with Gertrude Stein." In *The Creative Process,* edited by Brewster Ghiselin. New York: Mentor, 1963.

Raines, Howell. *My Soul Is Rested: The Story of the Civil Rights Movement in the Deep South.* New York: Bantam Books, 1978.

Ramírez, Rafael L. *Dime Capitán: Reflexiones Sobre la Masculinidad.* Rio Piedras, PR: Huracán, 1993.

————. *What It Means to Be a Man: Reflections on Puerto Rican Masculinity.* Translated by Rosa E. Casper. New Brunswick, NJ: Rutgers University Press, 1999.

Ramos, Henry A.J. *The American G.I. Forum: In Pursuit of the Dream, 1948–1983.* Houston: Arte Público Press, 1998.

Rivera, Tomás. *Y No Se Lo Tragó la Tierra: And the Earth Did Not Devour Him.* Houston: Arte Público Press, 1987.

Rodríguez, Richard. *Hunger of Memory: The Education of Richard Rodríguez.* New York: Bantam Books, 1983.

Rodríguez de Laguna, Asela. *Notes on Puerto Rican Literature.* Newark: Rutgers, the State University of New Jersey, 1987.

Rosenberg, Tina. "Machismo Gives Good New Laws a Black Eye." *New York Times,* June 20, 1998.

Rothenberg, Paula, ed. *Racism and Sexism: An Integrated Study.* New York: St. Martin's Press, 1988.

Said, Edward. *Culture and Imperialism.* New York: Alfred A. Knopf, 1993.

Sandoval-Sánchez, Alberto. *José, Can You See? Latinos On and Off Broadway.* Madison: University of Wisconsin Press, 1999.

Sharabi, Hisham. *Neopatriarchy: A Theory of Distorted Change in Arab Society.* New York: Oxford University Press, 1988.

Shockley, John. *Chicano Revolt in a Texas Town.* Notre Dame, IN: University of Notre Dame Press, 1974.

Sikora, Jacobo Schifter. *Amor de Macho: Lo Que Nuestra Abuelita Núnca Nos Contó, Sobre las Carceles.* San José, Costa Rica: ILPES, 1997.

————. *De Ranas a Princesas: Sufridas, Atrevidas, y Travestidas.* San José, Costa Rica: ILPES, 1998.

————. *La Casa de Lila: Un Estudio de la Prostitución Masculina.* San José, Costa Rica: ILPES, 1997.

Sikora, Jacobo Schifter, and Johnny Madrigal. *Hombres Que Aman Hombres.* San José, Costa Rica: ILPES-SIDA, 1997.

Silko, Leslie Marmon. *Ceremony.* New York: Penguin Books, 1977.
Silva, Helio R.S. *Travesti: A Inverçao de Femenino.* Rio de Janeiro: ISER, 1993.
Solas, Humberto. *Lucía.* Havana, Cuba, 1968. Film.
Steinbeck, John. *The Grapes of Wrath.* New York: Penguin Books, 1989.
Takaki, Ronald. *A Different Mirror: A History of Multicultural America.* Boston: Little, Brown, 1993.
———. *Strangers from a Different Shore.* Boston: Little, Brown, 1989.
Tiger, Lionel. *The Decline of Males.* New York: Golden Books Publishing, 1999.
Trujillo, Carla, ed. *Chicana Lesbians: The Girls Our Mothers Warned Us About.* Berkeley: Third Woman Press, 1991.
———, ed. *Living Chicana Theory.* Berkeley: Third Woman Press, 1998.
Ulanov, Ann Belford. *The Feminine in Jungian Psychology and in Christian Theology.* Evanston, IL: Northwestern University Press, 1971.
Vicente, Luciano Perena. *Derechos y Deberes Entre Indios y Españoles en el Nuevo Mundo Según Francísco de Vittoria.* Salamanca: Universidad Pontifica de Salamanca, 1991.
Villañueva, Alma. "Inside." In *Breaking Boundaries: Latina Writings and Critical Readings,* edited by Asunción Horno-Delgado, Eleana Ortega, Nina Scott, and Nancy Saporta Sternbach. Amherst: University of Massachusetts Press, 1989.
Villareal, Rosa Martha. *Doctor Magdalena.* Berkeley: TQS Publications, 1995.
Villarreal, Roberto E., and Norma G. Hernández, eds. *Latinos and Political Coalitions.* Westport, CT: Praeger Press, 1991.
Walker, Alice. *The Color Purple.* New York: Pocket Books, 1982.
Wolin, Sheldon. "Political Theory as a Vocation." *American Political Science Review* 63 (December 1969).
Woolf, Virginia. *A Room of One's Own.* New York: Harcourt, Brace, 1929.
Woolpert, Stephen, Christa Daryl Slaton, and Edwin Schwerin, eds. *Transformational Politics: Theory, Study, and Practice.* Albany, NY: SUNY Press, 1998.
X, Malcolm. *The Autobiography of Malcolm X.* New York: Grove Press, 1966.
Young, Iris M. *Justice and the Politics of Difference.* Princeton, NJ: Princeton University Press, 1990.
Zambrano, Myrna M. *Mejor Sola Que Mal Acompañada: For the Latina in an Abusive Relationship.* Bilingual edition, Seattle, WA: Seal Press, 1985.

Films

The Ballad of Gregorio Cortéz. Directed by Robert Young. PBS American Playhouse, 1992.
The Blood of the Condor. Directed by Jorge Sanjines. Bolivia, 1969.
Camila. Directed by María Luisa Bemberg. Argentina, 1984.
Like Water for Chocolate. Directed by Alfonso Arau. Mexcio, 1992.
Lucía. Directed by Humberto Solas. Cuba, 1968.
El Norte. Directed by Gregory Nava. Independent Productions, 1983.
La Operación. Directed by Ana M. García. Cinema Guild, 1982.
Operation Bootstrap. Directed by Carl Dudley. Universal Education and Visual Arts, 1964.
A Portrait of Teresa. Directed by Pastor Vega. Cuba, 1979.
The Salt of the Earth. Directed by Herbert Biberman. Independent Productions Corp. and the International Union of Mine, Mill, and Smelter Workers, 1953.

Index

—

213

About the Book

What does it mean to be a Latino man in the United States today? David Abalos shows how the traditional cultural stories—the male roles of the *mujeriego* (womanizer), the macho, and the patriarch—are becoming unlivable. Too many men choose manipulation, power, or violence in response, in an effort to restore the old order. But there is an alternative, argues Abalos.

Demonstrating that Latino men can participate in the creation of a new way of living, Abalos boldly reconsiders how the personal can be political. He redefines *machismo* as the pride in self that allows Latino men to choose and create new and better stories for themselves as faithful lover, as political innovator, as archetypal guide. And he shows how the transforming Latina/Latino family can generate a new and vital *comunidad Latina* in the United States.

David T. Abalos is professor of religious studies and sociology at Seton Hall University. His publications include *La Comunidad Latina in the United States: Personal and Political Strategies for Transforming Culture*.